NO ORDINARY INVITATION

Called to Live a Life of Eternal Purpose

FRANCEE STRAIN

WESTBOW
PRESS®
A DIVISION OF THOMAS NELSON
& ZONDERVAN

WestBow Press books may be ordered through booksellers or by contacting:

WestBow Press
A Division of Thomas Nelson & Zondervan
1663 Liberty Drive
Bloomington, IN 47403
www.westbowpress.com
1 (866) 928-1240

Scripture taken from the King James Version of the Bible.

Scripture taken from the New King James Version®. Copyright © 1982 by Thomas Nelson. Used by permission. All rights reserved.

ISBN: 978-1-5127-9522-6 (sc)
ISBN: 978-1-5127-9524-0 (hc)
ISBN: 978-1-5127-9523-3 (e)

Library of Congress Control Number: 2017910437

Print information available on the last page.

WestBow Press rev. date: 9/25/2017

DEDICATION

To my Savior—may You be glorified.

To those who love me and prayed this book to completion—thank you.

To my readers—may you RSVP to the God who loves you.

CONTENTS

CHAPTER 1

No Ordinary Invitation

THE INVITATION IS ISSUED

Imagine this. The gorgeous embossed invitation has just arrived in the mail. The recipient tears open the envelope and scans the card. She tosses it onto her desk and moves on to the next task. It came. She saw. She ignored it.

One month passes, and her desk needs a good cleaning. The stuff of life sure piled up in a hurry! She begins to sort through the mess, organizing, filing, and of course, disposing of some junk mail. And there it is: the invitation. She has been so busy that she has not even thought about it since the day it arrived. Thoughts and plans begin to formulate in her mind. She reaches for the phone and dials her coworker.

"Hello?"

"Hi. It's me."

"Hey, how's it going?"

"Pretty good. I have a question for you. I was just looking at the invitation for the banquet next weekend. Are you going to go?"

"I don't know. I have a lot going on next week. And by the time Friday night gets here, I'm going to be pretty tired."

"Yeah. I know what you mean."

"And besides, it's fifty dollars per person. And that's only the *start* of the expenses! I'd also have to find time to go shopping for a new outfit, get my hair done, and find a sitter. There goes another fifty dollars times three. It'll probably be boring anyway."

"Probably so. Events like this usually are. You know, if you aren't going to go, I probably won't go either. I really don't have that kind of money to spend right now, anyway. And besides, I have to get up early the next morning to help Joe with some yardwork before his brother comes to visit. Actually, I'm just going to decide right now. I'm not going to go; it'll be a lot easier that way."

"Well, I'm not going if you're not going! They probably won't even know we're missing. Two does not a banquet make!"

"So, what are you going to do instead?"

"I don't know. Probably watch some TV, eat some junk, and stay up way too late."

"Sounds like a plan. Well, I need to go. Another call is coming in."

"Okay. Talk to you later."

"Bye."

She tosses the invitation into the trash and answers the other call. Just like that, she moves on to the next thing, never giving the first thing another thought. And there it is. It came. She saw. She passed over it. In just a few moments, the invitee has made several excuses, and with her friend's help, has talked herself out of going. So many things have happened here in just a short amount of time, some of them nearly imperceptible. The recipients spurned the host and turned down the event because of their own plans and assumptions; however, it may have been the most wonderful and amazing event they had ever had the opportunity to attend. The expense may have seemed small when compared to the benefits gathered there. The guest list may have included people pivotal to their future careers and relationships. Also, the opportunity was taken away for their children to have a special treat, for their babysitters to earn money, and for their beauticians to improve their skills. Furthermore, the assumption that they would not even be missed at the event relegated them to an unimportant status. Shall I go on? The decision was theirs to make, the ultimate effect upon them alone, but they were impacting others all along the way.

Let's go a step further and compare this scenario to our spiritual lives. What do *we* do with the invitations that come to us—from believers, unbelievers, the poor, the needy, and God Himself? What excuses do we make so that we do not have to interact with these individuals and be part of what they are inviting us into? Regardless of the excuses we make, our refusals have consequences. A decision to avoid interacting with God or others affects not only them but also us. We miss blessings. We miss relationships. We miss opportunities to make an impact, both now and in the future. When it is all about us, we miss them. When it is all about us, we miss God.

THE HOST IS CALLING YOUR NAME

Have you ever been a contestant on a game show? I would venture to say that most of us have not been game show contestants, but the majority of us have probably seen them on television. Place your mind-set into a game show scenario, and envision the show taking place in front of you. You know how it is: people in the studio audience sitting on the edges of their seats, just waiting for their names to be called. They wait with sweaty palms and thumping hearts for the chance to win money and prizes and trips to Jamaica or other exotic places. The possessions they can gain, the vacations they can take, and the monetary amounts they can win are things that most of us can only dream about or experience vicariously.

What is it about things that makes people respond so eagerly? When people hear the words of an exuberant host inviting them to come to the front, they excitedly comply because it is expected that they do so. They go forward expecting to have the opportunity to win prizes as the host promised. The competition gets underway, and we watch and wait to see what the outcome will be. The crowd cheers or boos the contestants as the competition ensues. Our minds and emotions follow them through to the end of their game show runs—to happy victories or to heartbreaking defeats. The players will either rejoice in their winning or sadly trudge back to their seats, their opportunities over. The time of the invitation has ended, and they part ways with the host.

What motivates people to respond to invitations in life? Would we excitedly respond to an amazing invitation from an exuberant host, especially if it was to something so much better than the incredible prizes awarded on game shows? Well, we do not have to guess or imagine what we would do if this happened to us, because it already has. God is a host, and He has called us to come forward to receive amazing gifts. Now, understand that there are differences between this invitation and a game show invitation: God's invitation to us is not for a game or show—it is for real life! There is no competition to engage in. There is no loss, only winning. There is no sales tax to be paid on the earnings because everything He offers is absolutely free! We just need to get up out of our seats in the audience and become active participants in the events taking place in front of us. The rewards will be great, and there will be believers cheering us on. And after we have received our reward from this host, we will never have to part ways. The reward is eternal life with Him forever in heaven.

Since before time began, a call went out to you. Even in the midst of a crowd, God has been seeking your heart as an individual. An invitation was developed with you in mind. From the time that the foundation of the world was laid, Jesus prepared to die for you and for each soul that would ever live. His sacrifice was arranged before you were ever a thought—before a single soul had ever lived. He did this so that you might have eternal life. Have you responded to His invitation?

This call has gone out directly to you. It does not involve living vicariously through someone else; it involves you living directly. The rewards of answering this invitation are beyond anything you could ever imagine. God is offering you a most amazing prize: *the gift of eternal life.* This gift was given in the person of Jesus Christ, the Son of God. "For God so loved the world that He gave His only begotten Son, that whoever believes in Him should not perish but have everlasting life" (John 3:16 NKJV). God, the host of heaven, wants you to win in life, and He wants to give you a reward in heaven too. Eternal life is the prize that God will give us if we come forward to claim it. It is free for the taking to whoever wants it. Come and get it! Eternal life is an eternal prize!

As we look through the pages of the Bible, we repeatedly see that God is calling out for people to come to Him. Humans have needs, and He has the answer to all of those needs. Foremost, there is a spiritual need to be saved from sin, and Jesus's death on the cross provides for that need. There are also physical and emotional needs, and He will meet those too. He cares for our bodies and for our souls. He is the Source, the Provider, and the Sustainer. He is all that we truly need, and none other can ever compare. Have you come to have your needs met? Have you answered His call?

This book was written as the result of a call—an invitation that God gave to me. It was an invitation to obey, to believe, to walk by faith and not by sight, to pray more, and to learn and practice the truths presented here for myself. It was an invitation to persevere through the difficulties of life, health, relationships, spiritual battles, doubts, and fears. It was an invitation to ultimately know God more and to be able to confidently rest in Him. I recorded the beginning of this journey in my journal. The entry reads:

> May 16, 2012: Last night God told me to write, and it was not a dark and stormy night. I had had a long busy day, full of joy and pain, ease and difficulty, yet when I laid down to sleep, my spirit was stirred that now was the time to write my story, our story, His story. But where to begin? That was the question. Well, it began with excitement but was almost instantly extinguished by excuses that brought resistance, and those in turn were quickly extinguished by sleep. The next day, I "happened" to be at home. I filled my day with study and rest, work and coffee, mothering and dishes, to-do's and not-to-do's; all the while, the Lord's conversation with me from the previous night kept pushing to the forefront until I found myself seated with pen and paper in hand, prayers in my heart, and God's words in my mind. The words of Hebrews 13:5 and also more personal words to me were these: "'I will never leave you nor forsake you.' Never. In the midst of this process, the future that comes of it, the struggles you are currently immersed in." Even as I slept that first night and toiled the next morning, He never left me. His presence was with me, and He was giving me rest.[1]

This story is my story, not quite my complete memoir but more like an account of a lesson I had to learn the hard way, and at times realize I am still learning. Here is how my story is looking so far: I was a good student throughout my primary and secondary school years and also my college years (good grades, good study habits, good focus, good behavior), but what did I know about real life? I was about to find out. I was also about to learn what this phrase means: "Come unto me." Jesus spoke these three words in Matthew 11:28, and they can be pivotal in a person's life. Life is tough, full of difficult choices and devastating disappointments. Life is chaotic, wearing, and can exhaust us to the core. But life can also be rich and full and blessed beyond belief because Jesus has given us an extraordinary invitation to make it so—if we will come to Him.

So, let's journey on together. You see, this book is not all about the details of my life story; part of this story is *your* story too. How will our stories turn out? Let's search out an answer to that question as we go through these pages together and as we walk life's road.

As we sojourn through life, we will discover that we are students on a mission to find answers. It sounds like this could easily be accomplished in the Information Age, but I can honestly tell you, for me it has not been easy. I have had some issues along the way as a student of life and as a student of this small but powerful phrase that Jesus spoke. Despite what my school report cards and accolades show, I have discovered that I am a slow learner when it comes to grasping this simple phrase: "Come unto me." My heart resists, my mind resists, and my schedule resists. I delay the process of increasing my knowledge and claiming the blessings that could be mine if I would just come to Him. All it takes is a simple action, a simple response of "Yes, I'll come," but I drag my feet and ask for five more minutes of recess or else tell Him to "hold that thought" because I have to finish something else first. Hopefully one day soon, I will learn to respond quickly and then be able to give you a great report that I have gotten my grades up!

I hope that you are a faster learner than I am and that your response happens quickly and readily. I hope that you will decide to come. God invites you to eternal life through Jesus, His Son, and also to a temporal life filled with incredible blessings. I said yes to eternal life long ago, and I am currently learning how to say yes to the blessings that are available to those who continue to come to Him. In spite of the fluctuations of my human responses, I already know how things will ultimately turn out for me. You can know how your ending will look, as well. I am hopeful and prayerful about the choice that you will make so that we will both have an ending that can be stamped "well done!" It is time to make a fresh start, right now, today.

Even though not all things in our lives are good, we can journey on the path to a good ending. I invite you to join me. Come with me, and let's go to God. Right now you have a choice: continue reading or put the book down. I have invited you, not commanded you. You have a choice in the matter; you have free will. God has also invited you to do some things. He has also offered you a choice and the opportunity to use your free will. I hope that you will search out what it is that He has invited you to do. May you be inspired by these things, but more than just be inspired, may you act upon the invitations and be blessed. May you RSVP with a yes to God's invitations to you.

CHAPTER 2
Come Unto Me

REAL LIFE

The things that go on every minute of every day are things that I can barely comprehend. My heart is torn from my chest, wrung over and over until no more tears will come (or so I think, until the next terrible thing happens to me, or I hear about it happening to someone else). Abuse, murder, deceit, adultery, greed, corruption, terrorism, depravity, prodigals, and religiosity. Loneliness, fear, illness, pain, competition, disregard, slander, and hatred. And more and more and more. Then and now. Now and later. It is there all around me, in my life and in the lives of my family, friends, and neighbors. It inundates our world. There are accounts filling the pages of the Bible, the newspapers, the history books, and the personal journals people keep at their bedsides. Things like these have filled the lives of human beings since the Garden of Eden. Why? Why then? And more importantly, why now in our lifetime where we have to be affected by it? How can this even happen? Why is this even happening? More importantly, when is it ever going to stop? Because these things have been around for thousands of years, almost since the beginning of time itself, my guess is that they likely will not stop anytime soon. Actually, I can do better than make a guess, I can know that these things are not going to stop. The reality is that things are actually going to get worse before they get better, and the better is not going to come until time itself comes to an end. What an awful, hopeless scenario. Or is it?

It is not a hopeless scenario. There is hope yet. What! How is that even humanly possible? The answer is: it is not humanly possible. Something extraordinary has to happen. Something extraordinary has to happen to me, to you, to us, to them, both now and later. In the housing projects and in the new subdivisions. On the wrong side of the tracks and on the right side. In the hills of Hollywood and the gutters of Calcutta. In broad daylight and in the middle of the night. It is there. It is happening even now. It is the hope of God's presence, making its way into human lives and hearts and history. God said, "My Presence will go *with you*, and I will give you rest" (Exod. 33:14 NKJV). These words of God were spoken to Moses thousands of years ago as he led the Israelites, but they still hold true today because God does not ever change. He is with the ones who have chosen Him to be their God.

The questions of "Why, God?" and "How could you let this happen?" are soothed with the words of Exodus 33:14. "That's not good enough!" you may answer, and do so quite forcefully. "That's a fairy tale! A fantasy! A useless crutch!" I understand your viewpoint in spirit, even if I have not been exactly where you are. I understand why you would respond in such a way. Yet, these words of God remain true: "My Presence will go *with you*, and I will give you rest" (Exod. 33:14 NKJV). If these words go unnoticed, unclaimed, disregarded, disbelieved, and disowned, that does not make them any less true. When we let His presence pervade every part of who we are, we *will* find rest, despite what is happening and what will continue to happen in the world around us. This is an extraordinary thing. To be invited to claim these words is an extraordinary invitation.

YOU ARE PERSONALLY INVITED

Jesus said, "Come unto me" (Matt. 11:28). This phrase is not likely to be heard in modern times since we do not typically speak in that fashion anymore. Today, we would be more likely to hear the words "Come here." These two phrases appear to essentially be saying the same thing, but Old English versus Modern English tweaks the feel just a bit. However, Jesus was not constrained by Old English or Modern English, in fact, He did not even speak English! For our purposes, we will look at the three-word phrase, but know this: when Jesus speaks, His words are packed full of meaning, no matter what language you encounter them in. They were spoken nearly two thousand years ago and recorded for all the rest of humanity to have for the remainder of all time. He gave a timeless invitation to us that is for such a time as this. Let's open and read His invitation to us. This is no ordinary invitation!

In examining the phrase "Come unto me," we will find that we can interpret it as either a command or an invitation because we hear no inflection from an audible voice. Later, we will examine Jesus's intent in speaking these words, but for now we will look a bit deeper into the concept of invitations and how they vary from commands. An invitation can be given in a formal or informal manner, but the purpose is the same: to invite someone to come and participate in something. It is a notification calling someone to an event, with the hope that action will be taken to come. Although different types of incentive accompany various types of invitations, and thus, differing responses from the invitees may result, the host still expects to receive a response upon receipt of the invitation.

An invitation contains important information about an upcoming event whether the event itself is considered important or mundane. There is typically a *who, what, when, where, why, how,* and *RSVP* (French for "respond please"). The invitee is informed of why there is an event, when and where it will take place, and how the event will be conducted. There may be instructions given regarding preparation for the event so it will transpire as planned. These instructions may suggest dressing in a particular fashion or bringing a particular item to the event. And while there are formal rules for delivering written invitations, informal methods of invitation also exist, such as social media, face-to-face encounters, or over the telephone. However the invitation is delivered, the fact remains that the invitee has a responsibility to act upon it. The RSVP request expresses the host's desire for notification of attendance so that preparations for the event can be made in the best possible way and the invitee's presence will be expected.

We hold events for just about every occasion. We celebrate relationships, milestones, accomplishments, performances, and holidays. We also hold miscellaneous social functions that are important to us but are not placed on the grand scale of a celebration. Regardless of the occasion, the essence of an invitation is the same: there is a purpose and there is a motive. And whether or not an invitation is deemed ordinary or extraordinary, it still awaits a response from the invitee.

So, what invitations would we consider to be extraordinary? The ones calling us to cataclysmic events? A teenager might view an invitation to join the sports team or attend homecoming or prom as a cataclysmic event, but in the grand scheme of things, these are not typically such. Extraordinary invitations do not seem to happen too often. It seems that most invitations are given for mundane or ordinary reasons. They are important, yet they are routine in life. What, then, makes an invitation extraordinary? *Who* did the inviting, *what* we were invited to do, the expense involved, the time commitment involved, or that *we* were even invited? The main qualifier for these types of invitations is a significant, life-changing event that will make an impact for the remainder of a lifetime, even for all eternity.

What is the most extraordinary invitation you have ever received? To be a spouse? To go on a dream vacation? To accept a promotion? What event has impacted your life for the remainder of it? And has your life been impacted even further, into eternity? It has been, whether or not you were even aware. The Creator of the universe has asked each of us to spend eternity with Him, and this can definitely be considered an extraordinary and life-altering event. But the profound and lasting effect comes with the response; otherwise, the life-change will be incomplete. The choice is ours. If the RSVP given is a no, then life will take an entirely different course than if the answer is a yes.

When we receive invitations, our first thoughts may be to check our calendars and wonder what we should wear, but at other times, our thoughts are about whether or not we are obligated to go. Sometimes, honestly, we just do not want to go. Other times, we know without a doubt that we want to go but have to ask ourselves if we are able to go. Do the events coordinate with our schedules? Can we find babysitters or house sitters? Can we afford the costs associated with the events? And occasionally, we will just need to gather more information before we can make our decisions and give our RSVPs.

Once we have dealt with all of the questions and decide to say yes, it is then time to prepare for the events, if any preparations are necessary, that is. Sometimes, no preparations are needed; we can just attend as we are. Other times, there is not enough time given to prepare, so we do the best we can, and come when it is time. Our preparations may be physical, mental, spiritual, social, or emotional. There may be costs involved to our finances or our time. We may need to acquire new wardrobes, prepare food, gather some supplies, or wrap gifts. We may need to regulate our emotions so that we can function. We may need to steel our minds or calm our nerves. We may need to take some time for prayer, confession, and fasting. And while we are doing our parts, whatever they happen to be, the hosts are doing theirs. And eventually, we will meet together for the events, in whatever states of readiness we each happen to be.

The Bible is full of extraordinary invitations, some for other people and some specifically for us. Some of these invitations were for thousands of years ago, while others are for today or for the future. Some involve a time of preparation, and some are for us to act upon right now. As we examine these biblical invitations, we will discover that these are no ordinary invitations. God gave invitations that no one else could. The most extraordinary is the one to join our lives with His. Hopefully, we do not casually toss this invitation onto the desk with a halfhearted intent to come back to it later. And hopefully, we do not choose to ignore or discard it altogether.

I once hosted a tea party, mailing out elegantly-styled invitations with my home telephone number listed for the RSVP information. Of the nineteen invitations that were sent out, none of the invitees personally replied to me as I had requested. My telephone never rang. My ears never heard the words of acceptance or declination. The etiquette of a personal reply was lost. I wondered why things were unfolding in this manner. Apparently, I was not current on the RSVP methods of the day. Eventually, some of the invitees sent word to me via my daughter, either verbally or through social media; however, others did not even reply to her by the requested date. Finally, I had to attempt to connect with the unresponsive invitees so that adequate preparations could be made. After all of this, even after making multiple requests by voicemail and social media, some invitees still did not reply. I had prepared a feast, but it was turned down, ignored, and left waiting by the absentees. I learned afterward that some of them had excuses for why they did not attend: they were working, socializing, had the date wrong, and had never arranged for transportation to get to the venue. Other issues besides communication surfaced, as well. For example, some arrived at my home unprepared because they had not readied themselves per the instructions the event required. Things sure did not turn out as I had envisioned.

Initially, it was an upsetting situation. I had to decide if I was going to be offended that no replies were given to me and that the event went unattended by several people. I had gone to a great deal of work and made many sacrifices to do something nice for the invitees, but perhaps they just did not understand that or even care. I tried to be understanding of the situation, but this fact remains: those who did not attend definitely missed out on a grand event. Their chairs at the feast sat empty. Their portions went to waste. Their right to be there went unheeded. And most importantly, I missed their company.

If we look at this event through the eyes of a spiritual analogy, it would be like those of us who have chosen not to respond to the invitation to become God's children through the sacrifice of Jesus Christ. God has offered us the gift of eternal life in heaven, and a feast will be prepared for those who RSVP (see Matt. 22; Rev. 19). He has gone to a great deal of work and sacrificed much for us. And now, He is awaiting our response. He is willing to prepare a place for us all. Sadly, however, many of us will choose to be no-shows.

Many people are searching for another way to heaven besides Jesus. They are trying to alter the requirements for fulfilling the invitation. They want to enter on their own terms and in their own timing. They want a different dress code or a different response method. These who are trying to respond through improper channels or alternate methods will never be allowed entrance by the Host, though. And there are others who will experience this same outcome. These are the ones who are not making any effort at all to respond during this preparatory period. They will end up missing out on the opportunity and timing of it all.

We often flutter and race through life. We are caught up in our responsibilities, distractions, and selfish desires, and we take no thought for God or the consequences to ourselves. We do not closely pay attention to when we need to be ready, and so we end up being late. We then miss out on some of the benefits. And if we do not attend at all, we miss out on everything—the benefits of the event and the host Himself. What must God feel after all He has gone through for us? When He sees that everything He has offered to us gathers no response, or worse yet, is intentionally declined? He will miss the company of those who do not attend, but heaven's eternity will have to continue on without them.

There are no second chances. Once an event is over, it is over. My tea party was for two hours on one specified date. Excuses could not cover what had been done or left undone. I chose to offer grace and forgiveness to the absentees, but that day can never be redone. I am sad regarding what they missed that day in the realm of a good time and good food, but more than that, I am sad that I missed out on the pleasure of their company and giving them my best. Invitations are of greater consequence, though, in regard to God. He is preparing a feast and calling for everyone to attend. When everything is ready, He will call those who have responded favorably to come to the table. At this point, there will be no more opportunity for anyone else to choose to attend the feast. Once the door is closed, it is permanently closed. There is no "next time," nor can time be turned back. The event will only take place one time, and sadly, there are going to be some empty chairs at the feast. People are going to miss out on God's best. Please do not let your chair be empty. Experience the extraordinary. Experience eternal life.

CHAPTER 3

Great Expectations

COME TO RECEIVE

The word *come* is used frequently in language. If you were to do a word search and browse for book titles containing that word, you would find many. We also use *come* in many common phrases, such as "kingdom come," "come winter," and "come what may." All of these portray an expectation for the future. Our key passage for this book will be Matthew 11:28–30 where Jesus says, "Come unto me, all ye that labour and are heavy laden, and I will give you rest. Take my yoke upon you, and learn of me; for I am meek and lowly in heart: and ye shall find rest unto your souls. For my yoke is easy, and my burden is light." These verses indicate an expectation for the future: there will be rest for us after we have learned to wear the yoke of Jesus.

In the Greek language, *come*, as it is used in Matthew 11:28, means to "come hither!"[1] The exclamation point following these words indicates insistence, as when one is giving a command. There is also an invitation given in these words because there is the option to respond to or ignore the words. If the purpose and motive behind the words are unknown, the character of Jesus might be examined in order to determine if it is safe for the hearers to respond. Upon examination of His words, we see that safety is indicated, as is His character. He is wanting to give, and He is wanting to bless. When Jesus spoke the words "Come unto me," He was calling those who were in a state of weariness to come to Him for rest. He wanted to restore their souls. He had an expectation for the future: He wanted people to come and learn of Him and simultaneously have their burdens lightened and their expectations of rest met. Jesus had an expectation of what was to be done, but the hearers were allowed to exercise free will. The future remained to be seen.

WHAT'S IN A COMMAND?

Why are commands given as opposed to invitations? In researching the similarities and differences between the words *invite* and *command*, I found that a command has aspects of an invitation within it, but an invitation does not have aspects of a command within it. To *invite* is to "ask to do something socially"[2] without requiring that it be done. To *command* is to give a "directive" or "instruction"[3] with the expectation that it will be accomplished. In commands, we can see implied invitations, as there is a request to take action, but there is also an expected response: compliance. The purpose of issuing a command is to accomplish a goal that is within the commander's will. Commands are directions that are given authoritatively and are not typically viewed as warm and personal. Demands and domination can be a part of commands. Although both commands and invitations can be refused, a refusal is not expected or desired when a command is given.

Do people most often respond favorably to a command or to a request? When we hear someone say the words "Come here," what feelings stir within us? The answer seems to depend on the different tones that lie beneath the message, both in speech and in character. Even though this phrase seems to most frequently indicate a command rather than an invitation, depending on the tone of the delivery, the words may seem either harsh or inviting. The inflection in the voice can make the difference between feeling warmly invited or sternly commanded. At times, the words may be spoken with a tone of annoyance or a demand of compliance, tacking the word *now* onto the end as understood. At other times, though, the words might be spoken lovingly or excitedly as an invitation to share a moment with the one speaking the words. To give an example, the words can be said with the tone of "Come here, sweetie," or they can be said with the tone of "Come here, you naughty child!" Imagine a hand beckoning gently or a finger urgently pointing at the ground as the voice commands, "Come!" Is the speaker urging relationship or urging compliance, causing fear and resistance to stir within the listener's heart or peace? Thus, the attitude of the one speaking will convey the intent of either a command or an invitation.

And the types of responses from the listeners will be based upon what they hear.

It seems, attitudinally, that we are most likely to respond favorably to requests rather than commands. Why is this true? One reason is that being commanded affects our feelings. Our human natures frequently bristle at being told what to do. We would much rather do our own things and follow our own wills. We might comply because we have to do so, but inside, our hearts and minds resist. Regardless of our ultimate responses to a command and the commander, we do not like the fact that there is an air of authority over us and an expectation that we give a particular response in a particular time frame. Other reasons we might respond less favorably to commands rather than requests are because of the motives behind the commands and who is going to benefit from the commands being obeyed. Sometimes, commands are given to benefit the commanders and at other times to benefit the ones being commanded. So, when commands do not benefit us and our selfish natures, why would we want to follow them?

Some commands are given with underlying motives of cruelty, selfishness, and manipulation. The commander desires to exercise authority and maintain control over the one being commanded. Matthew 23 tells of an admonition by Jesus not to follow the evil examples of the scribes and Pharisees. They were being hypocritical because they were not doing the very things they were bidding the people to do. Jesus said, "For they bind heavy burdens and grievous to be borne, and lay them on men's shoulders; but they themselves will not move them with one of their fingers" (v. 4). Commands can definitely be unpleasant things that result in negative responses or no responses at all. When the expectations are not great, neither are the responses.

Some commands do not seem like good ideas to obey. Some scare us, and some seem impossible to heed. Goliath gave such a command to the Israelites when he called for a man to come and fight with him. He taunted the Israelites and defied the living God by saying, "Come to me, and I will give your flesh to the birds of the air and the beasts of the field!" (1 Sam. 17:44 NKJV). From a human perspective, this did not appear to be a good invitation to respond to—until it was realized that it invited God's power to come down. David knew that God was on his side, so he RSVP'd to Goliath that he was coming "in the name of the LORD of hosts, the God of the armies of Israel" (1 Sam. 17:45 NKJV). When David invited God's presence into the situation, God brought victory to His people. At times, God's children are going to be invited to do difficult things, but if He is issuing the command, then He is in the situation, and there is no need to fear. He is always present with His children and will help them to obtain victory, peace, and rest. He can give supernatural ability, amazing strength, unbelievable courage, the words to speak, and the faith to act. And when He does, giants fall.

Although both commands and commanders can be negative, and thus the responses to them be negative, this scenario does not apply in all cases. There are both positive commands and positive commanders. Positive commanders give commands that keep the best interests of the other in mind rather than self-interests. Examples of such commands would be those that are given in order to save someone's life or to express urgency in a precarious situation. I remember hearing a debate on television many years ago about whether parents should tell their children no. Some of the experts were saying that a child should never be told no. I recall a man responding to this advice by saying that if his child was going to touch a hot stove or run out into traffic, then he was going to tell him no. These would be circumstances in which commands would be to the recipient's benefit and the commander would have pure and selfless motives. Other examples would be when we are told to silence our cell phones during performances (because it teaches courtesy for the ones who are presenting) and when we are told to keep laws that benefit ourselves (e.g., speed limits keep us safe) and our society (e.g., speed limits protect both the lives and property of others). Positive responses can safely take place when commanders and motives are honorable.

God's commands should elicit positive responses from us because they are issued with the purpose of benefiting those who will heed and obey them. First John 5:3 (NKJV) says, "For this is the love of God, that we keep His commandments. And His commandments are not burdensome." God's love is not pharisaical. He is not issuing self-serving commands, nor is He issuing commands just for the sake of being authoritative. The things of God are not joyless and burdensome, and they are not intended to make our hearts heavy and loveless. On the contrary, we can joyfully obey God's commands with love in *our* hearts, knowing He issued the commands with love from *His* heart.

Because God gives us free will, we can choose to respond to His commands as though they are invitations rather than commands. This is not advisable, but it is possible. The best thing, however, is not to be flippant or callous upon hearing God's words or remain unfazed by them. His commands are instructions of things to be done for a purpose. He is not trying to kill our joy or limit our freedom; He is doing just the opposite. His underlying intent is for us to be blessed through right relationships with both Him and others. His commandments are all about love.

Exodus 24:12 says, "And the LORD said unto Moses, 'Come up to me.'" Moses obeyed this command and went up to Mount Sinai to receive the Ten Commandments from God's hand. If he had not followed this command, can you imagine the mayhem that would exist in the world today? People would have made a greater mess of things than they already have and likely would have destroyed the earth and one another by now. With these commands of God holding us to a particular standard and to prescribed methods of behavior, we find that things are better in the world than they ever would be without their existence. The commands were not given so that God could domineer over us and dictate our lives, but so that our lives could be peaceful and fulfilling, without damage to ourselves and others. And ultimately, He wants us to know Him, without anything standing between the two of us. His motives are pure and His character is honorable.

In Lamentations 3:31–58, we see in God's character that He is compassionate and not willing to afflict or grieve people, nor does He approve of subverting their cause. When He tells us to turn away from our sin and turn to Him, it is only for our benefit, so that He can forgive and pardon us and bring restoration to our lives. As it says in Isaiah 44:22 (NKJV), "Return to Me, for I have redeemed you." Following the commands of God will identify us as His people, the people who have chosen His one and only Son.

When we understand God's love and the reasoning behind His

commands, it will not be difficult to do as He has asked. But even when we do not understand, we can still unreservedly keep His commands because He is someone who is trustworthy and has pure motives. In Psalm 111:7–10, we find words about God's character and the benefits of keeping His commandments: "The works of his hands are verity and judgment; all his commands are sure. They stand fast for ever and ever, and are done in truth and uprightness. He sent redemption unto his people: he hath commanded his covenant for ever: holy and reverend is his name. The fear of the LORD is the beginning of wisdom: a good understanding have all they that do his commandments: his praise endureth for ever." I think these are some pretty good reasons to support the keeping of His commandments.

Jesus, like His Father, issued commands, all with the purpose of benefiting those who would heed and obey them. And there was not only benefit to others, but *great* benefit. He invited people to life, healing, change, and freedom. We can identify additional benefits from Matthew 11:28–29. Jesus told people, "Come unto me, all ye that labour and are heavy laden, and I will give you rest" (v. 28). The compliance with this command results in rest. Jesus also said, "Take my yoke upon you, and learn of me; for I am meek and lowly in heart: and ye shall find rest unto your souls" (v. 29). The compliance with these commands to take up His yoke and to learn of Him results in knowledge of Jesus and rest for our souls. He cares deeply for us. So much, in fact, that He died for us.

Here is a brief list of some of Jesus's other amazing commandments that also held within them an invitation to respond:

- He commanded the widow's dead son to return to life by saying, "Young man, I say to you, arise" (Luke 7:14 NKJV).
- He commanded Lazarus to be resurrected from the dead by saying, "Lazarus, come forth" (John 11:43).
- He commanded His disciples by saying, "Rise, let us be going" (Matt. 26:46), and they were able to continue in His company as He lived His last few hours on earth.

- He commanded a demon by saying, "Be quiet, and come out of him!" (Luke 4:35 NKJV), and a man was healed from demon possession.
- He directed people to "ask" and things would be given to them, to "seek" and they would find, and to "knock" and it would be opened to them (see Matt. 7:7).

Think of the tragedy and negative consequences that would have occurred had compliance with these commands been refused. Death, demon possession, and emptiness would have remained for the disobedient. These states would have then affected the people around them and created additional problems, such as grieving, lost relationships, loneliness, brokenness, and more. Thus, Jesus's commands affect not only the doers of the words but also those who are impacted by what is done. A prime example of this is Jesus's Great Commission. He instructed His followers with these words: "Go into all the world and preach the gospel to every creature" (Mark 16:15 NKJV). This command was not selfishly given so that He could boss us around and control our lives, but so that all people might know of His love and His desire to have a personal relationship with each one of them. How tragic it will be for others if we choose to ignore this commandment. We need to give people something to hope for, something great to expect. We need to give them Jesus and His love.

There are other commands in the Bible that can inspire and encourage us. First Corinthians 15:58 (NKJV) says, "Therefore, my beloved brethren, be steadfast, immovable, always abounding in the work of the Lord, knowing that your labor is not in vain in the Lord." As we are steadfast, immovable, and abounding in the work of the Lord, we will have the benefit of knowing that it is not for naught! Heeding His commands is profitable for us. Come expecting life, peace, healing, change, and freedom when you follow them.

Are we waiting in expectation of hearing a command? Are we always at the ready, listening for God's voice? Do we hear the commands that He has already issued to us in the Bible? Our obedient responses to these commands will affect our lives and the lives of others for the better, and they will also open us up to hear even more instruction from God. Important examples of obedience can be seen in the responses of the twelve disciples as Jesus called them to follow Him (Mark 3:13-19). He called; they responded favorably. And then they changed the world for Christ. If these twelve had disobeyed the call, our world would be quite different from what it is today. The cause of Christ would not have been advanced in the same manner. We would not have the life stories and examples of these twelve to learn and grow from, to follow, or to improve upon. What they did all those years ago still affects people today. Each life matters, and the action each person takes affects others either positively or negatively. Coming to follow Jesus will affect the legacy that we leave in this world.

WHY THE INVITATIONS?

Why are invitations given? There are many events to call people to attend, and there may be just as many motives behind the distribution of an invitation. Some of these motives are to manipulate, impress, share, bless, fellowship, fulfill an obligation, and continue a tradition. Although there are various reasons to give invitations, some things hold true in the distribution process. Typically, invitations are not given to all people but rather are addressed to a select person or group. The one giving the invitation is expecting a certain audience to attend.

Think back to your school days when party invitations were distributed. What effect did the receipt of an invitation have on those who received one and on those who did not? Was there ever a time when everyone but you received an invitation to the birthday party? Did this exclusion result in a huge blow to your self-esteem and cause you to deem yourself unworthy and unlikable? We are talking Charlie Brown standing there with no invitation while the others are gloating and making cruel comments about his exclusion. Can you relate? Or were you one of the privileged ones who did receive an invitation? Did you fret until an invitation was actually placed in your hand? Did you then proceed to gloat in front of those who did not receive an invitation, or were you simply relieved and thankful to have received one, and thus, humbly remained quiet? Did your spirit and esteem lift because someone thought you worthy or valuable enough to attend the party? Whether the results were this extreme in our childhoods or not, didn't we feel differently when we were invited as opposed to being left out and uninvited?

An invitation can carry quite an impact. The experience of not receiving an invitation can prove to be devastating, so much so that when my children were in elementary school in the early 2000s, it became a requirement that if invitations were going to be passed out at school, the entire class had to receive one. No one was permitted to be excluded. What was the purpose behind such a rule? There is power held by the presenter of an invitation, and there is power passed on to the recipient as well, but when there is no receipt of an invitation, a feeling of powerlessness results. This impact can be felt for years.

At times, we think we may be able to identify the motive behind an invitation, and so we rush to conclusions and judgments, especially when we are left uninvited. At other times, we are left puzzled and do not understand why we actually received an invitation. We are left to wonder if perhaps there was some mistake and we should not have received it. Things like this happen. I know. I handed out the wrong birthday card to someone once because she shared the same name as the intended recipient and their birthdays were close to one another. Oops. How would you like to have to say "Sorry, that is for the other Karen" as you ask for the card to be returned to you? I think I saw something similar in a Charlie Brown episode!

Were you ever the "new kid" at school? I was. I grew up in a military family and attended eight different schools before graduation. It was difficult moving to small towns where nearly everyone had been attending school together for their entire lives, and it seemed that the majority of the students were related to one another. This accounted for not being invited to some events because I was the outsider. Some people befriended me, but the friendships only ran so deep; when they had to make a choice between me and the old crowd, I was left standing alone and uninvited. Moving to a large city was also difficult. In this case, there were more people, and thus, more events. With more people came more cliques, and thus, more groups excluding me. But a wonderful thing happened in this large city: I became part of a church youth group. One of the girls threw a surprise party for me on my fifteenth birthday. The motive was to bless me, and bless me it did. I was unaware of the invitation because it was a surprise; nevertheless, it was there, buried under normal reasons to get me to go to my friend's house where the party was waiting. Will it surprise you to know that God has given *you* an invitation? It's true. He has. And it is not a mistake. You will never have to stand alone again.

When Jesus spoke the words "Come unto me" (Matt. 11:28), He was speaking to all people who labored and were heavy laden. These people carried the burden of sin and also the physical burdens of things like illness, poverty, rejection, rule-keeping, and oppression. Think about some of the different types of people that God called into His service or the different types of people Jesus interacted with during His years on earth. Some of these people were currently, or would later be, murderers, prostitutes, betrayers, persecutors of Christians, poor, and of no reputation. Yet, in spite of this, He called them all—because He loved them all. He does the same thing now; He calls us all because He loves us all. Will we be among the people that respond to Him, or will we walk away? Will we turn our backs to Him and close our ears? Will we busy ourselves with distractions so that we cannot hear His still, small voice whispering in the depths of our souls? Or will we come to Him to learn of Him, have our loads lightened, and gain rest for our souls? This is an extraordinary invitation that can cause us to expect great things because it is from someone who commands and invites with love.

There is no one else who can issue an invitation like this and no one else who can give the things that God can give. If others call us to come to them, their motives may not be pure. If others call us to come and work alongside them, they are likely not expecting to bear the heavy part of the load but are instead looking to divide their load in half. They get half and we get half—our load is not lighter than theirs, but their load is made lighter by us. The relationship is not wholly to our benefit, nor can we receive complete rest from this situation. With Jesus, however, things are different, *much* different. He wants to teach us, help us, and show us how things can be done better and easier. Why then wouldn't we want to take advantage of the help and instruction that He offers to us, and ultimately, the rest? Because sometimes we act like children.

There are times when we make our burdens into bigger issues than they have to be. We turn things into a drama, or we turn ourselves into drama kings and queens. Think about teaching children to clean up their toys. Do they usually want to do this when they are told to do it or even when they are invited to do it? Not very frequently, as far as I can tell. To them it seems like a nearly impossible task. But is it really all that difficult? We call them to us, and we help them in various ways as they go about completing the task. We teach them how to do it, speaking words of encouragement along the way, and occasionally even pitch in and put a few toys in the toy boxes ourselves. We have not asked them to clean up their toys in order to be unkind to them, we are just attempting to teach them responsibility. During this process, we have eased their burden and equipped them for handling their burden in the future. In spite of all this, they may throw a tantrum worthy of an Oscar, exclaiming that it is unfair. However, we know the underlying purpose, and with our guidance behind them, the chore actually turns out to be trivial.

Sometimes, however, the problem is not a refusal to comply; it is a refusal to accept help. Children may complete the tasks that they are given but stubbornly refuse help or instruction during the various stages of the completion process, even when things go awry. They insist on complete independence. Once again, we adults act like children when we try to shoulder most or all of our burdens in life and do not allow Jesus to help us with them. We work at things inefficiently and even take on additional burdens that are not meant for us to bear. We try to live life all on our own, playing the martyrs and refusing help from anyone, even Him. Jesus knows the purpose behind all things, has the techniques to deal with all things, and has the solution to every problem, yet we shun His involvement in our situations.

We commonly suffer in silence, although our suffering may be anything but common. Why won't we let Him help us? Perhaps we suffer like this because this is how we have been taught to suffer. Blatant messages and subtle implications surround us, telling us this is how things are to be done. We have been taught through words and experiences that we just have to pretend things do not bother us and move on. This is an incorrect line of thinking, yet this is so often what our minds follow, with our behaviors right behind them. But we can disregard all of this nonsense and examine the truth: we do not have to live like this! We *do not* have to bear our own burdens. We *do not* have to bear them in silence. We *do not* have to manufacture and carry our own faith to get through life. We can pray and ask for help and comfort. We can ask Him to give us faith or to increase the faith that we already have (Luke 17:5), even if it is as small as a mustard seed. Faith will come by hearing Him and heeding what He says (Rom. 10:17). Help will come by asking for it. Jesus offers to bear our burdens Himself! We can expect great things. We can expect great help.

We are old enough to choose wisely now, but do we always? Unfortunately, the answer is no. We have knowledge, skills, and maturity, yet our selfishness and self-protection remain, even to our own detriment. But we can learn to change, just as children can learn to make wise choices as they age. They can learn that their affirmative or negative responses will affect the outcomes of their days. They can learn to make good choices even when those around them are making poor choices. Maybe we should be mature like children and make wise choices! We *can* learn, just as they have.

Sometimes, we might hang our heads in shame, trudge our feet reluctantly, or come without wholehearted abandon. Days of pain will elicit a fight or flight response, and some days it will be both that happen. We will fail. We will falter. We will run away. We will fall. He knows all of these things about us. He knows our frame, and He remembers that we are dust (Ps. 103:14). His answer to our problems and our human condition is to give us His mercies, new every morning. He will always be there with His arms wide open, prepared to welcome us home, welcome us in, and enfold us with His love. Whatever our states of being or states of mind are, He calls out to us nonetheless. He wants us to come.

God only gives good things and perfect gifts, so there does not need to be any hesitation in coming to Him. We are told that when we come before the throne of grace, we will find mercy and grace to help us in our time of need (Heb. 4:16). Thus, when we hear the words of Jesus inviting us, we can come with expectation and hope. The words of Matthew 11:29 tell us that we will find rest for our souls. We do not have far to travel to get to Him since He is near to all those who call upon Him (Ps. 145:18).

God has invited us to great things—the ultimate invitation being to salvation through Jesus. This is an invitation to come and know Him and come and spend eternity with Him in heaven. Jesus Himself was the invitation. God sent Him to the world for whoever would believe in Him (see John 3:16). This invitation is an exception to the common rule of picking and choosing some people while excluding others. His invitation is open to all people, to whosoever will come. He said, "And I, if I am lifted up from the earth, will draw all *peoples* to Myself" (John 12:32 NKJV). It does not say that you will be drawn if you belong to a specific group, not just if you are a man or a woman, not just if you are a Jew or a Greek, not just if you are bond or free. God shows no favoritism (Acts 10:34). He wants all people to come to the knowledge of the truth and spend eternity with Him in heaven (1 Tim. 2:4). He does not wish to exclude us from His plans and His ultimate celebration.

In God's eyes, no one is any more valuable than another. We never have to worry about whether He wants us or not—we can rest assured that He does. He has proven this to us through His words and His actions—through His life, death, and resurrection. Christ died once, *for all* (Rom. 5; Heb. 2). If we RSVP, we are guaranteed to get into heaven. We will not be turned away because He does not turn away anyone who comes to Him (John 6:37). His intent is to bless us, and blessed we will be, *if* we respond favorably to His invitation. God is expecting us, but we have to let Him know that we want to come. Come expecting great things. Come expecting eternal life.

CHAPTER 4

Elemental Invitations

God gives us elemental invitations that metamorphosize into grand and glorious events. His power is incomparable. Every need that we have can be supplied by His hand, and He has invited us there to receive what we need. And beyond just meeting our needs for life, He has invited us to receive life itself. He sustains us with food, water, and rest in our human bodies, but more importantly, in our souls. Nothing is too trivial for Him, and nothing is too difficult for Him. He is all-encompassing, and He is available *to us*. He is the bread of life, the living water, and the source of peace, rest, and life itself.

People who lived during Bible times received invitations of various sorts that arrived through various methods, some ordinary and some extraordinary. When we examine their lives, we can see the hand of God at work. We can see how they were going about their daily business of living life and how God entered into their worlds with His supernatural power. They were given opportunities to respond, either positively or negatively. At times, they chose well, and at other times, they did not. Sometimes, the results of their positive responses came quickly and surely, but other times, they had to continue on in faith, waiting for the fruition (see Heb. 11). They were like us, and we can learn from their experiences and the examples they set.

THE CALL TO THE DEAD

Lazarus was not doing anything when his invitation arrived. He was getting nowhere in life. Actually, He was *dead*! But despite that he no longer lived and breathed, he received an invitation. This was a most extraordinary invitation, and it did not come in the mail! It was personally delivered by Jesus Himself.

John 11:1–44 gives the account. Jesus had been preaching in another town when word arrived that His good friend Lazarus was ill. Jesus did not immediately depart for the city of Bethany in order to heal Lazarus; instead, He remained where He was for two more days, finishing up what He was there to do. When it was in God's timing, and after the work had been completed in the place where Jesus was, He then traveled to see Lazarus.

When Jesus arrived in Bethany, He was greeted with criticism and the accusation that He was arriving too late because Lazarus had already been dead for *four* days! Count them—four. Four days of being dead. Four days that passed while Jesus worked and traveled somewhere else. But Jesus did not allow this unwelcoming reception to stop Him from delivering His invitation to Lazarus. He went to the tomb where Lazarus was buried, told people to move the stone away from the mouth of the tomb, and then proceeded with His commanding voice to issue an invitation for Lazarus to live again. Jesus cried out, "Lazarus, come forth" (v. 43), and Lazarus came out of the tomb. Here we get a really good look at what Lazarus was doing in life. He was dead in a tomb, sealed behind a stone, and bound in graveclothes. But extraordinary things happened when Jesus showed up on the scene. First of all, an invitation was given to a dead person. Second, God's resurrection power was seen. Third, a dead man got back to living his life. If this does not prompt us to come when God calls, I do not know what will!

God extends the same invitation to us that He extended to Lazarus. God is calling us to come out from death unto life—from spiritual death unto spiritual life. This is eternal life: to know Jesus Christ (John 17:3). No matter what stones are trapping us in life, no matter what we are wrapped up in and tied up in, no matter what stench we are covered with, no matter what cold darkness we are surrounded by, no matter how alone and laid out flat we are, no matter what others say about us, no matter how hopeless things look—even if it appears that our best days are behind us—He wants to free us from spiritual bondage and restore us to life and relationships. He wants us to be healthy and vibrant again, breathing and glowing, being and doing, loving and being loved. He wants us to *live*! He has placed the breath of physical life into us, but He also calls us to live with the breath of the Holy Spirit.

But does it ever seem to us, instead, like God is far away—in some other city or some other universe? Does it seem that He is ignoring both our pleas and the pleas of those who are telling Him we need help? Are we surrounded by people who are lamenting our situations? Do we have people in our lives who are like Mary and Martha, who accuse God of letting us suffer? Do they believe that if He was truly in our lives, things like this would not be happening to us? At one point, my son questioned why he should continue to pray for me when God was not giving me physical healing. Several people who are saddened by my chronic illnesses tell me that these illnesses should not be a part of my life. What do all of us honestly think and feel?

Does it seem like God is taking His time in getting to where we are and responding to our needs? Has it been more than four days—a lot more? Are we wondering whether He will ever come? Do we fear that He is too busy taking care of other things in other places to have any time for us? Do we think it is already too late and that the situation has passed beyond His power to help? Have we resigned ourselves to permanently live in our current states? Have we given up the fight? Have we stopped asking for help? Have we almost ceased to breathe? I have news for us— *good* news. We can change, although our circumstances remain the same. We can have a full and joyfully abundant life now—despite the pain— because Jesus came to give us that abundant life. It seems improbable, impractical, and impossible, yet it is true. But we have to make the choice to come out of the tomb and get out of those graveclothes. We have to come forth from the unpleasantness. We have to respond to His call to leave behind the things He wants us to leave behind, and *live*.

Job was not physically dead, but life as he knew it and the dreams that he'd had, they were dead. He wondered when all of his suffering would come to an end. He even wondered if his life itself might perhaps come to an end (see Job 7:3–10). He went through so many trials, losses, and pains that our minds can barely fathom how much he suffered. His life circumstances are not ones we would willingly choose; he did not choose them either. This man was in the throes of suffering, yet he did not forsake God; instead, he spoke to God, and God spoke to him. He recognized that it is God who has the strength (Job 9:19). After some time passed and some serious conversation with God took place, Job was then blessed beyond what he had been originally. His latter circumstances are ones that we would not mind experiencing. This man walked and talked with God and was richly blessed for it. He was a man who received another opportunity to live, with abundant life and abundant joy. Miracles are possible!

Our lives can appear dead to both ourselves and to others. There may be people missing the life they once saw in us. A few years ago, a woman said to me that she missed "the old Francee" (the person I was fifteen years prior to the start of my health problems). People may mourn because of our circumstances and the death of who we used to be, but I can guarantee that when Jesus raises us up out of this (in whatever way He chooses to do so, whether it is through healing, restoration, overcoming, endurance, strengthening, a changed perspective, grace to accept it, or some other method), we will be new, improved, different, and vibrant; and people are going to see a miracle! I am living proof! I am not yet physically healed, but people have seen miracles come from my life anyway. God is on the scene!

God is at work in the lives and circumstances of His children even when we do not see it, even when the darkness of the tomb envelops us. Even when we do not see His handiwork or feel His presence, He is there. Nothing is too difficult for Him. Nothing is impossible for Him. He can breathe new life into us and into our circumstances. We need to take some time to look around and see what God is doing in our areas of difficulty. Psalm 66:9 tells us that God holds our souls in life and does not suffer our feet to be moved. We do not have to be removed from the circumstances in order to endure or have hope; He will be our anchor right where we are. We are told to cast all of our cares upon Him because He cares for us (1 Pet. 5:7). He hears, He sees, and His divine purposes are continuing to be worked even as these circumstances swirl and linger around us. Psalm 69:15–18 says, "Let not the waterflood overflow me, neither let the deep swallow me up, and let not the pit shut her mouth upon me. Hear me, O

LORD; for thy loving-kindness is good: turn unto me according to the multitude of thy tender mercies. And hide not thy face from thy servant; for I am in trouble: hear me speedily. Draw nigh unto my soul, and redeem it: deliver me because of mine enemies." God will give us the strength to live and also endure whatever we encounter while we do. Nothing is dead when God gives it life.

There is freedom when we are unbound from the graveclothes. There is new breath breathed into us when we allow the breath of God's Holy Spirit to fill our spirits. His light illumines our paths. The wonderful music of His voice joins us and guides us on our journeys. There are beautiful things to open our eyes to in this world: His creation, His people, and His purposes. The newness He brings is like the fragrance after the rain, fresh and clean. Our hearts can begin to beat again and be filled with passion for the lives He has called us to live. Instead of tasting the bitterness of life, which to us seems like death, we can "taste and see that the LORD is good" (Ps. 34:8). Our vision will become clear when we see with His eyes. We will see that life is not over just because we are suffering and feel dead; we will see that we have not yet begun to live.

What is it like when people come back to physical life? In testimonies of near-death experiences, we often hear that people's perspectives are changed and that they value their lives more afterward. They realize that they have been given a second chance at physical life. When God brings us to spiritual life, we are being given a second chance as well. We are called to new life—abundant life. We have the opportunity to value life more than we did previously. We will receive forgiveness and a chance to start life again, without our pasts being held against us. We will have the opportunity to live holy lives this time around. We will have the opportunity to begin anew, redo some things, change our lifestyles, and mend our ways. This is not reincarnation, instead it is God incarnate, dwelling in us in the form of the Holy Spirit. Once we allow the presence of God to fill us, we will no longer be who we previously were.

Today is a new day, and we can live in a new way. God can help us to build new lives; we just need to come forth to receive help from His hand. We will not necessarily have our circumstances remedied or changed, nor do we need to; He can revive us in the midst of them and use them for our greater good. He can work all things according to His greater purpose and glory so that even the ugliest of things will produce tremendous beauty and magnificently display His power. Second Corinthians 12:10 tells us that we are strong in our weaknesses because God is strong through us. We can be active and live powerfully, even during our days of waiting for the graveclothes to be loosed. We can spend our days alive rather than dead. We can pray, hope, love, and persevere. Remember, too, that things can be accomplished even after delays, and sometimes the delays are exactly what are needed. And even if situations end in the opposite way of what we were hoping for and wanting, we can praise God anyway, because He is worthy to be praised at all times and in all circumstances. Regardless of the outcomes of the situations and His answers to them, we can come and be alive unto God. In Him, we can live and move and have our being (see Acts 17:28).

When we return to life, we will see that there are people who care about us and who need us in their lives to make a difference. They are people who prayed for us. They are people who have missed our presence. They are people we have yet to meet. When God moves in us, the wailing of their cries and the longing of their hearts will turn into cries of joy and longing for a similar move of God in their lives. We can put off the old man and put on the new because we are alive in God and His Spirit is alive in us (see 2 Cor. 5:17; Eph. 4:21–24). God can and will be glorified in our lives if we simply come to Him and let Him give us life! Come forth to receive it!

THE CALL TO THE HUNGRY

Jesus lived to do God's will and finish God's work, even saying that it was His meat to do it (John 4:34). To Him, it was as essential as His necessary food. And when it was time for Him to die on the cross, He gave His body as bread for the life of the world, that whoever eats of it will live forever (John 6:51, 58). He is as essential to us as our necessary food.

One particular day, Jesus taught a lesson for His followers. He knew where His disciples would be that morning and that they would have some needs. They had gone out looking for fish to feed hungry bodies, but

He went out looking for people in order to feed their hungry souls. The disciples had been out fishing all night and had caught nothing. Because Jesus cared for each part of the person, physical and spiritual needs alike, He told them to cast the net on the right side of the ship (John 21:6). They did as He commanded, and He then performed a miracle in response to their obedience: He gave them fish for their physical need. He then extended an invitation to them by saying, "Come and dine" (John 21:12). He met their physical need for food by cooking them breakfast, but there was an even deeper need that He met that day: their spiritual need. This particular time that they met on the shore was very significant. Jesus was showing Himself to them after His resurrection. Also, after breakfast, He called Peter into service for the kingdom, commanding him to feed His lambs and sheep (John 21:15–17). He also prepared Peter for the hardships to come and foretold his death. He then commanded Peter to follow Him. There would be people to spiritually feed from that point on, and Peter and the others had work to do. Jesus made provision for the spiritual hunger of all those He was leaving behind; we are among that number. He is ready and waiting to fill us.

Jesus told a parable about a king who made a marriage feast for his son (Matt. 22:1–14). When the host announced that everything was ready, the people who were invited chose not to accept the invitation to feast and celebrate. Some made light of it and went on their way, making excuses that they had somewhere else to be: some to their property and some to their possessions. Others harmed and killed the messengers who were delivering the invitations. As a result of the refusals, those who were bidden to the feast were found to be unworthy. They had not esteemed the feast or the host as important. Many were called, but few actually came to the table. Today, people give many excuses about why they do not come to Jesus: they claim that He is not real; they do not like His character; they do not believe they can be forgiven for the bad things they have done; they want to get cleaned up first; they do not want to change their lifestyles; they do not want to be disowned, persecuted, imprisoned, or killed for their faith; and the list goes on. We can come up with a seemingly endless number of excuses as to why we do not want to do something. And the truth is, there are just some other things that we would rather be doing instead of seizing the opportunities or fulfilling the obligations that stand before us.

As humans, we hunger for things—some that we actually need and others that we want. Sometimes, we do not even recognize what it is that we hunger for. We have physical needs that must be met, but we also have spiritual needs. Jesus said, "I am the bread of life. He who comes to Me shall never hunger" (John 6:35 NKJV). He taught His disciples to pray for their daily bread, and we can follow that same model of prayer (see Matt. 6:9–13). He wants to provide what we need, not only physically and materially, but also emotionally and spiritually, each day. He has exactly what our souls need, and these are the very things that we cannot find elsewhere.

Things are going to be really good for the saved once we arrive in heaven, but until that time comes, we can find goodness in the lives we live now. God gives us abundant lives by meeting our physical needs with necessary life provisions, but He also meets our spiritual needs day by day through His Word and the presence of His Spirit. He is able to provide for every need that we have now and for every need that we could ever possibly have in the future. He created everything, so He has everything at His disposal. He owns the cattle on a thousand hills, and every beast of the field is His (Ps. 50:10). He can supply all of our needs according to His riches in glory through Christ Jesus (Phil. 4:19). He can orchestrate miracles to take care of us just as He did for the people we read about in the Bible. For example, when the Israelites were wandering in the wilderness and were hungry and thirsty and their souls were fainting within them, they cried to the Lord, and He delivered them out of their distresses and led them forth by the right way. God is the same yesterday, today, and forever. If He could do it for them, then He can do it for us. Yes, He will satisfy our longing souls and fill our hungry souls with goodness (see Ps. 107:4–9).

Coming to God for our provision is an amazing thing and an amazing privilege. He meets emotional needs by providing us with relationships, with both Himself and with others. His people minister to us to meet our various needs, and He even uses unbelievers to do the same. He meets spiritual needs by sending His words to us in a multitude of forms (e.g., written, spoken, sung, dreamed). Anything that proceeds from His mouth is extraordinary—after all, it is *God* speaking! And what's more, He does not just send provisions and people and words to us, His very presence comes to abide with us! His Spirit testifies to our spirits that He is real. And what's more, He indwells us, teaches us, comforts us, and fills us.

Answering the call to come to Jesus is about more than satiating our hunger, gathering knowledge, passing time, or completing a to-do list; it is about building a relationship. The invitation to come and dine is not ultimately about food and drink for our physical bodies; it is about having our most basic spiritual needs met. He is alive—ready and waiting to commune with us as we seek Him through prayer, study, and worship. May we be able to say as Job did that we have not gone back from the commandment of God's lips, but we have esteemed the words of His mouth more than our necessary food (Job 23:12).

THE CALL TO THE THIRSTY

Have you ever been thirsty, truly thirsty and without life-sustaining water? Have you ever been spiritually thirsty and without life-sustaining water? I cannot answer the first question for you, but I can answer the second one. We all have the same answer to the second question. We have all been thirsty in a spiritual sense. What exactly does this mean? Humans all begin their existence in this state and have a need for the living water that God gives. Those who have not asked God to be a part of their lives have a spiritual thirst for this living water. People seek to satisfy their spiritual thirst in many ways, but it is God alone who can quench it. He has made provision all throughout history to do exactly that. Long ago, speaking through the prophet Isaiah, God voiced an invitation of provision for anyone who was thirsty to come (see Isa. 55:1). In more recent history, He sent Jesus directly to us to deliver the invitation and to take care of that thirst for us. This living water is eternal life and can only come from one source, the Source. Jesus said, "If any man thirst, let him come unto me, and drink" (John 7:37).

Jesus's invitation to drink is an invitation to salvation for all people.

Whoever is thirsty, and whoever wants to, can "take the water of life freely" (Rev. 22:17). This salvation is freely given through the gift of His grace. We do not, and indeed cannot, have anything to offer in exchange for it; it was already paid for by His blood. It costs us nothing because He paid everything for it by His death on the cross.

John 4:5–42 tells about a Samaritan woman at a well. This woman is an example of someone who was doubly thirsty. She was not just in need of water for her water pitcher, she was in need of water for her soul. By all appearances, she seemed to be thirsting for fulfillment in companionship, but because she was taking in the wrong things to satisfy her actual need (her spiritual thirst), she found herself parched by shame. At the well, everything changed for this woman, though, because it is there that she encountered Jesus.

It all started when Jesus asked her for a drink of water. This was not an ordinary encounter, and this was not an ordinary request. Jesus was speaking with a Samaritan, something that Jews did not do. He was speaking to a woman in public to whom He was not related, also something that Jews did not do. Furthermore, He was speaking to a woman who did not have a good reputation. I have heard some people say that they believe she was an outcast and was at the well during this particular time of day because of her sinful lifestyle. Yet, in spite of all these things, Jesus invited her to converse with Him. After she pointed out to Him that their two cultures did not mix and He was talking to a woman, He responded to her by talking about the gift of God and living water. She asked where He was able to get living water from since the well was deep and He had nothing with which to draw water. He replied that the water He possessed was not like the water in the well; His water was spiritual and it gave eternal life. She then asked Him for some living water. He told her to go and call her husband and come back to Him, but when she said that she had no husband, Jesus proceeded to tell her some things about herself that she had not revealed to Him (such as her current non-married living arrangement and exactly how many husbands she had already had). She started to suspect that something unusual was taking place and that Jesus was a spiritual person of some sort. The conversation turned to the topic of worship, and eventually, Jesus revealed to her that He was the Messiah.

After conversing for a time, the woman left Jesus, presumably to go and bring back her boyfriend to meet Him. Instead of immediately returning with this man, she extended an extraordinary invitation to the townspeople by saying, "Come, see a man, which told me all things that ever I did: is not this the Christ?" (v. 29). Physical thirst was trumped by spiritual thirst that day, and the water pitcher was left behind. As a result of this woman's invitation, many Samaritans came seeking what this woman had found and chose to quench their spiritual thirst as well.

From the Samaritan woman's viewpoint, Jesus's invitation could have been seen as a risky proposition. Would He still be there when she returned with her boyfriend, or was Jesus just playing a cruel trick on her? What sense did any of this make? Why had she just spoken with a Jew, a representative of the very ones who ostracized her? What was it about this man that caused her to react in such a way? This extraordinary invitation from Jesus was the reason for her behavior. This encounter resulted in a spiritual relationship being formed and a testimony of God's love for all people being displayed. Because of one person's actions and testimony, many Samaritans came to believe in Jesus the Messiah. People started their journeys when they heard a story about "some man" and eventually ended up believing in the best thing they had ever heard: the good news of Jesus.

Living water is like no other water, just as our spirits are like no other parts of us. Our physical bodies are capable of intaking water or any other number of fluids, but our spirits are made to be filled only with the spiritual things of God. Relationships cannot quench our spiritual thirst, nor can material things or physical pleasures. At times, however, believers wander after the things of the world, trying to quench their thirst. They eventually find themselves in the pigpen. And let me tell you, eating husks will make you thirsty. Yet even when we do these things to ourselves, Jesus still seeks us. Even in knowing everything about this Samaritan woman, Jesus did not condemn and avoid her. Although the people she lived among may have treated her poorly because of her sin, Jesus did not. He treated her with love. He gave her dignity, time, attention, and spiritual provision. This shows us that we can come to Him just as we are. We do not need to clean up first or cover up. Jesus seeks and saves the lost. He died to take away the sins of the world, including mine, including yours. His living water washes us clean and quenches the thirst we have in our spirits. Only He can satisfy us.

When the Israelites were wandering around homeless, God turned the wilderness into a pool of water and the dry ground into water springs (Ps. 107:33). He took care of the physical needs of His children, but He also did more: He took care of their spiritual needs by coming to dwell among them. Later in time, He sent Jesus to dwell among people and offer them living water. Jesus said that whoever would drink of the water that He would give them would "never thirst" and that the water would become a "well of water springing up into everlasting life" (John 4:14). Living water, that eternal life, is a gift of God. And once we drink it, we will never thirst again.

Just as this woman did, we can respond to the extraordinary invitation for living water, no matter what our reputations and circumstances happen to be. We can begin a relationship with Jesus by simply responding when He invites us. And He is inviting us at *this* moment. He wants to talk to us, answer our questions, and share His love with us and all those around us. He will bring about change. A vitality will well up within us. And because of His touch on our lives, new people will emerge. We can then extend His invitation to others by sharing what it is that He gives us and sharing what He does in our lives. We can cause people to thirst after what they see in us, and our testimonies can draw them to Him for salvation. We just need to come, and then tell others to come.

As we continue on through life, we need to remember to keep drawing from the well of salvation, to keep coming back to Jesus to have our spirits refreshed. We need this reminder because sometimes we will become thirsty and parched. As our lives demand more of us than we can give, we often give less of ourselves to Jesus for rehydration. At times, we go through wilderness or desert experiences and just feel dry. We feel burned-out and stretched thin. Our spirits feel empty and devoid of life. We lack refreshment in our souls. We may begin to wonder why we do not feel God's presence and why we hear nothing but deafening silence. We can feel ourselves shriveling, the life and joy draining from us by the second. It is at these times that we need to lower our water pitchers and submerge them in the well of salvation. We need to tell our forgetful brains and doubtful hearts that a well of life lives within us that has been buried under the accumulating dust of life. We need to ask God to restore the joy of His salvation to us (see Ps. 51:12), flood us with His presence, and pour His strength into us. He can enable us to joyfully draw water out of the wells of salvation (see Isa. 12:3). We will be able to say, "Behold, God is my salvation; I will trust, and not be afraid: for the LORD JEHOVAH is my strength and my song; he also is become my salvation" (Isa. 12:2). Drink deep and long at the well of the remembrance of Him, and then remember to tell others.

THE CALL TO THE WEARY

Have you found yourself nearing the end of your energy supply? Are you past that point and already running on empty? Forget the running; are you dragging yourself through, day after day after day? Do you want the world to stop so you can get off it for a while? Do you wish it would all just end? Are you consumed by bitterness? Are you tottering on the edge of a nervous breakdown? Are you feeling joyless and unfulfilled and wondering if there is something wrong with you? Are you wanting to go away somewhere where no one knows who you are? Are you wishing to go to a different church where you can sit and be fed and truly worship rather than run helter-skelter, taking care of everyone else's needs but your own? Are you wishing you could just start over? Are you wishing you could reinvent yourself? Are you regretting that you ever said yes to this or that? I have had every single one of these thoughts and many more.

Sometimes we find that we are about out of strength and energy and have nothing left in our reserves to fuel us. We feel trapped in never-ending marathons of trials and relationships and often find ourselves wishing to escape the course so we can rest. At times, these wishes are truly a need and not just a want. King David formulated some words thousands of years ago that seem to echo in our hearts and minds today. He said, "Oh that I had wings like a dove! for then would I fly away, and be at rest. Lo, then would I wander far off, and remain in the wilderness. ... I would hasten my escape from the windy storm and tempest" (Ps. 55:6–8). We all want to run away at times. And we are not the first ones to think like this—we are just the current generation who is doing so.

We can become so tired that we feel we just cannot take it anymore. We wonder if there is anyone who will allow us to rest, if there is anyone who even calls us to rest. It is easy to feel like this because more often than not, we are told to "get to work" or to do something where work is implied. How many parents tell their children to go do their chores? And what about the honey-do list? Even being asked particular questions calls us to work and not to rest. "Did you get that report done?" "Did you do your homework?" "Did you drop off the dry cleaning?" Even the dentist tells us to do something: schedule our biannual appointments and remember to floss each day. Although these are the frequent words and cares of life, there are actually a few times when we are told to take a break.

Sometimes, people recognize the need for rest and say or do something about it. When friends see our marriages headed for trouble, they might tell us to find babysitters and have date nights. When our health is in trouble, our doctors might tell us to slow down or lower our blood pressures so that we don't have heart attacks. When we see loved ones headed for burnout, we may encourage them to take some time off. Sometimes, we might even talk to ourselves if we recognize that we have problems. We might tell ourselves that we need to take breathers or take some time to clear our heads. There are times when we are under great deals of pressure, self-inflicted or otherwise, and we know that we need to rest our minds. Some of the pressures imposed on us by ourselves or others are totally unnecessary. We are good at digging holes for ourselves and then making them deeper and wider until there seems to be no way out unless someone comes along to save the day. That someone who can save our days and save *every* aspect of our lives is Jesus. He tells us to come to Him and rest.

The disciples had been out on journeys where they were preaching, healing, and casting out demons. And when they returned to give a report to Jesus about what they had done and taught, they were still surrounded by people (Mark 6:1–13, 30). While they spent time talking with Jesus and debriefing after their demanding days and heavy workloads, the needy people kept coming. There were so many of them coming and going that the disciples did not even have time to eat. Jesus stepped in to help the disciples by saying, "Come ye yourselves apart into a desert place, and rest a while" (Mark 6:31). He invited them to get away from the crowds so that they could rest from the demands of ministry. He knew that His followers needed some downtime so that they could be rejuvenated and refilled for the future demands of life and ministry. At times, we too need a break from people. Some are needier than others, but all of them put a drain on us. If we do not take time to rest and refill, then we will soon run out of substance to pour out into their lives. Caregivers have to take care of themselves so that they are better able to take care of their loved ones. We need rest and nourishment of both the physical and spiritual kinds.

Weariness can settle into our bodies, our minds, and our souls. We likely know how to rid our bodies of physical weariness, but how do we rid ourselves of mental and spiritual weariness? We do this by going to God for rest. If we are running around under the label of a nominal Christian, we will not find this rest. Rest comes to those who genuinely live for Him, to those who have taken Christ's message into their inner beings—into their very cores. We need to take on the mind of Christ; otherwise, we might practically make ourselves crazy with our human thoughts. Our thoughts need to come under the captivity of Christ. If we do not think like He thinks, then life will be very difficult. We will always feel like we are fruitless and unproductive, like we are working without winning. We will feel like we are stuck in changeless routines and will find ourselves asking, "Is this all there is to life?" If we do not *come* to Him and access a better way to live, then we will not be able to *go* very well through life.

We can literally drive ourselves to utter exhaustion and collapse—physically and mentally. We need someone to essentially and quite literally say to us, "Give it a rest." We need to be told to cease our incessant activity and curb our insatiable drives to do more and be more. God has, in effect, given us an invitation to do exactly this, *to give it a rest.* We can stop doing what we are doing and find a better way, His way. In Jeremiah 31:25, God said, "For I have satiated the weary soul, and I have replenished every sorrowful soul." Weariness needs to be washed away—our health and our lives depend upon it. We can accomplish this by allowing God to be our satisfaction and our restoration.

Occasionally, we will have seasons in life (e.g., milestone events, critical health problems, tragedies) where we are going to be weary for a while. Eventually, things may settle back down and we will be able to return to some semblance of normal life or else learn how to create a new normal. Other times, though, our lives will not ever settle down, nor will normalcy return. When this is the case, we may find ourselves resting inadequately unless we do something to intervene in the cycle. If we choose to continue without intervention, our health and lives will suffer. So, if there is any way we can possibly control the situations, then we need to get off the type A personalities and onto the type B. If we do not intentionally work at this, then our stress hormones will be elevated while our minds spin and spin. We will be running endlessly at the extreme. We will not eat well, sleep enough, speak civilly to our loved ones, focus on truly living, give tasks our undivided attention, or take care of the bodies God has given us. We may think that we are quite adept at multitasking, but we are actually quite good at destroying our bodies and our very selves in the process. Our bodies can only take so much. They will break down, and so will we. And we might even burn dinner.

Yes, I have burned many dinners because my attention was divided among a multitude of other things rather than being focused on the task at hand: cooking. I abandoned what I was supposed to be doing in the kitchen at that moment so that I could work on other tasks. I came back to a mess, and my family and I had to pay the consequences. You can ask my husband about a marinara sauce-decorated wall I happened to create. You can ask my children about my famous burned grilled cheese sandwiches, repeatedly served! Nothing like service with a grimace! It has resulted in a standing joke that if I am going to make grilled cheese, it is going to end up burned. Someone needs to sweep in and rescue me, and thereby, rescue the sandwiches and my family. Either we need Grandma here to make the sandwiches, and make them edible, or I need to learn how to focus on what is important: serving a decent and uncharred meal to my family. If I am not present in the moment, then negative consequences arise. If I ignore the steak that tells me to flip it now, then I am going to end up with shoe leather. If I ignore the Savior who says "Come to me," then I am going to go hungry, thirsty, unrested, and without all of the other things that He offers me in His invitation. If I do not rest and focus as my body and spirit need, then my life will look and taste about as appealing as char.

Always being plugged in and in a perpetual state of motion is not how we were created to be. We were created to need times to simply "be." Doing too much takes a toll on the physical body, emotional well-being, and spiritual growth. Being so busy with other things that we neglect focused quiet times is dangerous on many levels. Just as driving without sleep is dangerous, so too is traveling through life without spiritual rest. Rest is important. But this rest does not mean we are muddling through life or just subsisting, traveling without a destination in mind or proper course headings; it means we are doing the things God has called us to do and being the things God has called us to be. We should be living and moving intentionally. We should be bearing fruit, but only after we are cultivated and nourished properly. It is important to take time to be still rather than be continuously running around in hyperdrive, overextending our brains, bodies, and spirits.

In 2002, I lived this exact scenario, the one about running around continuously in hyperdrive, overextending brain, body, and spirit. Yes, I remember it well; it was like one big blur of non-stop activity. I remember often having the thought that I just wanted to stop and get off the world for a while. I vividly remember standing on my back porch, looking up at the sky and talking to God about that very thing. I told Him that I needed change, and I asked for His help, something along the lines of "God help me, I know I need to change." I knew I needed to change. I desperately wanted to change. And change I did. But not by the method I would have chosen. I hit burnout and my health crashed. I was bedridden. My world stopped, and I had no choice but to get off it. I could not work, could not minister, and could not even care for my home or the people in it. So, are you curious about what my thoughts were as soon as I crashed? Can you guess what I said? I said, "I want to get back to it," meaning that I wanted to get back onto the crazily-spinning world I had just exited. Why on earth would I think like that!

Humans are so fickle and wishy-washy. We want what we do not have, and then when we *do* have it, we do not want it anymore because we want something else instead. Despite our natures, the decision to come to Jesus should not be approached in such a manner. Our eternal destinies and the destinies of others depend upon us not being this way.

During some of my speaking engagements, I use a visual aid to make a spiritual analogy of what my life was like in 2002, leading up to my crash. I prepare a basket beforehand that is filled with items representing my life. I place my Bible in the very bottom of the basket and then proceed to cover it up with symbols of my life: a church bulletin, a running shoe, a teacup, a book, a piano figurine, my calendar, pictures of my family, a feather duster, a volunteer certificate, and more. I begin the presentation and pull out the items one by one to demonstrate the things that I did with my time. And there in the bottom, finally, at long last—buried among the comings and goings of my life—is my neglected Bible. This analogy is a perfect representation of how I consistently lived my life. I was busy doing many things: good things, important things, and necessary things. However, I was not doing the most necessary thing: spending time with God. Yes, I was doing many things for God, but I was operating on autopilot (what I have termed "function mode"). I knew how to get the job done and was doing it in my own strength, without the undergirding of prayer or guidance from God. I was doing so many things that I was not doing any one thing well, and definitely none to the best of my ability. I sure did not have a good spiritual fill-up to accomplish those things. I played pretend. People thought I was so good, so capable, so talented, and so amazing; but here I was: faulty, empty, prayerless, and running on fumes. On the outside, I appeared to have it all together, but on the inside, I was falling apart. We can look very much alive as we flit from place to place but in actuality be breathing shallowly. We can be running on our own breath rather than the breath of the Spirit. We may come to God as a last resort rather than a first resource, but it should not be so. It is best to avoid such scenarios because whether we are walking in the Spirit or not affects all other realms of our lives.

We do not need to be running all around the country in full-time ministry like the disciples were in order to be in need of rest. We saw from their story that needy people were right there waiting for them on their doorstep. Depletion can come from anywhere, from anyone, at any time.

Sometimes, we are caught off guard by situations, and there is nothing we can do to prepare for them or rest from them; however, for much of the remainder of life's dealings, we do have the ability to rest so that we can face the situations with something left in our storage tanks. We, like the disciples, need downtime so that we can worship and still ourselves before God. We need time to think about our lives and listen to His voice regarding them.

I have often heard that we should make time for rest within the course of each day. Even a few minutes will benefit us. The same holds true for taking time to be with God. Any amount of time that we can spend with Him will benefit us and bring quietness to our spirits. It is important, on many levels, to take this time to rest. We need to decompress, talk through our troubles in prayer, count our blessings, refocus our minds, and prepare to do our best for God and others when it is time to step out again.

Spending time with God will prevent our lives from becoming filled with anxiety, recklessness, weariness, pride, or any other negative things that do not invite His presence. We can counter these negative things with intentional acts that invite His presence, such as stillness, the study of His Word, taking on the mind of Christ, worship, and prayer. And one important thing that we can do during these times of rest is examine our lives to see if the things we are doing are eternally significant. We need to be aware of when we are lading ourselves with burdens that accomplish no eternal purpose. We need to make sure we are not adding more to our agendas than what God desires for us to have on them. We need to know what sucks us in and pulls us away from God. During these times of reflection and rest, we can prepare ourselves to do kingdom work, to do things which are eternally significant and which will leave a lasting legacy.

We must remember to allow all parts of our beings to rest. We accomplish this by stepping into God's presence rather than into what the world offers us and labels as "rest." Relationally, we need to let love govern all that we do. Emotionally, we need to cultivate the fruits of the Spirit and receive the love God offers us. Mentally, we need to remember the reason for our existence. Physically, we need to have good diets, get exercise, rest adequately, and prioritize our schedules. Spiritually, we need to read the Bible, pray, worship, fellowship, meditate, and serve. Resting thoroughly will benefit us and all those around us as we operate the way God created us to.

We can combat weariness by thinking about these facts: God is our strength, God is our power, and God makes our way perfect (see 2 Sam. 22:33). I can relate these words to my own life because I am not my strength and power, nor do I make my way perfect; I do quite the opposite: I often make my way messy, *very* messy. Thankfully, the Lord gives strength and peace to His people (see Ps. 29:11). We will find rest when we fill our minds with Him rather than with obsessive thoughts of fear, failure, and worry. And if we are willing to take the time to lay our burdens upon His shoulders and be taught a better way, we will be refreshed, renewed, revitalized, and educated about how to do things in His strength rather than ours. At times, we may be rescued entirely and have the burdens completely taken away; other times, the burdens remain, but He is there to help us carry them. No matter how long, how far, and how difficult our journeys are, God will help us complete them, and not just complete them, but excel at doing so. He will strengthen our spirits with His supernatural power so that we can meet the challenges of life.

When I examine my life and the experience I had in 2002, I see that I did learn a lesson from the rest that was imposed upon me, but the lesson did not always stick because I did not always stick to the lesson. I readily admit that there were times that I failed to spend sufficient time with God and instead ran around frenetically. Periodically, I still struggle with this. Is there shame in admitting this? Yes. Do I want anyone to know this about me? No. But here it is. The truth. Now you know. And do you know what else? I am *forgiven,* and my shame is removed! I thank God for His mercy, grace, and forgiveness, and for never giving up on me even when I throw His yoke off and proceed without Him. He patiently waits for me to return to His side to join Him in the work. He waits for me to allow Him to be the strength and guidance for my life. The ability to rest and the ability to work come as results of being filled by Him. I hope to one day leave a legacy of having done the eternally significant things that God called me to do.

God is always at work around us, so we do not need to be wearing ourselves out by trying to do His job. Whether we see the evidence or not, He is up to something. We do not need to be worn down by fretting, because He is perfecting our ways. He is faithful and is going to complete the work that He began in us (Phil. 1:6). We should trust in His work, and ask for the power to keep believing and to have more and stronger faith. Although our outward man is perishing, our inward man can be renewed day by day. Our afflictions are but for a moment, and they work for us far more exceeding and eternal weights of glory. Because of this, we should not focus on the things that are seen but rather on the things that are *not* seen, for the things that are seen are just temporal, but the things that are not seen are eternal (see 2 Cor. 4:16–18). God is eternal and His power is eternal, and it is this power that can ignite us and carry us through.

Because God is with us and God is for us, we will always be sufficiently cared for in every part of who we are. When we come forth to receive His life and His rest, we will never have to thirst again, never have to crave another's love, never have to collapse in weariness, and someday, will never have to cry again. His provision is great and His provision is all-encompassing. He is our sustenance for life. He is a place where we can rest as we journey. He is a place where we can linger when we are weary. We can draw deeply from the well of His salvation. In His presence, our souls can be rested and replenished, and then we will be able to rise up and go through all the days ahead of us. May coming to Him be elemental to our lives.

CHAPTER 5

Hide and Seek

We look in every cupboard and under every table. We look around every corner and through every window. We go searching, calling out for someone or something to answer us. We rush here and there, trying to beat the timer before it is all over and we have lost. We think we know what we are looking for, but we get distracted looking at other things along the way. We find disappointment when things are empty. We find joy when we find what we were ultimately seeking. We play the game of hide-and-seek, sometimes doing well at it and other times not.

We sometimes treat life like a game of hide-and-seek. We have something in mind that we are searching for. We think that important things can be left undone while we chase our targets. Sometimes, we do not want to play by the rules. We act like the consequences do not matter. There are some times when we do not even want to play at all. We hide from it all, hoping that nothing and no one finds us. But God is looking for us, and He knows exactly where we are.

THE CALL TO THE HIDDEN

Moses was hiding from Pharaoh, the king of Egypt, after killing one of Pharaoh's men. He fled to Midian where he took up residence, married, and became a shepherd for his father-in-law (see Exod. 2:11–25). Exodus 3:1–22 gives the account of when Moses experienced an ordinary day that turned extraordinary. One day while he was tending the flock, he heard his name being called out from a burning bush. He did not know it, but he had just received an invitation to respond to God, the One calling his name. Moses had a choice to make about how he would respond. Would he answer the call, or would he run from the unknown? He decided to approach the bush, and thus, God. His response was, "Here am I" (Exod. 3:4). He then had a conversation with God and was called to a task: to deliver the Israelites out of slavery in Egypt. With God's help, he completed the monumental task. Later on, as Moses was leading the people toward the Promised Land, God said, "Come up to me" (Exod. 24:12). Moses responded to God's call and went up to meet with Him on Mount Sinai. He talked with God and learned what was expected of the Israelites. He was given the Ten Commandments at this time. When he went back down the mountain to share God's commandments with the people, he found them worshiping idols. He became angry with the sin of the people and broke the tablets upon which the commandments were written. At this point, Moses could have quit his leadership position and hidden himself far away from such corruption, but instead, he continued to lead the people and continued to listen for God's voice.

After this, Moses received another calling and another opportunity to go up to meet with God on the mountain. When Moses returned to the camp this time, the Israelites got to hear God's words and they got to see God's glory shine upon Moses's face (see Exod. 34:29–35). They also received another opportunity to possess the Ten Commandments and follow the true and living God rather than idols made with their own hands. Where would more than a half-million people have been without the obedience of this one man?

What do we do when God calls *our* names? At times, we go into hiding rather than respond to Him—sometimes physical hiding, sometimes emotional hiding, and sometimes both. When things are bad and things are hard, when we are deeply hurting or when life is overwhelming, we lock ourselves away from the realities of the situations and from the very thing that can help us to come out of them. We tend to isolate ourselves in a myriad of ways, such as staying home, cramming our schedules, or not answering our phones. We try to handle things on our own. Perhaps it is because we do not trust others. Perhaps we think that no one can understand or truly help us or make a difference in our circumstances. But God sees us, all of us. "Behold, the eye of the LORD is upon them that fear him, upon them that hope in his mercy" (Ps. 33:18). No creature is hidden from His sight (Heb. 4:13). Since there is nowhere that we can go to be hidden from His Spirit (see Ps. 139:7–10), there is no point in trying to hide. We should just come.

There was a time in my city when budget cuts were made to the property crimes investigation unit. The local news stations were broadcasting that the police did not have the resources to attend to property crimes. The broadcasts went on day after day after day. Shortly thereafter, property crimes increased. The news stations were then reporting on the crimes while continuing to mention that there were few resources to address the problem. When some of the victims were asked what they would do as a result of their losses, they said that since nothing could be done by the police, they were not even going to report the crimes. They suffered the losses of their items without requesting the help of those who knew how to handle such situations.

Other victims, however, became proactive and took matters into their own hands, planning to deal with any future criminal activity on their properties. They were not going to stand idly by and let this happen to them again. They invested in home security in varying forms: locks, guns, alarms, security cameras, and the like. The waiting began. Isolation took place. Mistrust grew. People hid in their homes, trying to deal with the problem on their own, just waiting for the thieves to show up. The neighborhood residents did not request help from those who could truly assist them in this situation but chose instead to hide within fortresses of their own making. Sometimes, we do the same thing when our problems escalate. We go into hiding and do not concern God with our problems. We invent our own solutions. We put up our own defenses in preparation for the next evil thing that will come our way. But we do not need to hide away from God, thinking that it is useless to request His help. We are not unloved. He is not lurking in the shadows, waiting to terrorize us or steal from us (that is what Satan does). God has all of the knowledge and all of the resources in the whole universe at His disposal. He is able to help us. And furthermore, there are never any cuts in the services He offers. He is always available and willing to help us; we just need to contact Him and ask for that help.

I once heard a story about a woman who had lost everything she owned. At this point in life, she and her three dogs were homeless. Since this had happened to her, she believed that God hated her. She was hiding herself away from God. But then some Christians entered her life and told her that God loved her. God found her where she was hiding, and He declared His love for her. He loves us too. He is *for* us!

I have heard of many people who will not approach God because they believe that their sins are too awful to be forgiven. They try to hide their sins and their shame from Him. They find it impossible to believe that God could ever love them, but their beliefs are contrary to the truth. God has been searching for and calling out to the guilty (which is all of us, by the way) since the first humans were on earth. Adam and Eve had walked in daily communion with God until they sinned. When they realized what they had done, they hid themselves from Him. God knew full well what they had done, and still He sought for them. He was seeking to have a relationship with them, just like He had done all the days prior. He went looking for them, calling out to them even though they were hiding in their sin, their failure, and their fear (see Gen. 3:1–21). God went looking for us, too, sending Jesus to find us and rescue us from our sins. When Jesus was nailed to the cross, so was the debt of our sin (Col. 2:14). Forgiveness has been made available to us because God sought the hidden. Rather than remain covered in our sins, we can come out of hiding and be covered by His forgiveness instead. And what's more, we can hide His Word in our hearts to avoid sinning against Him in the future (see Ps. 119:11). Be found hidden with Christ in God (see Col. 3:3).

THE CALL TO THE SEEKERS

There were those who were self-motivated in their coming; they came seeking Jesus without having received an invitation to come. There were others who came seeking Jesus because God was drawing them at this particular time. The news of Jesus spread across the miles, and people came to see what they could see, hear what they could hear, and get what they could get. All types of people came seeking Jesus. There were individuals and crowds, people of low reputation and those who occupied high positions. All of them were seeking something: help, answers, miracles, signs, the satisfaction of their curiosity, and more.

People came from many places, from every quarter, when they heard about the things He did (Mark 1:45, 3:8). Luke 6:17–19 says that Jesus stood in the plain and was joined by "a great multitude of people out of all Judaea and Jerusalem, and from the seacoast of Tyre and Sidon which came to hear him, and to be healed of their diseases; And they that were vexed with unclean spirits: and they were healed. And the whole multitude sought to touch him: for there went virtue out of him, and healed them all." People came to the temple early in the morning to hear Him (Luke 21:38). People stayed late in the day out in a desert place in order to hear Him speak, even missing their evening meal (Mark 6:35–36). People tried to detain Him as He was heading to other places by inviting Him to stay longer (John 4:40). A great multitude came to Him because they had seen the miracles that He had performed on the diseased (John 6:2, 5). Crowds followed Jesus from place to place, even anticipating where He was heading and racing to get there first. They went chasing after Him in boats when He was not where they thought they would find Him (John 6:24–25). Some people were making preparations to come and take Jesus by force to make Him king, to make Him into a political messiah who would deliver them from their Roman oppressors (John 6:15). There were also negative people in the crowds, such as the Pharisees, who came seeking to stir up trouble with their questions and false accusations.

Some accounts are given of seekers who wanted something very specific from Jesus. A woman with an issue of blood sought to touch the hem of His garment for healing, and when she did it, she was made whole (Luke 8:44). A rich young ruler was seeking an answer to his question of how to inherit eternal life, and Jesus gave him the answer (Matt. 19:16–22). Nicodemus, a Pharisee, came to Jesus at night in order to speak with Him about spiritual things. Nicodemus received quite a spiritual education that night (John 3:1–21). A leper came to Jesus seeking physical healing, and he was compassionately healed (Mark 1:40–42). Bartimaeus, a blind roadside beggar, went seeking for Jesus in the only way he was physically capable: he called out for help as Jesus passed by. When Jesus became aware of this, He commanded that Bartimaeus be brought to Him. Bartimaeus came in response to the summons, and he was then invited to let his petition be made known to Jesus. The result of his obedient response to Jesus's command was the receipt of his eyesight (Mark 10:46–52). All of these seekers received what they came seeking.

Some people who came were not seeking Jesus for themselves but were seeking Him for others. Jairus was seeking help for his dying daughter (Luke 8:41–56). A man was seeking healing for his demon-possessed son (Luke 9:42). Four men carried their palsied friend who was in need of healing. These four men were so determined to help their friend that when they could not get near Jesus because of the press of the crowd, they found another way: through the roof (Mark 2:3–12). A nobleman asked Jesus to come and heal his son who was near death (John 4:46–50). The needs of all of these men were urgent, so they went to where they were sure they could receive help. They definitely received the help they were looking for: it came in the form of miracles, performed by the Son of God!

While some people were simply curious about who this man was and what He was doing in their region, others came seeking proof of *who* He was, proof that they could see and touch. They wanted evidence of God. In Luke 19, we read the account of Zacchaeus, the one of short stature who is best known as the "wee little man." He wanted to see who Jesus was, so he went to great lengths (or should we say great heights!) in order to see Him. Zacchaeus ran ahead of the crowd and climbed a tree so that he could get a look at Jesus as He passed by. When Jesus saw him in the tree, He told him to come down. Zacchaeus RSVP'd joyfully and "made haste, and came down" (vs. 6). Jesus then went to Zacchaeus's house to visit with him for a while. Zacchaeus found salvation and subsequently, made some changes in his life: giving to the poor and righting some wrongs. All of this came as a result of searching for Jesus.

Some people came because they had heard a story about Jesus. Nathanael was seeking Jesus because Philip had invited him to come and see for himself that the prophesied One had arrived (John 1:45–51). John the Baptist sent two of his followers to ask Jesus if He was the One that they were waiting for (the prophesied Messiah) or whether they should look for another (Luke 7:18–19). John 1:35–42 gives the account of two of John the Baptist's disciples following after Jesus when John announced that Jesus was the Lamb of God. One of these two followers asked Jesus where He was staying. Jesus invited him, "Come and see" (v. 39). The two stayed with Jesus that day, and after spending time with Him, realized who He truly was. Afterward, one of them (Andrew) went and told his brother, Simon Peter, that he had found the Messiah. They could now discontinue their search for the Messiah because He had been found; He was indeed Jesus the Christ.

And one day, the Messiah was seen walking on the water in the midst of a storm (see Matt. 14:22–33 NKJV). The disciples were in their ship when a boisterous storm came up. Suddenly, Jesus came walking toward them on the waves. We find that Peter sought proof of Jesus's identity as he said, "Lord, if it is You, command me to come to You on the water" (v. 28). There was an "if" in there, and "if" means uncertainty. But even though Peter was doubting, questioning Jesus's identity, and testing Him, Jesus extended an extraordinary invitation to him by uttering a single word: "Come" (v. 29). Jesus invited Peter to get out of the boat *during a storm* and then walk to Him *on the water.* Jesus granted the request of this seeker rather than telling him to be quiet or to avoid the risk and stay in the boat.

Think about how *we* act in regard to storms and what we are told to do when there is one. People are telling us to get *out* of the water, not get *into* it. Lifeguards, the National Weather Service, and the National Oceanic Atmospheric Administration all give warnings to get out of the water because of storms, high tides, and dangerous currents. When there is lightning, we are told to stay away from water. When we are at the public pool and a storm is approaching, we are told to get out of the water. When we are in a boat and a storm comes up, we tighten our life jackets to keep us safe in case we end up going overboard. A ship's crew will batten down the hatches and make things secure on the ship when storms threaten. For the most part, we try to get out of the storm if we are at all able, and if not, we try to remain safe while we are within it.

There are many dangerous scenarios that can occur in life, and usually we take steps to prepare for them, including finding ways to try to protect ourselves from them or avoid them altogether. But this is not what we find Peter doing. He was not busy putting on a life vest or securing the ship. He was not writing out his last will and testament. Instead, we find him making a request of Jesus to come to Him on the water, and no one, to our knowledge, was telling Peter to get out of the water and stay away from it.

As a mom, I know what would be going through my mind in a case like this. Preserve. Protect. Be wise. Don't play with fire (or in this case, water). As someone who has seen what storms do to people and objects, I would be looking for shelter and seeking safety, calling 911, and scrambling to save lives and perhaps the photo albums. As someone who is not a great swimmer, I sure would not be making plans to get into the water under such conditions. And even if I was a great swimmer, I imagine that common sense would kick in and steer me away from such a daring feat. Yet, here we see a man whose focus momentarily shifts away from *what* is going on around him to *who* is right there in front of him. As a result of acting on Jesus's invitation, Peter saw, as did others, that this one walking on the water was indeed the Son of God. And as a result, they all worshiped Him. And this was not the only miracle to which these disciples were exposed. A miracle had preceded the invitation to come onto the water: Jesus Himself was walking on the water! Another miracle occurred when Jesus and Peter got into the boat: the storm immediately ceased. There had also been another miracle shortly before they took ship: Jesus had fed a multitude of five thousand people. Miracle after miracle after miracle. Seeking the Son of God will give you amazing and miraculous proof of who He is!

There were obstacles, distractions, and delays for those who were seeking Jesus, yet, they continued to seek. They did not let the obstacles prevent their coming but instead found a way to get to Him, even if it was unconventional. They tore up roofs, climbed trees, came under cover of darkness, sent others in their steads, and more. Imagine what would have happened if these seekers had not come to Jesus: no healing for themselves or their loved ones, no restoration to life, no miracles, no meeting the Savior of the world. Although there were naysayers who questioned Jesus's ability and authority, to those in need, it did not matter; their faith was proven. And through their acts of faith, God was glorified and people were resurrected, healed, and forgiven. The seeking was worth what they found.

Even after Jesus's death, people continued to seek Him. When Peter and John heard that Jesus was resurrected, they went to the tomb seeking proof. They found their proof in an empty tomb. They went away believing, with an amazing story to share with others (see John 20). Afterward, they went to find Jesus in Galilee where He had said He would meet them following His resurrection (Matt. 28:16). They were able to see the living proof they sought!

I have seen a phrase on Christmas merchandise that says, "Wise men still seek Him." The foundational reference is to the wise men who were seeking Jesus around the time of His birth, the ones who traveled many miles in order to worship Him and present Him with gifts (see Matt. 2:1–11). The reference for today's usage of the phrase is that wisdom is indicated if we are spiritually seeking Jesus. We often put great emphasis on this story, focusing our thoughts onto it to see how we might apply the concept to our own lives. What does it mean today for us to seek Him? And will we be wise enough to do it? Will we do it even if it involves much time and great distances? What gifts will we present to Him when we find Him? These are important questions for us to answer, not just at Christmastime, but every day of the year.

Another example of a wise seeker is the Queen of Sheba. She demonstrates a great way to seek out God. She came seeking confirmation of the things that she had heard about Solomon's kingdom and his wisdom. She wanted to see for herself and either confirm or disprove the things that she had been hearing. To do this, she traveled a great distance and then spent time searching out Solomon's kingdom and asking him questions (see 2 Chron. 9:1–8). Because she sought, asked questions, listened, and learned, she saw for herself the greatness of this earthly king, and through him, the greatness of God. She then blessed God once she saw His love for His people evidenced in Solomon's life. Just think, if we were to live right, we would cause people to seek God. They would come for answers and proof and find them. They would come looking for what we have and find Jesus!

God is a seeker too. He is seeking our hearts and relationships with us. He knows what we need and is able to do miracles to meet our individual needs. Many examples of His individualized care have been recorded throughout history—in the pages of journals, newspapers, biographies, history books, and the Bible. Sometimes, the care has come in the forms of jobs, material goods, miracles of healing, or someone's arrival at just the right moment. I have seen provision for my family that has ranged from things as large as a house and land to as small as a pair of toddler's socks, some contact lenses, and a few words on a page. I am quite sure, too, that there are other larger and smaller things of which I may never be made aware. May we be seekers of God's kingdom and His righteousness, and He in His divine wisdom will provide what we *need* (Matt. 6:33). May we come to Him as a new pursuit or as the culmination of what we have been searching for all along. Let us not hide from His light and His love. "Seek the LORD while He may be found, Call upon Him while He is near" (Isa. 55:6 NKJV).

When we seek God, we will find Him. When we go to where He calls us, we will find Him there. He does not invite us to places where He is not. He does not call us to do something where He is not right there to help, protect, and deliver us. If we are searching for Him, then we are going to find Him. If we speak to Him, then He is going to speak to us. We may not hear His voice directly in our ears, or even in our spirits, but He will reveal Himself to us in some way; we just have to be willing to look, listen, and wait expectantly for His response.

THE CALL TO THE TREASURE SEEKERS

During the nineteenth century, some Americans came down with gold fever and rushed off to find riches. The power of gold, greed, wealth, and vain imagination caused them to leave behind their established lives, their families, their responsibilities, and sometimes their common sense. Today, we still have a touch of gold fever, although we may go searching for riches that are in the shapes of green dollar bills, wealthy spouses, brand-name clothing, sports cars, and big houses instead of little gold nuggets lying in the creek beds of California. We still do some prospecting, but it is of a different kind. We are working the angles, working the schedules, and biding our time. We are looking for the ins, schmoozing, and playing the games. But sometimes, our plans are changed. Either we bring about the changes in our own lives, or they are brought upon us by an outside force. Someone or something changes our circumstances.

It is commonly said that money is power, but it is also said that knowledge is power. This is most definitely true if we gain knowledge of Jesus. When we discover the real Power of the universe, things change. We can have a life-changing experience by agreeing to allow the King of all kings into our inner circles. We discover that it is He who owns all of the riches in the entire universe. It is He who should be pursued. We can shift our focal points from "me and mine" to "Him and His." When our pursuits change to seeking Jesus, the treasures we find in life are shaped like love, joy, strength, peace, and rest.

There is an account given in the Bible of a rich young ruler who asked Jesus what he could do to inherit eternal life (Matt. 19:16–22; Mark 10:21). He received an unexpected answer from Jesus that he did not like, so he decided to turn down Jesus's offer and walk away. Jesus told the man to go and sell all that he had, give it to the poor, and then come to take up the cross and follow Him. The gist was that he needed to let go of the temporal in order to obtain the eternal, to serve God rather than possessions. It appears that the man was hoping for a different sort of invitation—one that did not involve sacrifice or a lifestyle change. He much rather would have offered his previous works and his good-looking past instead of his belongings. From this account, we learn that we are not to love anyone or anything more than Jesus. And although our codes of conduct may seem pretty good, Jesus wants more than that—He wants our hearts. He does not care about our money; He cares about our souls. He wants us to come and follow Him. He is the true treasure, and the things that He gives, which are not always material, are the things that matter. We should be willing to let go of everything we have so that we can grab hold of the better things that God has for us.

Holding on to anything that God asks us to release is like wearing a yoke of bondage. This is because we are tied to something rather than being free in Him and what He desires for our lives. We need to have hands and spirits that release what the natural man desires to hold on to. We should be rich toward God: in word, in deed, in time, in possessions, in all that we have and are. And when we are, we will be blessed beyond measure. It is better to be a doorkeeper in God's house than to live in the tents of wickedness (Ps. 84:10). To be doing something basic and unglamorous, yet be in God's presence, is better than to be rich and have everything but Him. Even if we are poor according to the world but rich according to God, we are truly rich.

So, what is Jesus saying when He asks us to come and take up a cross? Does this sound like a good prospective activity? Does this sound like a treasure and a road that leads to riches? It does not. At this point, we just need to walk obediently because God has spoken and not be concerned about any potential benefits of our obedience. We need to come, and come expecting to have to take up a cross. We may not even know ahead of time what the cross is going to be, but we still need to come. In addition to coming obediently, our minds should be prepared with a realistic perspective: what He calls us to do may not be easy by human standards. Will this end up turning some people off and cause them to turn away? If we look at the story of this rich man, obviously the answer has to be yes, yet, Jesus still asks people to follow Him. He wants true followers, not lukewarm, namby-pamby, uncommitted, wishy-washy, half-baked, for-the-sake-of-convenience followers. He does not want people latching on to Him thinking that He is a genie or a get-rich-quick fix to their lives. What type of people are we? Deep down, what type do we want to be?

When we look at how Jesus lived and correlate that with how He asks us to live, we see that it is not all about the money. We are to do things of eternal significance while here on earth. We are to lay up for ourselves treasures in heaven, where moth and rust do not corrupt, and where thieves do not break through nor steal (see Matt. 6:19–21). Jesus's life on earth was completely about eternal significance. He did not come to have servants and be served; He came to serve and to give His life as a ransom for many (Matt. 20:28). It was about Him giving, not Him taking. He gave everything He had to us poor sinners when He took up His cross. He was not seeking fame and fortune and popularity; He was seeking the treasure of human souls, our souls. And through His sacrifice, He has made us rich. Second Corinthians 8:9 (NKJV) says, "For you know the grace of our Lord Jesus Christ, that though He was rich, yet for your sakes He became poor, that you through His poverty might become rich." He left the treasures of heaven to seek us; may we leave the treasures of earth to seek Him.

Jesus invites each of us to take up our cross and come after Him

(Matt. 16:24; Mark 8:34). This is an invitation to give our entire selves to Him and submit to His call on our lives. Jesus was obedient unto death on the cross, and as we imitate His life, we too should be obedient to Him, to the death. We need to let our wills die and live in His will instead; this is what it means to take up His cross.

Jesus wants everyone to be with Him for all eternity. His desire is to save all people (1 Tim. 2:4); He does not want any of us walking away. He is "not willing that any should perish, but that all should come to repentance" (2 Pet. 3:9). He wants to give us things that are valuable and imperishable. He wants to give us eternal life and eternal love. He wants to make the riches of His glory known unto us (see Rom. 9:23).

If we come to Jesus to ask what is necessary to follow Him, we should be prepared for His answer. Are we wondering and worrying if Jesus will ask us to give away everything we own? He may ask us to; He may not. But since He gave us His all, does He deserve anything less from us? Possessions ultimately do not matter, yet we have such a difficult time letting go of things. We are so attached to our belongings, and often this is where our loyalties lie, but we should be giving our loyalty to Jesus, not to things. We need to make up our minds to prioritize Him over riches or over anything else that might hold us back from lives totally committed to Him.

Does all of this mean that we should not have riches? No. Some people from Bible times (e.g., Job, Abraham, Solomon) had many material blessings and great wealth. But the important thing is that they gave their faith to God. It is not about the money; it is about where our allegiance lies. We are not to place anything above Him. We cannot serve both God and wealth (Matt. 6:24). As it says in 1 John 2:15, "Love not the world, neither the things that are in the world. If any man love the world, the love of the Father is not in him." We need to go where God wants us to, even if it means not having an ounce of wealth to our names. When we choose to follow where He leads us, we will have made the better choice and will become rich in spiritual ways.

Jesus invites us to come to Him because He has things that we need. He shed His own blood for our souls: to give us forgiveness, redemption, and a way to be with Him forever. He will fill those who hunger and thirst for righteousness (Matt. 5:6). He will give the water of eternal life (John 7:37). He has the words of life (John 6:68). The treasures of wisdom and knowledge are hidden in Him (Col. 2:3). Yes, there are treasures waiting to be found in Christ; we just need to seek for them. God says, "And you will seek Me and find *Me*, when you search for Me with all your heart" (Jer. 29:13 NKJV). To me, that sounds like an extraordinary invitation!

God gave us Jesus so that we could have life and life eternal. He truly is the only source of real and abundant life (John 10:10). Nothing else can offer that to us; everything else takes from us. Seeking life and abundance in other places actually steals from the abundant life that God desires for us to have. Second Peter 1:3–8 tells us that Jesus can give us everything pertaining to life and godliness. His eternal things are not like our temporal things. The things of this world pass away, decay, and are destroyed, but the things of God endure forever. There are some things that can only come from Him: He gives us mercy through His resurrection, He gives us hope and an inheritance in heaven, He keeps us by His power until the end of time, and He gives us joy that allows us to rejoice despite our trials. We should seek the Lord while He waits for us to find Him. He is near and waiting to pour blessings into our lives. His storehouses are full of treasures that will make our lives abundant. And *He* is the greatest treasure of all.

CHAPTER 6

Lost and Found

We lose all sorts of things in life: money, homes, jobs, loved ones, health, quality of life, and sometimes even life itself. We also find all sorts of things: happiness, the loves of our lives, the perfect jobs, and sometimes even our car keys. But have we ever found the most important thing, the thing that we can never lose: the salvation of our eternal souls?

THE CALL TO THE LOST

There were specific events for which Jesus came to live on earth. He was given an invitation by His Father to be the Savior of the world, and He responded favorably to the invitation. He prepared for the event of saving the world by His first advent: "For unto you is born this day in the city of David a Saviour, which is Christ the Lord" (Luke 2:11). During the course of His ministry, Jesus clarified why He came and why He did not come. He said He did not come to call for the righteous or to destroy people's lives; instead, He came to preach, to call sinners to repentance, and to save lives (see Mark 1:38, 2:17; Luke 9:56). Jesus came into many cities, and He came in with the intent to minister (Mark 10:45).

As Jesus traveled around, He gave people His time, and He gave them Himself. He did not blow through town like a whirlwind, forcing and rushing His way through. While He was going along His way, He focused His time and attention on the people He encountered. He sometimes spent all day healing the crowds although He could have done it in a single moment with a single word. He saw that the crowds were like sheep without a shepherd, and thus, had compassion on them (Mark 6:34). He gave people His personal touch. He asked them of their faith, asked what they wanted and needed, and took time to encourage them. And then the healing came.

We see Paul's words exemplifying how Jesus lived: "We then that are strong ought to bear the infirmities of the weak, and not to please ourselves. Let every one of us please his neighbour for his good to edification. For even Christ pleased not himself" (Rom. 15:1–3). The underlying reason why Jesus lived like He did was that He came "to seek and to save that which was lost" (Luke 19:10). He came *unto us*! He did not come for Himself and His benefit, but for us and our benefit. Jesus offered life and help to the people He encountered during His lifetime on earth, and His offer still stands today. Let the love of Jesus find you, wherever it is that you are in life. Let Him shepherd your wandering heart and lead you safely to your eternal home.

Jesus is not only our Shepherd but also our High Priest, the Mediator between us and God (1 Tim. 2:5). Because He is holy, He was able to victoriously do away with our sin by dying on the cross for us. And because He did this for us and then was resurrected from the dead, we can overcome sin and emerge victorious through His power. His sacrifice gives us access to His Father, His power, and His kingdom. Jesus calls each of us to salvation. The wonderful truth is that the lost sheep (us) can be claimed if they want to be claimed! When we come, we will discover that we are welcomed, loved, and valued. Jesus came for us—will we come to Him?

All of the preparations for us to be found have been made, and the barriers that would separate us from God were removed when they were broken down at the cross. We now need to make our way over to His side, walking past those broken barriers instead of repairing them. A simple yes will do. The fighting in our hearts can stop and we can be at peace, if only we will come. We can stop wandering aimlessly through life like lost sheep. We can instead let Him minister to us, heal us, and save us. That is what He came to do, and we are who He came to find.

THE CALL TO THE GRIEVING

Grief can overwhelm us, and at times, we can become lost in it. Our hearts can break and bleed and cry out for relief. Our hearts can burn with questions hotter than Death Valley. "Why?" "Why God?" "Why are those three young boys going to be left without a mother?" "Why did he do that to me?" "Where *were* You when that was happening?" We can cry so many tears, inside and out, that we become dehydrated. Our throats become dry from crying, from screaming. We wander alone in deserts of pain and sadness, feeling like the vultures are circling overhead, their dark shadows coming for us next. So many unanswered questions. So much hurt. "Why?" "What good is there in all of this?" "What good is going to come out of this?" Our focus wanders from the well of water directly in front of us, to the blur of the heat waves rising from the burning sand all around us, to the pain of the scorching heat, to the howling of the desert wind. Our focus shifts to the pain and away from what can soothe the pain. But there is someone who can help us return from these perplexed states and find healing: God. We can mimic some of the words King David spoke in Psalm 25:16–18, asking for God to "turn" to us and "have mercy" on us because we are "desolate" and "afflicted"(v. 16). When the troubles of our hearts have grown, we can ask that He would see our afflictions and pain and then deliver us. And if we are in a state of grieving because of our sin, we can ask for His forgiveness (vv. 17–18). Calling out to Jesus is a good thing to do because He was acquainted with grief (Isa. 53:3). He knows what we are going through.

The Bible tells us about some women who were grieving because Jesus had just been crucified on the cross. They were headed to His grave to prepare His body for burial, but instead they encountered an angel who invited them to "Come, see the place where the Lord lay" (Matt. 28:6). This was an invitation to a *past tense* event, to see the place where His body *had* been. Jesus was no longer there because He had risen—He *is* risen! Talk about a cure for their grief! Talk about a cure for ours!

Immanuel. God with us. This is one of His names, one of His amazing characteristics, and one of His precious promises. He has said that He will never leave us, nor forsake us (Heb. 13:5). When our hearts are heavy and our spirits are wounded, Immanuel. When our minds swirl and whirl in chaos and questions, Immanuel. When nothing makes sense and all hope seems lost, Immanuel. Storms rage. Dreams die. Immanuel. People leave. People die. Immanuel. Homes are lost. Possessions ravaged. Immanuel. Days are long. Nights are longer. Immanuel. Pits are deep. Scars are deeper. Immanuel. No one even understands our pain and the depths of it. Immanuel. In this name, there is hope and there is rest. Immanuel. Comfort can be found in knowing that we are not alone in what we are facing. We can rest, assured of His promise to always be with us. And because God always keeps His promises, we can cling to this name for all we are worth. Immanuel. When we are lost, we can find Him: Immanuel.

THE CALL TO THE RIGHTEOUS

God has a purpose in mind when He calls His children to come to Him, and when they are living righteous lives and come in obedience to His summons, amazing things can happen. We can examine some biblical examples to learn what these purposes are and to see how significant the outcomes of obedience can be.

God commanded Noah to come so that he could obtain salvation from the destruction of a worldwide flood. Even though Noah had no idea what a flood was because it had never rained upon the earth previously, he obeyed. The means by which his salvation would come was through the building of an ark, another thing that he had no prior knowledge of. When he was finished building, the Lord said to him, "Come into the ark, you and all your household, because I have seen *that* you *are* righteous before Me in this generation" (Gen. 7:1 NKJV). Noah believed that God was going to do what He said He was going to do. Noah entered the ark. God shut the door. And the rains began. Noah's righteous obedience resulted in the saving of his life and the lives of his entire family (see Gen. 6:8–8:22). Because this family chose to come when called, they did not perish in the floodwaters but instead rested safely in God's care. And because of Noah's obedience, other people came into existence who lived righteously and changed the world for God.

Moses was called to deliver the Israelites from slavery in Egypt. Joshua was called to lead the Israelites into the Promised Land. John the Baptist was called to preach repentance and prepare the way of the Lord. Peter was called to lead the church as it was being established. Paul was called to travel and preach. These were people who followed after God's calls on their lives. They chose to live for Him, and He did great things through them to affect the lives of many others. God's name was made known, and people came to know His love.

These aforementioned followers of God had different abilities and tasks, but they were all invited to be part of God's kingdom work here on earth. It is exciting to realize that those of us alive today have the same opportunity since God still invites people to be part of His kingdom work. God has bestowed many gifts within His people that, when melded together, create a magnificent and multi-talented body, able to do great things. He created people with the gifts of design, music, smithing, preaching, teaching, healing, horticulture, nurturing, administration, prophecy, and many, many more—all for His purposes and just as He was pleased to make them. He calls us to be obedient to His plans and tasks for us while we live out our lives, and using these gifts is part of that obedience. Imagine the great things that individual members of the body could accomplish through righteous living. They could affect the whole body, and ultimately, all peoples of the earth for the sake of Christ. God's children can accomplish great feats while they wait for His return.

Someday, the call to obedience will change into the call to come home. There will be a second advent by Jesus when He will come to call those who have been claimed through salvation. He will take His children to be with Him forever, and they will get to inherit the kingdom prepared for them from the foundation of the world (Matt. 25:34). He did His part to invite us: He lived righteously and purchased salvation at the cross. And now we just have to do our part: accept the salvation offered to us. This salvation replaces our unrighteousness with His righteousness. Are we ready to make the great exchange, to take on the righteousness of Christ so that we are ready for His second advent?

Jesus will fulfill His promises, and He will fulfill the hopes and expectations of those who wait for Him. Yes, He *will* come again. He is currently fulfilling His part as host and is making the final preparations for His children. It is a blessing to be invited to such an incredible place, and there is nothing to keep us out but our own refusals to enter in. His kingdom is not surrounded by a moat or guards or signs that tell us to keep out. He *wants* us to come to Him and to come into His kingdom. I will be going to that great feast because I am a recipient of salvation. I have taken full advantage of the free gift that has been offered to me—eternal life. My name is on the guest list, recorded in the Book of Life. I will be dressed in His righteousness alone because I have done as it says in Philippians 3:9: "And be found in him, not having mine own righteousness, which is of the law, but that which is through the faith of Christ, the righteousness which is of God by faith." I hope that you will RSVP to get your name on the list while there is still time. Please get all dressed up in His righteousness with someplace to go: the Marriage Supper of the Lamb!

THE CALL TO THE UNINVOLVED

Some of the men that Jesus called to be His disciples were fishermen. These fishermen, Peter, Andrew, James, and John, were not engaged in the kingdom work that Jesus had in mind for them but were instead engaged in their daily tasks, taking care of their earthly lives and earthly responsibilities. They were just going about their ordinary days of fishing and repairing nets, until Jesus suddenly entered their world and asked them to follow Him. Jesus invited them to become something new, to come and let Him make them into "fishers of men" (Mark 1:17). They were given an invitation to change not just their careers but their entire ways of life. Their responses to His invitation were immediate. They left their nets and boats, their livelihoods, their coworkers, and even a father—all to follow after Jesus (Mark 1:18, 20). They became well-acquainted with God's Son and were given lessons and opportunities unlike anything they had ever known. The results of their positive RSVPs were that the world was eternally impacted and changed for Christ.

Saul (later known as Paul the apostle) was actively persecuting Christians. One day in particular, he journeyed toward Damascus to persecute more of them. As he began his travels that day, he thought his lifestyle was right and perfect and that he was doing what God wanted him to do. But, contrary to his beliefs, Saul was not engaged in the work of God's kingdom—he was actually destroying it. In his misguided mind, he thought he was doing the right thing by stopping those who followed Jesus. These people believed that Jesus was the long-awaited

Messiah, but Saul believed that they needed to be brought back to the tradition of waiting for the Messiah to come. As Saul was traveling, Jesus suddenly appeared to him in a blinding light. Jesus confronted Saul and questioned him. He gave Saul an invitation to examine what he was doing and realize he was acting wrongly. Saul chose to accept the invitation and then changed how he conducted his life. Once he understood his misbehavior, he repented and became a great missionary for Jesus (see Acts 9). He chose to move from pursuing his own interests to pursuing God's interests. And with the proper guidance in his life, he did amazing things for God's kingdom. Because he said yes to God's plan, the world has never been the same since.

Amazing things happen when people respond favorably to the hand of God moving upon their lives. As we have seen from this small sampling of men, a day can begin without a person being involved in God's kingdom work. By day's end, however, everything can change and there can be involvement. I have personally experienced this phenomenon. God has invited me several times to become involved in specific things. I can even recall some of the exact dates and the very details of what I was doing when He spoke to me. I remember how the days began without my involvement in particular areas of His kingdom work, but by the time the days ended, I was involved.

The first time He invited me into His kingdom work was at the point of my salvation. Some of the other times of invitation were when I was not involved in the things I was supposed to be or when He simply wanted to grow me. One example is January 10, 2003. This was a time when God called me to follow Him into a whole new way of life. He simultaneously called me out of children's ministries and music ministries and into women's ministries instead. I had not been deeply involved in writing or speaking or ministering to women prior to that day, but then God spoke to me through His Holy Spirit and asked me to come and take part. I was called into the unknown but had the assurance of His presence with me. The things that I had known and done since my teenage years were set aside as He called me into new ways of serving in His kingdom. Around two o'clock that afternoon, it was as though I became a whole new person, with a new identity and a new agenda. Because I responded favorably, He has been teaching me through the years and equipping me to change the world for Christ.

I would like to ask you if you are involved in the work of God's kingdom. Have you said yes to His invitation? I invite you to come and follow Him, and help me change the world for Him. This is our time, in our generation, to impact the world for eternity. Get involved in the work of His kingdom and you will never be the same again!

THE EXTRAORDINARY CALL TO US

The invitations that God has issued to us are no ordinary invitations; He has called us to extraordinary things. He has called us to do the unexpected. He has even called us to do the humanly impossible, with the aid of His power. He has called us to live above social norms. He has called us to take the hard road and the narrow path. He has called us to deny ourselves and live for something and someone other than ourselves. He has called us to be His and His alone. He has called us to real love.

Jesus has called us to come to Him, to take His yoke upon us and learn from Him. What an extraordinary invitation and opportunity that has been given to us. When we come to Him, He supplies our physical and spiritual needs for each task, and this is how we are able to accomplish what He asks of us. When we choose to wear His yoke, we will find that it involves service, not pew warming. His yoke is to teach us to love: to love Him and to love others. If we do not have love, we are nothing. If we do not abide in Him, we can do nothing; but *with* His help, we can change the world. If we are yoked to Him, then we will be able to do extraordinary things. We can do all things—not some things, *all things*—through Christ who gives us strength (see Phil. 4:13). We should tuck this away in our hearts and minds so that when we are going through hard times, we can pull it out and remember its truth. Take comfort. Take heart. Take these words to heart. And remember, He will never leave us nor forsake us. Once we are found, we can never be lost again.

CHAPTER 7

Needy

IT'S WHY WE COME

We have examined reasons for why people came to Jesus in the past and will now examine why people still come to Him today. Although there are many detailed reasons, the underlying one is that people have needs only Jesus can meet. Some things are different today than they were back then, but other things, such as the nature of the human heart, never change. We come forward to obtain something from Him that we seek, to satisfy something in some part of who we are, whether in the spiritual, physical, relational, mental, or emotional realms of our beings. And because we are coming to the Lord of all the universe, we will find that these things can be satisfied. He created us. He designed us. And He knows exactly what we need. Our God is JEHOVAH, and He is the Most High over all the earth (Ps. 83:18).

Following is a sample of benefits that come from God's hand which meet the needs we have in each part of our beings:

FOR SPIRITUAL NEEDS

1. *We can be saved.* Our biggest need, whether we realize it or not, is the salvation of our souls. We cannot save ourselves, nor can we ever be good enough to enter heaven on our own, and that is precisely why Jesus came (Matt. 18:11; John 14:3). Jesus is the only way to have eternal life and be with God the Father (see John 14:6). When we accept who He is and what He did on the cross, we will receive salvation. In the future, our salvation will bring us eternal rest for our souls when He says, "Come … inherit the kingdom" (Matt. 25:34).

2. *We can have life.* Besides eternal life, we can also have the abundant and Spirit-filled life that Jesus came to give (John 6:63, 10:10, 14:16; 1 Cor. 12).

3. *We can be forgiven.* We cannot effectively or completely clean ourselves up without Him, but if we confess our sins, He is faithful and just to forgive us of them and to cleanse us from all unrighteousness (1 John 1:9). He provides ultimate cleansing and will remember our sins no more; they will be buried in the depths of the sea and be removed as far as the east is from the west (Mic. 7:19; Ps. 103:12).

4. *We can know God.* We can find proof of who He is. We can see His works all around us in creation. We can discover that He wants to be involved in our lives and have relationships with us. We can be in direct communication with Him. In the past, people needed a mediator to go between them and God for communication and for teaching. The mediators (e.g., prophets and priests) communed with God, interceding and inquiring on behalf of the people, and then relayed God's messages back to them. Today, we can know the final Mediator, Jesus, and because of Him, we can know God firsthand.

The greatest evidence of God's desire for us to know Him and be in relationship with Him was the sending of His Son. While Jesus was on earth, He mediated between God and men. He taught the people what God wanted them to know, and He communicated with God about the people. Then, His death on the cross served as the intermediary sacrifice that made a way for us and God to be together. And now, Jesus ever lives to make intercession for us (Heb. 7:24–26). When He returned to heaven, He left the Holy Spirit to dwell with us. We should be taking immediate advantage of this access to God and learning what He wants us to do in life. We can receive instruction on what to do today and what to do next. If we are listening to His voice, we will gain words of great wisdom to help us make the best choices.

5. *We can be established in our promised land.* The Israelites were offered an inheritance, and they were told how to claim it. God wanted to gift them with life and land, homes and crops, the removal of their enemies, and the

methods to build relationships. However, they did not take advantage of the offer to the extent that they could have and should have. We should learn from their example and from their mistakes. When we do not act now, we may miss the opportunity altogether. When we do not drive out the enemies of our souls (e.g., procrastination, negative thoughts and emotions, selfishness, self-reliance, or lust) while we have the chance, they will coil and wait for the perfect time to strike, later rearing their ugly heads in attempts to destroy us. They will exert their wills over ours and threaten God's plans for our lives. If we do not deal with these issues, there will be detours and delays in entering into all that God has for us at the time He wishes us to have it. We cannot sit around inactively, yet be expecting the extraordinary. We need to walk forward in faith, believing in what God has said and can do, and then we will arrive at our promised land victoriously.

We need to work at living life *with* Him and *for* Him. Proverbs 13:11 (NKJV) says, "But he who gathers by labor will increase." We need to cooperate with God so that we can grow, be equipped, be supplied with what we need, and be firmly established. Rather than building foundations on grains of sand that can slip through our fingers, we need to let our foundations be rooted and built up in Him so that they are as solid as mountains. May our roots go deep—all the way to Jesus—and the Highest Himself will establish us.

6. *We can find a purpose for living.* By choosing to serve God, we come under His yoke rather than remaining under Satan's yoke, serving other gods, and ultimately the god of this world, Satan himself. And rather than seeking to make a name for ourselves, we can choose to know Jesus and glorify *His* name. God has a purpose for choosing to give us a particular calling in life, and we are to use that calling to be fruitful for His kingdom. We should strive to make a difference in this world, and in the one to come, by touching people's lives with hope, love, and the good news of salvation. The things that we do in accordance with His purpose will have a lasting result. Being fruitful will bring us into God's presence and deepen and strengthen our relationship with Him.

7. We can be an instrument of change in this world. Upon becoming children in the family of God, we are grafted into the vine and become part of a living, breathing, powerful thing—God's very presence. As we stay connected to Him, we will gain equipping and strength, wisdom and guidance, assurance and comfort. He will become our life source, a part of each breath that we take in and each one that we breathe out. He will become our all in all and give us everything that we need. He will move *in* us and *through* us while we are abiding in Him, and He will enable us to do above and beyond all that we ask, think, or imagine (see Eph. 3:20). He is where our strength lies, and He will fill us with His power so that we can accomplish all He has for us to do. He will do great things *for* us and will do great things *through* us so that *He* can be glorified and people can be drawn to Him. We will never be the same after we have encountered God in such a way, and those who encounter Him through our lives will be changed as well. Great and mighty is His name!

Jesus said, "You did not choose Me, but I chose you and appointed you that you should go and bear fruit, and *that* your fruit should remain, that whatever you ask the Father in My name He may give you" (John 15:16 NKJV). Abiding in the vine and being fruitbearers will change the world, although how much the lives of others change is not for us to say. Our task is to represent Jesus and minister to people as God desires us to. We can help people understand that they have been chosen by God and have been invited to dwell with Him forever. There is no one considered to be insignificant—all are special and all are loved. We need to make sure people know this.

FOR MENTAL NEEDS

We can come directly to God to be taught by Him and gain knowledge about Him. When Jesus was teaching, people came; and when people came to Him, He taught (see John 8:2). He was willing to share knowledge with those who were seeking it. There is a benefit in our day because we can seek His knowledge and be taught by Him at any time. In contrast, during Jesus's lifetime on earth, people could only come to Him when He was physically there. They did not have His words recorded in the

Gospels, and they did not have the Holy Spirit because it had not yet been given. Their only recourse was to take what they could get, when they could get it, and sometimes that involved a great deal of traveling and an investment of quite a bit of time. Yet here we are in the twenty-first century, potentially surrounded in our own homes by a stack of bibles, living a short distance away from a church that has its doors open (perhaps every day of the week), connected to the internet with His words at our fingertips as quickly as we can type, and we act like Sunday is all that there is and we had better take advantage of what we can get in an hour. But realize this: He is available to us daily, hourly, moment by moment, *now*! Anytime we want to access His teaching, and there is the freedom and availability to do so, we can access the Bible. But even if we are unable to access these words, we can pray and be taught by the Spirit. We have the opportunity and privilege to know God's words. We can come before the throne of grace at any given moment and then go out again with those words and that grace in our minds, hearts, and lives.

We can discover mental strength and peace by coming to learn of God. He can give comfort and knowledge that will cause our minds to be at rest even in the midst of chaos. Can our minds grasp this amazing God, the God who rules over the raging seas and calms the waves, who created and owns the heavens, who has an arm that is mighty (Ps. 89:9, 11, 13)? How utterly astounding to realize that this same God *loves us*. We will find stability in Him when we take time to learn how great He is, how much power He has, and how very involved in the intimate details of our lives He is. "When He gives quietness, who then can make trouble?" (Job 34:29 NKJV). God gives sleep to His beloved, and He blesses His people with peace (Pss. 29:11, 127:2). This peace is otherworldly and incomprehensible, but it can be ours when we ask Him for it. We do not need to be anxious about anything; we just need to pray. God can do anything, so there is no need to fret. We do not even need to worry about when the times of persecution come. The Holy Spirit will give us the words that we need to speak (Luke 12:11–12), and no one will be able to pluck us out of God's hand (John 10:28). There is peace in believing the words that Jesus prayed to His Father, because we have the same Father— and He said that all things were possible for God (Mark 14:36). It is all about having the perspective of His truths. When we make up our minds to know God, how we handle life will entirely change.

If we find ourselves in an unbearable situation and think that we cannot remember His words, the Spirit will bring things to our remembrance. Or if there is ever a time when the words do not seem to be enough, we can ask for help from the Spirit to have more faith to believe the words. He can help our unbelief, and He can add to our faith.

We can come to have our questions answered by God and to be guided through life. We can gain knowledge, direction, and clarity when we are seeking His thoughts. We can gain an understanding of who we are in Christ and then inquire of God about how to live our lives based on what He reveals to us. Focus can be sharpened as we gain God's perspective on who we are and why we exist. It is important to learn about the traits we should possess as Jesus's followers and also discover the gifts and abilities with which we are individually endowed. May we purposely take on the mind of Christ, letting His thoughts become our thoughts, and may these thoughts in turn influence our behaviors.

FOR RELATIONAL NEEDS

God has always wanted to be in relationship with us. Even before the time of Creation, He had already made a plan for His Son to come to us to make relationship possible. Jesus then made the choice to lay a foundation for relationship when He agreed to come to earth and die for us. Now we have a choice to make: we get to decide if we want to enter into relationship with Jesus. We have the final say about whether this building project continues.

While Jesus was on earth, He was building relationships. He walked along, specifically calling twelve men to enter into relationship with Him and become His disciples. He spent time with them, teaching them and investing in their lives. He was with them in good times and bad. For instance, one night while the disciples were in a ship and experiencing a time of great storm and great fear, Jesus joined with them. There He was, walking upon the water, straight into their crisis (see Mark 6:48). But Jesus also traveled from place to place, teaching and ministering to other people besides these twelve men. He united with people—regardless of their statuses—in whatever circumstances they were going through. And He still wants to join with people today.

God has drawn us with loving-kindness (Jer. 31:3)—greatly shown as Jesus was lifted up on the cross to draw all people to Himself. If we choose to enter into relationship with Him, then His Spirit will be available to intercede for us in prayer and to remind us that we are indeed God's children (see Rom. 8:16, 26–27). When we come to Him, He comes to us (James 4:8). And once we are with Him, nothing can ever separate us from Him (see Rom. 8:31–39). In Him, we will find a friend who sticks closer than a brother (Prov. 18:24).

God is approachable because the sacrifice of Jesus paved the way. The walk of suffering that Jesus took to the cross gives us the opportunity to walk with Him on streets of gold. We can come and experience communion with Him. We can give Him the worship that He deserves. We can bask in His presence, and indeed, be filled with His presence. We can offer or receive a new song. We can talk to Him in prayer, and listen for Him to speak to us. "O come, let us worship and bow down: let us kneel before the LORD our maker" (Ps. 95:6).

When we summarize what we are here for and what we need to do in life, it is pretty simple: we are to love the Lord our God with all that we are, and love our neighbors as ourselves (see Matt. 22:36–40). We were not created to be alone; we were created for relationships, with Him and with others. We can love Him and love others because He helps us to do these things. He gives us the capability to live out His perfect plans for our lives. And when we are in relationship with Him, we will experience love, fulfillment, joy, hope, and strength. We will be made rich, and the lives of others will be made rich, too, because of Him in us and Him through us.

FOR EMOTIONAL NEEDS

We can find fulfillment and have every emotional need met through God. We can find hope, joy, comfort, peace, and relationship. And we will find the truest and purest love of all when we find the love of God. We are greatly loved by Him, and that love can be poured out from us into the lives of others. "Beloved, let us love one another, for love is of God; and everyone who loves is born of God and knows God" (1 John 4:7 NKJV).

Listening to God's voice and surrendering ourselves to Him enables us to live in such different ways than does proceeding in our own strength. God's rest teaches us to emote differently and to have divinely-altered perspectives. When we surrender our minds to the mind of Christ and choose to walk in the Spirit rather than the flesh, our emotional states will become ones of joy and balance. Even when we pass through distressing and traumatizing times, our emotions can be expressed in godly ways. God created us with emotions, and we are permitted to express those emotions, as long as we do it in ways that are not sinful. When we express our emotions in negative ways, and when we allow the negativity to remain within us, that is when we will experience problems; that is when our representation of Jesus ceases to be seen and when our rest and strength diminishes. Negative emotions do not bring us rest; instead, they leave us in active and perpetual states of discomfort. They bring us anxiety and agitation and keep us from experiencing the healing of our wounds. Let's look briefly at a few of them that we frequently need help to overcome.

Being rigid, being wound too tight, and refusing to move out of our comfort zones are not behaviors that are going to give us the rest that we need. When we are inflexible, bitter, angry, prideful, and tense, we have a tendency to grumble about the little things. When we grumble, we are not at rest. Our inner feelings are going to pop out and inform everyone of our grumpy attitudes. During the period when we are experiencing unhappiness, we are not experiencing God's peace, joy, and contentment. We need to get rid of the grumbles and not be grumpy grapes. It is important to get a handle on our emotions because before we know it, one negative emotion will breed another, and then all together they will influence our behaviors. And then those who happen to be nearby will have to be on guard.

Anger will affect our manners of expression. It will make us rough rather than gentle, and prideful rather than humble. Things will not be restful if we are snapping or are even on the verge of it. Things will not be restful if we are allowing anger and bitterness to grow. Our minds will obsess, our hearts will pound, and our emotions will fluctuate as we plot and plan our revenge. What we need in these circumstances is forgiveness. It is vital. It will come to us from God only when we have given it to others (see Matt. 6:14; Mark 11:26).

Focusing on our difficulties, rather than on God's character and promises, will not allow us to rest. Anxiety is an opponent that challenges our faith; it crushes and steals it. Instead of adding to our lives, anxiety takes from them. We will waver back and forth if we are not sure of who God is. When there is unrest in our hearts, it showcases our unbelief. Anxious and fearful hearts will not be listening for answers to prayer, and they will have difficulty even formulating any prayers. Fear and anxiety will eclipse God's power. And just like an eclipse, the more His power is hidden, the darker our days become. We need to calm our hearts with truth and trust. God has said that when we call to Him, He will answer us and He will be with us in our times of trouble (Ps. 91:15).

We can look at biblical examples of people who discovered these truths of God's presence and God's help. Jonah, for example, knew the true source of hope and help. He said, "When my soul fainted within me, I remembered the LORD; And my prayer went *up* to You, Into Your holy temple" (Jon. 2:7 NKJV). The book of Psalms is full of David's prayers that were voiced in difficult times. Job had a conversation with God during a time of intense suffering. Jesus prayed before His crucifixion and also at many other times throughout His life. These men did not bear their burdens in silence, and they did not bear their loads alone. They needed rest for the distress in their souls, so they came to God through prayer, crying out for help. Their words went farther than their physical bodies could go; their prayers went all the way to God Himself. And because of those prayers, God intervened. These men learned more about God as He taught them during their trials. They had their expectations of being helped met, and they found the rest their souls had sought.

We need to take time to rest so that we have opportunity to accept the healing that God wants to give. Jesus has been called the Balm of Gilead. When we are in the depths of despair, He will place a healing balm on our hurts and remind us that we are loved. We can also find healing from sin and its consequences as we accept the gift of His grace. He is greater than the circumstances that we face and greater than the sin that tries to destroy us. We simply need to let Him tend to our wounds. He is able to bind them up because He is mighty in power (see Ps. 147:3, 5).

Allowing God to help and heal our emotions will allow us to persevere. Resting and trusting in Him will remove a huge load from us. When He shares our pain, we will truly be comforted. Having His support will reduce our stress levels. He will provide a peace that passes all understanding (Phil. 4:7). It is not denial. It is not false hope. It is true comfort that strengthens us and helps us endure in this life, no matter what has happened in the past, what we live in today, and what will come our ways in the future. He is the Ancient of Days, and He is the contemporary. He has always existed, and He is here with us now. He is the everlasting God, and He will be with us throughout our futures.

Psalm 142:1–7 is a good passage to read when feeling overwhelmed. These verses tell us that we can cry out to God and let Him know about our complaints and the trouble in which we find ourselves. He knows our paths. He is there for us when and where no one else is, even if it is the middle of the night and we are at our absolute lowest points. He is our refuge. He is our deliverer. He is going to bless us. Instead of letting our hearts be troubled, we should focus on our belief in Him and know that He is preparing a place in heaven for us (John 14:3). Better days are coming.

God has created us as amazingly intricate and complex creatures with so many pieces and parts, with so many expressions and actions; may all of them be true and beautiful representations of who He is, seen by all those around us. For a watching world, may we be pictures of love, beauty, and grace, from the inside out.

FOR PHYSICAL NEEDS

Sometimes, our lives are literal messes; however, they do not have to remain so. Our lives can be improved on various levels when we allow God to get involved. Job said, "You have granted me life and favor, And Your care has preserved my spirit" (Job 10:12 NKJV). God can do the same for us that He did for Job: grant us life and favor and preserve our spirits. We can receive the abundant life that He offers, starting now;

there is no need to wait until eternity. Being given spiritual life will affect change in our physical lives. His Spirit will direct us in how to live. If we need to change, He will be there to help us do it. In some instances, we can make fresh starts and get our lives turned around. In other cases, however, we will be unable to change the circumstances. Yet even if we cannot, we can be thriving where we are rather than just surviving. We do not have to remain in our circumstances unchanged; God's power can be invoked and a difference made. We can be "strengthened with all might, according to his glorious power" (Col. 1:11). The change can course through our veins and touch every part of who we are, even if our circumstances remain the same.

God is able to meet our physical needs and may even do it in ways that we never asked, thought of, or imagined. I could share many, many stories with you of evidence from my own life, and I have also heard and read about so many others. It is astounding the things that God can do for His children! The blessings can come from the most unlikely of places—from believers and unbelievers alike. God worked through Pharaoh, the heathen ruler of Egypt, in order to bless the Israelites and meet their needs. Pharaoh spoke to Joseph, saying, "And take your father and your households, and come unto me: and I will give you the good of the land of Egypt, and ye shall eat the fat of the land" (Gen. 45:18). We are significant to God and He is going to take care of the things we need. He cares for all of His creations; He even values each little sparrow—and we are of more value than many of them combined. He knows when each one of them falls to the ground (see Matt. 10:29, 31). They have no worries as He provides for them, and He cares even more for us. Think of it this way: God cares for the birds and for the people watching them! Yes, God can give of His riches and of the good of the land to supply every need that His children have.

We can receive rest in our weary bodies. Remember the rest offered to the heavy laden in Matthew 11:28. During times that we need help, when we are in distress, when we have circumstances come crashing down upon us, He is there. When we are persecuted, when we are imprisoned, when our life is threatened, He is there.

Job experienced so many challenges that wore him down. The

changes in his life touched him physically and then sank deep into his being; his mind, emotions, spirit, and relationships were all affected. He was devastated and bowed down in the dirt. He was in a sorry state of being and a somewhat sorry state of mind. Hope seemed lost. He could not help himself. He did not have the strength of stones or brass or any other resource to remedy the devastation in his life (Job 6:11–13). He needed God's help and would not have rest until he allowed God to give it to him. And then, there was God. God touched Job's life, and Job was able to get up and move forward. And like Job, we no longer have to lie there on the ground, defeated by the heavy loads of life; God can step in and make our burdens lighter too. Yes, the help of God can be found in us if *He* is found in us. He will give us grace and strength when we hope in Him and choose to walk uprightly. We can pass through our daily trials with strong and hope-filled hearts.

IT'S WHY HE SUPPLIES

God wants us to be overcomers, and He will help us with His mighty hand and outstretched arm. He can meet *whatever* needs we have, in ordinary and even extraordinary ways. He will send us the help, supplies, and strength that we need in order to accomplish the things that He has called us to do—take note: the things that He has called us to do, not the things we have invented for ourselves that do not fit into His plans. Also take note: He supplies our *needs*.

God met the needs of the Israelites in extraordinary ways. He worked a miracle by bringing down the walls of Jericho; He can do the same in our lives if we follow His ways. No walls are too high if God is on our side! To us, it is unknown exactly what will transpire in our lives and when, but we can know that God is good, and He is working something good—in His way and in His timing. We can safely arrive in our promised land and take possession of the things that God desires for us to have. We can live and love, work and rest, having peace in who He is.

When the Israelites prepared to cross the Jordan River so they could take possession of the Promised Land, their leader Joshua spoke to the three tribes who were going to remain behind on the other side of the river. These tribes were going to be away from the visible presence of the Lord and away from the remainder of the congregation; thus, Joshua cautioned them and said, "But take careful heed to do the commandment and the law which Moses the servant of the LORD commanded you, to love the LORD your God, to walk in all His ways, to keep His commandments, to hold fast to Him, and to serve Him with all your heart and with all your soul" (Josh. 22:5 NKJV). In dissecting this verse, we can see a way to establish our lives and order our priorities. There are six verbs of instruction that will be beneficial to maintaining a relationship with God: *do, love, walk, keep, hold,* and *serve.* If we *do* the commandment and the law, *love* the Lord our God, *walk* in all His ways, *keep* His commandments, *hold* fast to Him, and *serve* Him, then we will remain on the correct path as we live for Him. These are the things that He wants for us because these are the things that we need.

CHAPTER 8
There Is No Present like the Time

We have examined people of the past. We have looked at people of the present. Now let's consider the importance of the present in regard to the future. The present time is something precious that we so often take for granted, yet it is so very important to our lives, both now, and for our lives to come. Time is a gift to us. And because our time is so precious and important, the time involved in accepting invitations needs to be given careful consideration.

When to come. That is the question. What is the duration of an invitation? Invitations do not last forever; they have expiration dates. They apply to a specific event at a set time. Even if they are given with a flexible window for the timeline, there is usually a roughly-held ending time in mind. If someone says to you, "Come see me sometime," he or she is implying that it should be done while both of you are still living. Based on other information you may have discussed, you may be able to glean even more extensive details on how long that invitation will be open. It is prudent to act upon open-ended invitations in a timely manner, before the circumstances change. Do not delay and miss your opportunity.

Jesus's invitation to come to Him is no exception to the structure of an invitation—there is an ending time in mind. His invitation has remained open longer than most because He wants all people to come to repentance and not perish, but there *will be* an end to His invitation someday. The invitation will end when the necessary things prophesied in the Bible have come to pass and God the Father calls for the end of all things. Although the event that He is inviting us to is going to last for all time—for eternity—there is a limited amount of time that the invitation will remain open and RSVPs be accepted. The time before the doors of heaven are shut is decreasing by the moment. Jesus's invitation is to live forever in heaven, but the invitation to enter heaven does not last forever.

Jesus has promised so many wonderful things, but we need to make Him our own in order to claim these promises. These things are available for life in the present and for life after death, but they are based upon the condition that we come now to accept His death, burial, resurrection, and forgiveness. This is a decision that each of us must make, and do so before it is eternally too late, due either to our death or His return. So to answer the question of when to come, the answer is: *come when you are called, before your death, before God calls for the end of time.* An RSVP to Jesus's invitation is of utmost importance, it is even urgent, because no one knows the day or the hour that time on earth will end. All we can rely on is this exact moment of existence, and what we choose to do with it has eternal consequences.

Salvation was spoken and confirmed; we should not neglect it. But if we do choose to neglect it, we will not escape what is to come. Indecision or delaying a decision is, in fact, still a decision; it is a *no*. If we die without having said yes to Him, then it will be too late for us to be admitted to the event. We will be unable to give any excuses. We will be unable to ask for more time or another chance. Everyone must stand in judgment and give an account for his or her life, and what has already been done is all that can be done. Please do not neglect your opportunity to be saved. Life passes by quickly and we do not have any time to waste. We need to take care of what matters while we still can, and where we are going to spend eternity is definitely something that matters.

With an invitation, there must come a response, and not giving a response is still a response. The response to the invitation will have ramifications, just as there are consequences to every choice that we make. If we overeat at Christmas and gain two pounds, it may seem inconsequential, but if we do this year after year, before we know it, we will find that in ten years we have gained twenty pounds. A little bit compounded adds up to a big amount as time passes by. Many little noes to God are still one big no. A little attitude each time eventually builds up into one big resentment and rebellion. Our hearts will be hardening over time until they are standing up in defiance. Things do not have to get to this point, however. Different outcomes can be achieved based on making different choices at the beginning or making course adjustments along the way. If we have told God no in the past, we currently have an opportunity to tell Him yes. We can alter our courses now and ultimately, for all eternity. One of His RSVP numbers is "For whosoever shall call upon the name of the Lord shall be saved" (Rom. 10:13).

CONSIDER THE PRESENT

God has invited us in our lifetimes to receive the gift of His salvation, love, and presence. He draws us to Himself through multitudes of ways. He may draw us with words through things such as the Bible, a pastor's sermon, a song, or a conversation with a believer. He may draw us through the supernatural with things such as miracles, visions, dreams, and signs. He may draw us through creation with beauty so stunning that we are awestruck and our hearts have to worship. He may draw us through the actions of others. He may draw us through gifts or talents that He has given to us or someone else. But no matter which methods He uses to draw us, He draws us with loving-kindness because He has loved us with an everlasting love (Jer. 31:3). His most amazing and sacrificial representation of this love was expressed when Jesus was crucified on the cross. Before Jesus died in such a horrible way He said, "And I, if I am lifted up from the earth, will draw all *peoples* to Myself" (John 12:32 NKJV). His very death draws us to life. This was His purpose for coming to us: so we could come to Him.

Today is a gift of opportunity to come and speak with God in prayer. We are able to pray at any point in the day to accept the gift that God offers us, but since we do not know what will happen in the next moments of our lives, we should not delay something as important as coming to God. There are no guarantees that we will make it past the morning, until our lunch hours, or through the night. We need to act now, while we still can. We can pray right now to accept His invitation. There is no better time than the present. Today is the day. Will today be *your* day?

CHAPTER 9

Refusing Excuses

THE REFUSALS AND THE LACK OF RSVPS

Sending out invitations is definitely an interesting thing because the host or hostess does not know if, when, or how the invitees will RSVP. Although I have hosted a variety of events, I have found the behaviors of the invitees to be similar. Some politely reply with a timely yes or no. Some call at the last minute to see if they can squeeze in. Some tell me they are going to attend but never show up (some have legitimate reasons for their absences while others have simply changed their minds). Some never answer the invitation at all, nor do they show up, and I am left to wonder why. And then there are other invitees, though rare, who are party-crashers; they never answer the invitation yet show up on my doorstep, expecting to be included in the event. What are the reasons the invitees do not RSVP to me but still expect to be included? What motivates people to behave in such ways, and what does such behavior do to a host or hostess? I do not know the answers to these questions for certain, but I can imagine what they might be, based upon my personal experiences and the thoughts I have had regarding events to which I have been invited.

There are so many matters in life that can keep us from good things, enjoyable things, and the company of those we enjoy. Sometimes, the cause can be an unforeseen scheduling conflict in the form of a trip to the emergency room, unexpectedly having to pick up a sick child, or a babysitter's last-minute cancellation; but sometimes it is just our own selves that keep us from these good things because we simply do not RSVP. I imagine that we all have found ourselves at one time or another not giving an RSVP because of disinterest, preoccupation, forgetfulness, disliking the type of event, or feeling uncomfortable with the crowd that is going to be there. Other times, we have justifiable reasons for not attending events (e.g., physical limitations, lack of training, financial restrictions), but we still neglect to give our RSVPs. Although these are legitimate excuses for not attending an event, they are excuses nonetheless. Thus, we can see that many things, from any and every angle, can keep us from replying to the hosts. But whatever the reasons, the results are the same: the RSVPs are missing and so are we.

At times, we make assumptions about what an event will be like and decide not to go based on those assumptions, never even giving it a chance. But the reality is that we do not know everything that will happen at the event. Life is just not that predictable. We do not know every word that will be spoken, every interaction that will take place, or every associated detail. For example, who wants to go to Financial Aid Night at the high school? Or any financial meeting, for that matter? It does not sound like a fun use of time, but valuable information will likely be disseminated at that meeting. And who knows, there might even be cookies afterward. (There were. They were chocolate chip! *And I got the most amazing photos of the sunset over a nearby lake!*) We try to determine what events represent and then make decisions based on whether or not we deem them important enough to attend. On occasion, our judgments are off. The truth is, some events are beneficial, important in concept, maybe even essential; and despite the perfunctory things, they provide us with opportunities to interact with others who may need our presence there. And above all, even without the cookies, these events provide us with opportunities to show others the love of Jesus.

As a hostess, I am grateful for those who RSVP as I have requested, even if they are declining the invitation. I appreciate the common courtesy of a reply, but I also realize that there are those who have no idea that they are supposed to give me an answer, regardless of which it is. When people show up that I did not anticipate, it disrupts seating and supplies, but I still allow these non-responders to enter my home rather than turn them away. Because I know these people, I do not deny them access to the event. We have developed relationships, and I do not hold their lack of RSVPs against them; I know that they are not perfect, and they surely know that I am not, either! We have established an unwritten set of rules: they do not reply, but I still let them in the door.

Things work quite differently with strangers, though, both for my events and in the spiritual realm. Just as I will not allow strangers into my home because they were not invited and because we do not have relationships that precipitate us being in the same dwelling together, so it is with God. Imagine what it must be like for God. Just as I value a stranger as a person, God also values each person; yet, just as I cannot allow a stranger to enter my home, He is unable to allow those who have not developed a relationship with Him to enter His. You can probably understand why I cannot allow strangers into my home, but do you understand why God cannot permit strangers into His? There have not been relationships established between them, everything has been one-sided. They have not given their RSVPs. They have not contacted Him through prayer to say they want Jesus to be their Savior so they can come into heaven. They will not come to Him so they can have life. These strangers have not come properly prepared by knowing the Host, and thus, they cannot join in the festivities. Their lack of responses to God when invited equates to refusals of relationship.

We are not His friends if we do not do as He commands (John 15:14). And if we are not His friends, He cannot allow us into His eternal home. Luke 13:25 tells us that one day He is going to shut the door. Strangers will then be trying to get in, but because their names are not written in the Book of Life, He will have to tell them that it is too late for them and that they must depart because He never knew them (see Matt. 7:23). On the other hand, those who have previously chosen Him will come from the north, south, east, and west and will get to sit down in the kingdom of God (Luke 13:29).

RESISTING A REST: EXCUSES FOR REFUSING TO COME

Sometimes when we receive invitations, we base our RSVPs on whether or not we are obligated to go. We sometimes whine or groan the words "Do I have to?" We sometimes even ask this same question when we are presented with invitations from God, even the one given to us in Matthew

11:28–30. People have resisted coming to God almost since the beginning of time. They have resisted His plans, His ways, His commandments, and even His love and blessings. The question "Do I have to?" becomes a perfect example of resisting God, and in the case of what these verses offer, resisting a rest.

Why do we ask if we "have to" come? What causes us to resist coming to God? The reasons are many and varied, but they seem to fall into some common categories. Let's look at a few. (1) Perhaps it is because of how we develop our personalities. How we think, feel, and perceive the world around us affects how we pass through this life and how we relate to others, including God. We have tendencies, and we allow tendencies to control our choices. (2) Perhaps it is because of circumstances or experiences. Our current or past situations affect how we view God and whether we see Him as a good guy or a bad guy. Our circumstances and experiences influence our perspectives, and at times, even change our personalities. All of this, in turn, transfers to our decision-making processes which influence whether we come to God or not and receive His rest or not. (3) Perhaps there are some influential factors that we value, such as things and people, and when they become a part of the mix, they can cause us to reconsider our choices or even dissuade us. We want to please them and serve them, and they can become distractions and excuses for why we are not turning to God. Simply put, the people we are, the people we are trying to be, and the people with whom we live life can cause us to refuse to come. We end up with obstacles in the way: thought processes that interfere, spiritual issues that stump us, and relational influences that inhibit. As a result of these obstacles, every part of who we are can be found to be resistant to coming to Him, and thus, resistant to being truly able to rest.

The scope is much grander than this, of course. There are so many particulars that can hinder and even stop us from coming to Jesus (or from returning to Him), even though He is the best medicine for what ails us and is the best healer of our wounds. Think of a scenario where a child is aided with medicine, has a splinter removed, or has a wound cleaned. Fear and resistance are frequent behaviors in these instances, even though something beneficial is being done for the child. When the caretaking is complete, the caregiver might say, "See how easy that was?" We can be just like the child in these scenarios, fearful and resistant. In reality, it is so easy to come to Jesus, and that is the absolute best thing for us to do, yet it seems difficult and even undesirable for some reason. But if we would only come to Him, we would find good things. We would receive the best care that we have ever experienced. Our hearts would be captured by love and filled with peace if we drew near to Him rather than ignoring, resisting, or abandoning Him.

BEHAVIORAL REFUSALS

Because of our behaviors, we can be our own obstacles in coming to God. Our personality make-ups, our quirks, our attitudes, our perceptions of life, and our physical and spiritual prioritizing can cause us to keep away from God. Some of us prefer to search for our answers outside of God because we think that another way will be more to our liking. We can often be stubborn, selfish, fearful of the unknown, and resistant to change. At times, we may be fearful of changes or be uncomfortable with having to do things in new ways, but at other times, we just have poor attitudes and simply dislike change for change's sake. Even when we are presented with opportunities to change for the better, we resist. Some people absolutely refuse to change for no other reason than because they scorn God. There are heartbreaking situations where people not only refuse to change but abandon God altogether, never to return. Whatever the reasons are, we have commonalties in our refusals: they all stem from the root of our sin natures. We do not want to submit to anyone else because we want to do what is pleasing to us. People began behaving this way shortly after they began to walk the earth. In the Garden of Eden, God's commands were resisted as fruit was eaten from the wrong tree (Gen. 3). Later in time, God pointed out a place for His people to rest, but they refused His invitation (Isa. 28:12). Jesus experienced the same problems as His Father had: people became resistant to His teachings and left Him. Jesus even asked His disciples if they were going to leave Him as the others had (John 6:60–67). Resistance was a reality then, and it is still a reality today.

The way we arrange our schedules and our life goals can be reasons why we do not come to Him. We like our plans, and we like making them. We like to be the ones in control. Our pursuits become central, and we become preoccupied with our lives. We may find ourselves buying into the lies that happiness comes from pursuing things like possessions, relationships, financial security, or success. We engage in these pursuits because of our desires and sometimes out of obligation. We do not want to be still because then we will seem unproductive and ineffective, and that is not something that is expected of us. The ideas of productivity and effectiveness are found in our society and may even have been drilled into us by our families as we grew up. We know we have to get the job done, and we know precisely how to do it. We are the focus, so we are the obstacle in coming to God.

Truly there are many things that compete for our time, and we may find ourselves rationalizing that it is "just this once" or that it is the only time we have in our schedules to do the activity. We may find that we give up church attendance and Bible study time so that we can watch the local and then the national news, or maybe sitcoms full of foul language, perversion, and crude humor. We may spend hours every day with screen time but only spend minutes in prayer, if even that. We may avoid our quiet times because there is a load of laundry to do or maybe an infomercial to watch about the latest beauty treatment. I think it is genuinely sad when I can find time to weed my flower garden but not find time to spend with God. I have truly reached a low if I would rather pull weeds than spend time with God! Somehow we find time to do everything else except walk with Him. He gets put at the bottom of the list. He is not our top priority because someone or something else, even a thistle or a dandelion, occupies His rightful place.

The availability of so many activities can be an obstacle, a curse rather than a blessing. We run our children and ourselves from event to event to event. We neglect the spiritual training and Christian fellowship we should have because there is a game, tournament, competition, or recital that conflicts with when the church doors are open or when we could be doing family devotions at home. These pastimes fill our schedules to overflowing. They divide and conquer our families as they send each member in different directions and exhaust us to the core. We want our children to have the best, be the best, and experience the things we never had the opportunities or funds to do as children. Are these things wrong? Are sports and music and hobbies wrong? No! It is what we do with them and how we prioritize them above God and His desires for us that is the problem.

Here is a perfect example of my imperfection—if I had to give it a name I would call it "My Eight Days of Unrest." My family went away on an eight-day vacation to visit relatives. They went without me because my health did not permit me to travel at that time. In a way, this meant a vacation for me too. Less cooking, less laundry, less commuting, and so on. So, did I have an eight-day vacation like my family did? No. Why? Because I did not rest. I compiled a to-do list that grew by the day instead of shrinking. I fully anticipated that God would speak mightily to me while I had eight days to be alone with Him, but then I only took the time to be still before Him twice. I prayed quickly. I did my devotions quickly. Why? Because I had stuff to do! I did not have time to come to Him; there was a list beckoning me. I let *its* voice drown out *His* voice. I know now that I did not use my time wisely. Did I need to scrape the limescale off my shower walls? Did I need to organize my workroom? What significance did those two activities have? What did they do to shape my character and prepare me to be more serviceable and effective for God's kingdom? Even three days of illness that slowed me down during this time did not serve as much of a motivator to deepen my relationship with God; instead, I trudged from room to room doing "stuff," all the while feeling crummy. I did not come to Him, nor rest in Him. Opportunities were lost during those eight days, never to be regained.

Those are very difficult words for me to write, and that is a painful experience to remember. Thankfully, though, God's mercies are new. I moved on into today, praying to learn more of Him, praying to remember and learn from my past mistakes, and hoping not to squander or resist future opportunities to come to Him and rest. And as a side note, I recently had the opportunity for another eight days of rest as my family had to make a trip without me, and I am happy to report that I did much better this time! I learned from my past mistakes and made better use of the opportunities that God presented to me during this time. Thank you, God, for another opportunity—and for the growth!

Our definitions and pursuits of success can be obstacles that keep us from God. Our success-driven society encourages us to try to make the most of the opportunities that we are offered in life, and we try to pass this concept on to the next generation as well. One of the opportunities that is offered to us lately is evolving technology. We invest our time and money so that we can have the best or most current technology, but sometimes we misappropriate it, and sometimes it becomes a distraction to us. We spend hours texting, checking our social media pages, and playing games instead of kneeling before the Father with our eyes in the Word and our hearts listening to His messages. We want to try out all of the latest fads like fitness apps, pinning, and online shopping, yet we do not spend that time or use those things to minister to others and may even be doing them in lieu of what God has asked us to do. But technology is not the only place of opportunity and distraction. There are also the money-making places, the gym, and the social functions. But these are not the places and things of true success. A life lived with Jesus is the way to be successful. The "me" in "Come unto me" means Jesus and not any of these other things or places. He is the opportunity that we should make the most of! We have been given great gifts and a forum to make a great impact; may we send out His Word and His light in whatever our hands find to do. Being successful in His eyes is true success.

Besides trying to make the most of our opportunities, we try to make the most of our stuff. At times, we pursue material things rather than our Maker. Possessions can distract us, deter us, and even completely prevent us from coming to God. Money can be such an issue if it is allowed to draw one's focus. Jesus spoke of wealth and told us that we cannot serve both it and God. He said, "It is easier for a camel to go through the eye of a needle, than for a rich man to enter into the kingdom of God" (Matt. 19:24). This is true because when money gets put before God, it creates self-reliance. A friend of mine often asked for prayer for her relatives. They were wealthy and believed that they had achieved this status on their own, and thus, did not have a need for God. And remember the rich young ruler whose wealth became an obstacle to a life spent following God and serving others. It made him sad to think of parting with his wealth, so he decided to keep it instead. He left Jesus behind. He left others behind.

And he left without choosing eternal life (see Matt. 19:16–22). It has been said that our checkbooks show where our priorities are. We can become so consumed with our earning, our spending, and our debt that we do not spend time with God; or we can be ashamed of our spending and debt and avoid Him because of it. Where does our treasure truly lie?

Redirecting where we focus and also viewing what we have as belonging to Him and being for His use will definitely make a difference in how rested we are. Gratitude and contentment can lighten our loads. Our eyes can be opened to see those in need and how we can be a blessing to them. Joy and blessing will fill our hearts as we give rather than receive. And when we realize what truly matters, and receive that truth into our souls, we will find that we are satisfied. Truly, God is all that we need. May we learn to be satisfied with having it all!

MENTAL REFUSALS

Our perspectives and our worldviews can become obstacles that cause us to resist a rest. A personality trait that can be an issue is perfectionism. The set of standards that we impose on ourselves and others, or that others impose on us, may prevent us from resting. We may be guilty of imposing undue pressure on ourselves and thinking that we can never be good enough. We may have faulty thinking and believe that God is putting extreme and unrealistic pressure on us because that is what others have done to us. We may have an inaccurate or incomplete understanding of His grace and think that we have to clean ourselves up first before we can come. We may put pressure on ourselves to be more than it is even possible for us to be. Something that can help us through this obstacle course is to realize that only *God* is perfect, and only *He* will ever be perfect. Accepting this knowledge can remove a great burden from our minds and shoulders. We can adjust our worldviews so that they contain an understanding of the completeness of Jesus's sacrifice for our salvation. We can come to Him to confess our imperfection and acknowledge His perfection. We do not have to work to gain His favor; He has given us His grace. We can see ourselves as God sees us: dearly loved and lavished with grace. We can see ourselves as what God wants us to become: His dear children.

The way we think about time, and how things should happen in relation to it, can prevent us from resting. Impatience can present quite an obstacle. It is becoming more difficult for us to wait as the years pass by. We live in a "now" society. We are becoming accustomed to and even expectant of instant gratification. Remember in grade school how giving and taking cuts in line were the norm? Even as children, we wanted to get to the head of the line as quickly as we could. Today, there is fast food, high-speed internet, no-wait reservations, expedited shipping, and so much more, all to accommodate our desire to have things *now*. It seems that patience is becoming a thing of the past. People are becoming more and more impatient the longer that they have to wait, even if the wait time is, in reality, quite brief. Some may give up and walk away after just a few minutes of waiting, if they even make it that long. Others may loudly complain about having to wait, and they plow ahead when it is not their turn, disregarding and cutting off others in the process. We see an increase in road rage, but this type of behavior is not just reserved for the roads. We see people trampled during Black Friday retail events. We see people run over in crosswalks when red traffic lights are disregarded. This impatience has transferred over into our spiritual lives as well.

We see waiting as a waste rather than a blessing. This, in turn, leads us to think that stillness and rest are undesirable, and thus, God's perfect plan for us is skewed. Waiting times seem like such a waste to people who are accustomed to being active, productive, and organized. People such as these may wonder how they could even possibly be still. They do not have the patience to be still and learn how to rest. A good aid to help us adjust such a perspective is Psalm 37:1–11. These verses talk about trusting, waiting patiently, not fretting, delighting in the Lord, committing our ways to Him, and waiting on Him to bring things to pass. We should read this passage. Now.

EMOTIONAL REFUSALS

Emotions can be obstacles that cause us to resist a rest. Many times it is the negative emotions, such as anger, fear, and bitterness that obstruct the pathway to God. We may be disappointed in Him and our circumstances.

We may be frustrated at His timing. We often have a fear of the unknown. We fear rejection in relationships, careers, and things we undertake. We may fear that God will reject us once He knows our true identities. We may fear that our standards and expectations do not line up with His. We wonder if we will have to give up some things we love or perhaps have to change our lifestyles because they do not line up with what God expects. Our emotions become entangled in our thoughts and subsequent behaviors, and rest becomes elusive.

We can be such negative people and allow our negative emotions to keep us from responding, but we can also be hindered by positive emotions. We may be content with how our lives are right now and not want to change them. We may be so happy in the company of particular people that we neglect taking company with God. We keep processing our emotions, but we neglect to process the quietness, rest, and relief He can bring us. Feelings are not necessarily our friends in such cases. The focus should be on loving God with all of our hearts, minds, souls, and strength, and then loving our neighbors as ourselves. When He is the first priority, everything else will come into alignment.

SPIRITUAL REFUSALS

We have priorities in every area of life (e.g., schedules, relationships, finances) that affect the things we pursue and the plans we make. Things like what we wear, how we look, our hobbies, our children, our social statuses, being the best at work, escaping debt, and having clean houses can consume our thoughts. The cares of life can become our top priorities, moving God to the bottom of the list. And when God is not our top priority, we will not be coming to Him first and may not even be coming to Him at all. As a result of this, we will not be living in ways that will bring us rest.

We become so focused on our frantic pursuits that we neglect the most important things—our relationships with God and others. We tighten our control on our lives (or so we think), and we let go of God and others in the process. We may find ourselves thinking that there is contentment found in things other than God. We want food sacrificed to idols rather than the food He supplies. We try to be independent and self-sufficient. We run all day, toss and turn all night, and sometimes never pay any mind to God. Instead of giving Him what He requires of us, we make our own ways, our own rules, and our own traditions. We try to be everything to everyone else but Him. All in all, these things are distractions to us. Eventually, we will become overwhelmed by the cares of life rather than by the grace of God.

Oftentimes, we place our goals and priorities ahead of His and on our own timetables rather than His. We are actually quite adept at putting God last in our lives. We spend time with Him if and when we get around to it, after all of our other obligations are taken care of, and yes, even after recreation is done first. Ouch! We see it happen in society as stores are not closed to observe a day of rest. Community events like marathons and national athletic competitions are scheduled during typical church hours. We see these events pulling at the lives of believers. Church services are even cancelled at times so that they are not competing with these non-spiritual events. Are these events wrong in and of themselves? No. Where the problem arises is the prioritizing of these things above God. This is definitely a touchy area, and I can imagine some blood pressures rising even as I sit here and type this. Know this: I am not casting stones (I am just as guilty as the next person); I am simply stating that this is the truth of what we do. *His* goal and priority is to love and care for us, while *our* priorities are ourselves. What *we* want is what *we* want, when *we* want it, and this "it" may have absolutely nothing to do with God. We each have to ask ourselves, "Is my first thought Him or me? Do I do what makes Him happy or what makes me happy?"

And then there is that problematic pattern that all humans encounter: sin. Sin can be an obstacle to us because we can be bound in it, whether as a believer or as an unbeliever. This bondage will not allow us to rest, no matter how the sin is manifesting itself, whether it is being done in public or in private. The consequences of our sin will hound us, and the memories will torment us. The apostle Paul talked about doing things in the flesh that his spirit did not desire to do, and vice versa (see Rom. 7:14–25). The flesh and the spirit war against each other. It is a constant struggle for us between two options: to live for God or to live for self. In our minds, we may want to live for God, but our flesh wants to live in sin.

From birth, we are burdened and yoked by the domination of a sin nature and will remain that way until we are set free by Jesus's salvation. But sometimes, even after that release from eternal condemnation, we do not allow ourselves to be released from the bondage of sin and its power over us during our earthly lives. We sometimes remain chained to our guilt and do not want to be unchained from it. When we continue in bondage, we do not have freedom from the shackles of our pasts, the broken laws, the awful memories, or anything else connected with sin. Good news, though! The Bible tells us that there is no condemnation for those who are in Christ Jesus (Rom. 8:1). However, we have to get into Christ Jesus to apply this principle. We have to stop resisting the rest that He offers. We need to allow Jesus to fight for us and rescue us. When we become believers, we are released through the power of Christ's forgiveness and the chains fall off. And since we are free from these chains, I suggest that we do not put them back on again! When we have been forgiven, we have freedom of access to God, and it is up to us whether we take advantage of that privilege or not.

Saul, also known as Paul the apostle, is a great example of someone who was set free from bondage (see Acts 26). He was so caught up in his ways, his knowledge, his pride, his reputation, and his hatred for Christians that he morphed into someone who was fighting against God. Saul changed his ways, however, when he accepted Jesus's invitation to come and be a part of something great for God's purposes: the evangelization of lost souls. What could God do in *our* lives if we came to Him?

That is a good question to ask ourselves, and so is this: When are we going to come to Him? The longer we stay away, the more we miss out on peace, comfort, help, and rest. Staying away means that we are conducting life on our own, using our own wisdom. Those are both scary thoughts! Is it smart to use our intelligence rather than God's? Let's see. Do high grade point averages, college degrees, music classes, foreign language studies, job training seminars, church retreats, business conferences, specialized workshops, independent studies, in-depth research projects, and the abilities to comprehend and memorize lengthy training manuals place our knowledge above God's? Absolutely not! Even after all of that learning, we still barely know anything, while God knows everything about every field of knowledge that exists. He is an expert in *all* fields. We most definitely need Him in our lives!

RELATIONAL REFUSALS

We can be making good progress as we travel through life, removing some obstacles as we go and even coming to a point where we acknowledge that "life is not all about me," but then people enter the scene of our lives, and that has the potential to change everything. God made us for relationships, but there is a correct time and place for those relationships and they are supposed to line up with God's design. People—even good, wonderful, relationally-healthy people—can become deterrents on the pathway to God. On the other hand, sadly, we may surround ourselves with those who do not encourage us to follow Jesus and may even discourage us from doing so. Popularity becomes what concerns us. Popularity with people, believing the popular ideas of the day, and following pop culture will all find us trending away from Christianity. We become susceptible to being drawn away from God if we do not guard our hearts. We may begin to compromise because we do not want to lose our places in the cliques by acting differently than the other group members. We do not want to be known as one of those "crazy Christians" or be known as too uptight to have a good time. We have reputations to uphold, after all; or so we think. This is when the trouble starts. This is when we have to choose which burden to bear: the burden of popularity or the burden of propriety. This is when we have to decide if our priority is popularity or God.

The first ridicule of my faith that I remember experiencing was in the fifth grade. My best friend told me that there were comments going around that I was weird because I went to church even on Wednesday nights. In high school, I was known as a prude and a wallflower. I remember people being shocked that I did not drink, swear, or party. The comments and questions continued on into adulthood, and they likely will continue for the remainder of my life. We may be ridiculed by our family members or coworkers. We may find ourselves to be the brunt of the jokes around the water coolers or at the family picnics. And then there is the media. They do not typically portray Christians in a good light, and we have to deal with the fallout of that. When people learn that we are Christians, they may presume we are boring, snobby, judgmental, or pharisaical. The comments can begin to fill our ears and affect our reputations. They can sting and wound us. But despite being surrounded by this verbal unrest, we can be at rest in our hearts when we settle the questions of *whose* name we want to be called by and what names we are willing to be called in order to glorify God's name.

When we love our families and friends and want to be part of their lives and activities more than we do God's, we have an obstacle that keeps us from moving to where God wants us to be. He wants us to love them, but He also wants us to love Him. We are to place God first in our lives and make Him the priority over others. We have to make a choice as to what and whom we value most. And when we value Him first, we will then value others, and our priorities will properly fall into place.

When we do not love Him enough, we stay safe and comfortable and do not cause any issues. We place the details of our relationships with people above our relationships with God. Our spouses may be unsaved, and so to avoid friction with our loved ones, we avoid God. We may have a desire to grow in our relationships with God, but if our spouses do not, we just let God drop from our calendars, eager to please our spouses rather than God. Decisions are made to forego a deeper relationship with God when that is what make things cozier and where the least amount of resistance is encountered. The best thing for us and them, though, is God. When we have the love of God poured into us, we can love our spouses more purely and deeply. It is important to consider the choices we make because we may be affecting people's decisions regarding eternity.

Another difficult familial aspect is that some people are disowned by their families for choosing to follow God. This was the case for a friend in high school. She wanted to follow Jesus but knew that her family would disown her if she did so. She had a decision to make, and make it she did: she chose to remain with her family and not follow Jesus. These are not easy choices to make. They are not light, and they are not inconsequential. God wants us to love other people. He has commanded it. But He wants our love and loyalty to be to Him first.

If we truly knew God and followed His plans rather than avoiding or resisting Him, things would be better for us. If we treated one another well, things would be better for us. Yes, we still live in a world of sin and suffering, but why not control and repair the things that we can. One person truly can make a difference, and one person focused on Jesus truly can change the world.

Jesus made a difference, and if we are striving to be like Him, then we will make a difference too. Imagine the tragic end that would have been met if Lazarus had resisted and said no to Jesus's command to come out of the tomb: he would still be in the tomb and less people would have come to believe in Jesus.

Look at the lives of Mary and Martha (see Luke 10:38–42). Mary sat and learned at Jesus's feet while Martha ran around, cumbered with much serving. Martha was letting the supper dishes keep her from the Bread of Life. When she complained that her entertaining plans were going awry without Mary's help, Jesus said that Mary was doing the better thing. Imagine what Mary did in life with the knowledge that Jesus gave her and the effect of His presence upon her spirit; imagine what Martha could have done.

Look, too, at the disciples. They changed the world for Christ, but if they had resisted Jesus's command to get away and rest a while, they would have hit burnout instead. And what about the others who chose to listen—what if they had resisted? People would have remained unhealed, hungry, thirsty, demon-possessed, overburdened, and joyless. All of the focus in these instances was on listening to God and doing as He asked, and lives were changed as a result. Father God, please help us to stay focused. It is not about us; it is all about you. Always. Help us change the world for you!

How long will it be before I come to Him? What is keeping me from coming forward? Pride? Shame? Procrastination? I do not know. Let me think about that, would you! Undoubtedly, we all have plenty of excuses: we will do it when the children are grown, when our to-do lists are finished, when we retire, when we get some time off, when we attend the retreat next month, when our spouses go to church with us, etc. But we do not need to wait to come to Him. He is there for us today. Now. Right now. So, when are we going to come to Him? All we need to do is

102

decide to do it and then act upon our decision. It is not difficult. One small step is all that it takes to get onto this path; we just need to take that first step. "Draw nigh to God, and he will draw nigh to you" (James 4:8). Step to Him; He is right there. Step into His presence, into His arms, into His wisdom, light, love, and life.

THE RSVP

Commands and invitations always invite us to make a choice, to exercise the free will that we have been given. What will we do with our opportunities? How will we respond? We can have excuses for refusing, but we can also refuse excuses. It is all about our attitudes and our choices. We each can predetermine what types of reactions we are going to give when we are asked or told to do things. We can be the type of person who always says, "No, I'm not going to do it." We can be the type that always says, "Yes, Lord. Whatever you ask, I will do." Or we can be that person in-between, the one who evaluates each case before saying yes or no. Who will we choose to be, and what will we choose to do?

Responding favorably to the invitations of God is an opportunity, not an obligation. Free will gives us the opportunity to choose God's will, but it also gives us the very opportunity to say no to Him. Once the invitation or the command is given, it is our choice as to how we respond or even if we respond. If we want to go to where He is, we need to take action. It is our turn.

ALL ALONE TO HIM ALONE

What do we do if no one goes with us? We go anyway! It is a fact that not everyone will choose to come to God. Moses proved this point when he gave an invitation to the Israelites, asking for those who were on the Lord's side to come and stand by him. This was to prove who was for God and who was not, to see who wanted to follow and obey Him and who did not. Some came to Moses's side, showing their acceptance of God's authority, but others did not (see Exod. 32:26). Yet whether or not anyone else goes, *we* need to go. We are the only ones who are responsible for ourselves, so when He calls to us, we are the only ones who can make the choice to go. The Bible tells us that each one must give an account (Rom. 14:12). It is not a family thing, a couple thing, a best friend thing, or a group thing; no, it is none of these. It is an individual decision that each one of us alone can and must make. When we take the first step, we will be on God's side and will obtain eternal life. After that, we will never be alone again because He will always remain with us.

God chose us and invited us to be with Him, and now we get to choose Him and invite Him in return. He has invited us into His life, and we can invite Him into ours, choosing Him to be our Savior! It does not matter what others do, say, or think about our decision to choose Him, because whatever we do needs to be done unto the Lord and not unto men (see Col. 3:23). While people may be looking only at our outward appearances, God is looking at our hearts (see 1 Sam. 16:7). Make these words of David's your own: "Behold, I come ... I delight to do Your will, O my God, And Your law *is* within my heart" (Ps. 40:7–8 NKJV).

Before Jeremiah was even formed in his mother's womb, he was chosen to be a prophet of God. God called him for a purpose, and Jeremiah chose to answer the calling. After he said yes, his life was comprised of many years of ridicule, rejection, imprisonment, and dismissal, just to name a few of the difficulties. But in the midst of the hardships, the importance of the call remained and so did the One who had called. The verses of Lamentations 3:55–58 demonstrate an invitation from Jeremiah to God and an RSVP from God to Jeremiah. Jeremiah called to God from the dungeon, asking that God would not hide His ear from his breathing or his cry. God heard Jeremiah's voice and drew near on the day that Jeremiah called for Him. God told him not to be afraid. Jeremiah recognized that God pled for his soul and redeemed his life. Although things were not good, God remained. Jeremiah chose to remain with God, as well, and fulfill the purpose for his life. And just as God knew Jeremiah's name and had plans for him, He also knows our names and has plans for us. He knit us together in our mothers' wombs (Ps. 139:13). He has divine purposes for each of us, but *we* have to choose to accept Him into our lives so those purposes can be activated and accomplished. He invites us to come to

Him to be saved, helped, prepared, and sent out. Will we accept what He offers and offer ourselves in return?

So often I hear phrases and see merchandise telling people to "dream," and dream we do. We sometimes have huge dreams and make grand plans, yet they are not *His* dreams and plans for us. It is fine for us to dream big, but we need to be sure to align ourselves with what God wants to do through our lives. Creativity came from Him in the first place, so to fall back on His resources while we use it is the best route to go. God has large and magnificent plans for His people, but oftentimes we do not realize the scope and magnitude of those plans. Sometimes we even have difficulty believing that these things can be realities in our lives. But remember, God is able to do above and beyond all that we ask, think, or imagine.

As we step forward, it is important to commit our plans to God. We need to remember to seek discernment and direction when obstacles come, for they surely will. Obstacles are not necessarily closed doors that should stop us in our tracks, rather, they should cause us to seek what God is saying at this point in the process. If we ever feel overwhelmed by the large plans that God has for our lives, we should just trust Him step by step, day by day, and we will be fine! We need to be encouraged and take courage. Think on the grand things that He did through people such as Noah, Moses, Esther, Paul, and especially Jesus. God is working, seen and unseen, on a future timeline beyond our scope. It is astounding to realize and accomplish the things that He has for our lives. We cannot even begin to imagine, but we can know that just as He laid out paths for these biblical people from before the time they were even conceived, so He has done for our lives. Life with Him will be incomparable!

God may call us to enter into new and different roles that are completely unfamiliar to us, and we will be called to minister in some way because of what we experience and where we go. We may have times of ease or times of great difficulty. There may be storms and trials; there may be days of peace. Our stations and statuses may change. We may need to step up or step out—out in faith or out of the way. But whatever needs done, the things to which He calls us will result in new opportunities to commune with Him. We will learn greater trust and dependency and also how to develop a vibrant faith. Our callings may be any number of things, but our responses should not vary. When God calls for us, we need to answer and allow Him to present us with our new opportunities and instructions. Just as Abraham trusted and went forward, despite being unaware of where he was ultimately going (see Heb. 11:8), so we need to trust in God's plans and promises to get us where we need to go. "The steps of a *good* man are ordered by the LORD, And He delights in his way. Though he fall, he shall not be utterly cast down; For the LORD upholds *him with* His hand" (Ps. 37:23–24 NKJV). Take action, and watch God act! Step out with Him; He is holding you securely in the palm of His hand. All to Him alone gives Him the glory alone.

When God calls us to come, the best thing to do is come. If we refuse His invitations, we are going to miss out on something, perhaps something as big as being part of a miracle like Peter was when he walked on water or like Moses was when he parted the Red Sea. We are to be faithful to God and His callings on our lives, and when we are, He will use us to do great things. So, may we do more than just receive the invitations that God has given to us— may we actually act upon them. May we RSVP with yeses.

CHAPTER 10

Seeker-Friendly

METHODS FOR COMING TO HIM

So, if we are interested in coming to Him instead of refusing, what exactly do we do to make that happen? We simply respond by telling Him that we accept His invitation to come. The first step may look different for each of us depending upon what we are doing in life at the moment we decide to take the first step, but all of us will take a step of faith and a step of action. We may surrender our wills, leave something else behind, make time to come, prioritize Him, or simply say, "Yes." Each one of these steps moves us forward toward Him. We must come purposely and diligently seeking Him. We must step forward to receive God's mercy by accepting the sacrifice and payment made by Jesus on the cross. Titus 3:5 (NKJV) says that it is "not by works of righteousness which we have done, but according to His mercy He saved us, through the washing of regeneration and renewing of the Holy Spirit." God is a rewarder of those who diligently seek Him (Heb. 11:6). We must simply believe that He is the way, the truth, and the life. If we will confess the Lord Jesus with our mouths and will believe in our hearts that God raised Him from the dead, we will be saved. For with our hearts we believe unto righteousness, and with our mouths confession is made unto salvation (Rom. 10:9–10). Step one is to take the first step.

After we have accepted the initial invitation to eternal life, there can be an expansion of the quality of our lives now. We can experience abundant life no matter what our life circumstances. Each part of our beings can come to God. We can develop full and vibrant relationships with Him through the following areas:

1. *Prayer*

   This is a time to talk to and listen to God. He wants to talk to us about some things, and He wants us to talk to Him about some things. We can allow the cries of our hearts to be heard, and we can hear His in return. The expressions from our souls may include the extremes of sorrow and elation, tears and joy. We can approach Him humbly and honestly.

2. *The Bible*

   The words we see on the pages before us were spoken by the very mouth of God, specifically in communication to us, breathed out onto paper for our knowledge and benefit. We should take time to read, study, and memorize His words so we can understand how He desires for us to live. The Bible itself is an invitation to learn about the life of Jesus—its words are His words, full of His character. John 14:23 teaches that if we love Jesus, we will keep His words. John 15 talks about abiding in Jesus and what will happen as we spend time with Him: prayers will be answered, fruit will be produced, capability will be given, joy will be experienced, we will be guided into truth by the Spirit, and we will continue in His love. We are invited to great things and great love.

3. *Worship*

   We can worship God with our whole beings: minds, bodies, and souls. We can invite His presence. We need to recognize that we are sinful human beings and He is the Most High and Holy over all the universe. We need to approach Him with a reverent attitude. We can praise Him with our hearts through words, music, expressions of adoration and thanksgiving, and also with obedience.

4. *Music*

   We can listen to uplifting songs about God and even compose some of our own. Psalm 95:2 says, "Let us come before his presence with thanksgiving, and make a joyful noise unto him with psalms." God inhabits the praise of His people (Ps. 22:3). It is precious to enter into His presence, and it is precious to invite His presence to be with us. My favorite musical invitation to God is to sing the words of the old Latin hymn popular at Christmastime: "O Come, O Come Emmanuel." I think some Christmas songs are great any day of the year! We can enjoy the gift of music, but even more the presence of God.

5. *Meditation*

We need to take time to actually think about God, taking time for stillness by setting other things aside and actually being physically still and quiet. King David spent much time thinking about God. He said that he would meditate on God's precepts and regard His ways (Ps. 119:15). He said he would meditate on all His works (Ps. 77:12) and on the glorious splendor of all His majesty (Ps. 145:5). He remembered God while he lay in his bed, and he thought about Him in the night watches (Ps. 63:6). All throughout the day, and until our eyes close in sleep, we should take time to process the words of God, recognize His character, and ponder His works.

6. *Fellowship*

We need to spend time in a church setting with the body of Christ, His church. The church may be indoor, outdoor, magnificent, or underground—the physical locale does not matter when the Spirit of the Lord comes among His people. We can put the previous five suggestions into practice as we meet together. Also, we should take time to talk about the Lord. Malachi 3:16 tells us that what His loved ones say about Him will be recorded: "Then they that feared the LORD spake often one to another: and the LORD hearkened, and heard it, and a book of remembrance was written before him for them that feared the LORD, and that thought upon his name." Our prayers can join in agreement with others as they are offered up to Him. Discipleship in a group setting can encourage us in our relationships with Him as we see how others live their lives with Him and for Him. Sharing testimonies of our blessings with one another gives encouragement and helps us to cultivate grateful hearts. Gathering together gives us an opportunity to both give and receive support. We have opportunity to rejoice with those who rejoice, and weep with those who weep. Where two or three are gathered together in His name, He is there in the midst of them (Matt. 18:20). If we invite His presence, He will surely come to be with us; there will definitely be *strength* in these numbers!

7. *Ministry*

We need to come to Him so that we can go in service to Him and others. We should offer ourselves as living sacrifices that willingly yield to Him and His plans for our lives. When we give ourselves to the work of God, we can point others to Him and bring Him glory. We can use the things that we do in life as opportunities to minister in Jesus's name and to be a witness for Him. We can glorify God in our bodies and our spirits by doing everything for Him (1 Cor. 6:20). As it says in Colossians 3:17 (NKJV): "And whatever you do in word or deed, *do* all in the name of the Lord Jesus, giving thanks to God the Father through Him." He can and will do great things through our lives if we allow Him to do so.

OUR STATUS

Well, now comes another one of those tough questions we each must ask ourselves: What is my level of commitment to God? Is it platinum, gold, silver, bronze, honorable mention, participant, observer, or less? How much of ourselves will we give to God and the work of the kingdom? How deep, wide, far, and long will we go to be His? How much of our hearts will we give to Him, and how much of His love will we allow to flow through us as we go about living our daily lives?

King David was a man after God's own heart (1 Sam. 13:14; Acts 13:22). He lived within God's presence, with a heart that was committed to living for God and following His plans. Upon examination of David's prayer found in Psalm 25:1–22, we can see that he used all seven of the methods noted earlier to come to God. He used *prayer, scripture, music, worship, meditation, fellowship, and ministry.* He took time to adore God, confess his sins, show gratitude, and humbly ask for what he needed. He asked for things such as God's help in ruling the kingdom, deliverance from his enemies, to be unashamed of God, to be shown God's ways, to learn God's paths, to be in the truth, and to be a man of integrity and uprightness. He asked for God's tender mercy and loving-kindness. He sought God's involvement in every aspect of his life. I would say David gets the platinum-level medal. May we strive to do the same. All of our hearts, all for Him, all for forever.

We have the same opportunity and the same privilege of coming to God that David had. The ways in which he approached God are some great techniques that we would do well to emulate, especially if our desires are to become people after God's own heart. As David came to spend time in prayer, scripture, music, worship, meditation, fellowship, and ministry, he did it with a particular manner. (1) *He came by lifting up his soul.* He had many weights upon him: he was in trouble, in distress, desolate, pained, afflicted, and his heart was full of troubles. He brought these things to God, seeking help with them all. (2) *He came without shame.* There were definitely things in his life to be ashamed of, but he came anyway because he knew that God is forgiving. (3) *He came because he claimed God as his salvation.* He knew he was secure in God's love. (4) *He came because he trusted.* He waited on God, always keeping his eyes on Him, knowing that He would rescue him. (5) *He came because he was wise.* He recognized the benefit of keeping God's covenant and laws. There were many aspects to David's life and a great number of things going on within each aspect, but there was also a great investment in his relationship with God. He lived and moved and had his being in God. His relationship with God made a difference in the world around him, and it continues to do so today. May we come to God in the same ways, and may our lives make a difference far into the future. May we:

1. Come with lifted souls. We need to come to God with our hearts, not just our lips and actions (see Matt. 15:8–9). We can come to Him no matter how we are feeling inside, no matter our hearts' conditions; He is able to handle it and act according to our needs. We can come to Him whole-heartedly, half-heartedly, or with broken hearts. If we have experienced tragedy, betrayal, discontentment, unfulfillment, or disappointment, we can come. If we are having the best times of our lives, we can come. If we are numb and do not even know what to think or feel, we can come. We can come to Him with our sorrow, when our hearts are broken and aching, because He is the Healer and the God of all comfort (2 Cor. 1:3). He binds up wounds and is near to those that are of a broken heart (Ps. 147:3). We can come to Him with our joy or lack thereof, whether we are rejoicing again or begging to have the joy of our salvation restored to us. We can share and exult in our victories with Him but also invite Him to share in our sorrows. We should come expectantly since deferred hope makes a heart sick (Prov. 13:12). We need to recognize His goodness and His hand in our lives to bring joy and triumph to us. Know that He gives good things. If we open our mouths wide, He will fill them (Ps. 81:10). We can be hopeful even if today looks hopeless, because we have a living hope, not a dead one. The name of this hope is Jesus.

We need to come to Him during our times of desperation, when we are out of time, options, help, and hope. When we have come to the end of ourselves and have nothing else to cling to, we will find Him there, waiting for us. No matter how low we are or how exhausted and beaten down we have become, we will find that He is there. He is with us in the pit, when we are overwhelmed and feel farther from Him than we ever have before. When life is overwhelming and we do not know how we can possibly continue on, He is there. His presence will go with us through all of our desperate times, and He will give us rest in the midst of them if we simply allow Him to do so. Even when the circumstances do not change, we can find rest in Him. Even when the circumstances change faster than we can handle, we can find rest in Him. He is the unchanging one who can help us in any and every circumstance. This God is *our* God—our rock, our anchor, our hope and stay.

2. *Come without shame.* We need to come to Him with our guilt. We do not have to remain at a distance because of who we are and what we have done. I have heard of many who believe that God could never forgive them for their misdeeds. But they are not the only ones with misdeeds; the Bible tells us: "There is none righteous, no, not one" (Rom. 3:10). The remedy for all of us is to confess our sins, and He will forgive us. Jesus is the only one who is perfect. We all have things to be ashamed of, but once we are forgiven, Jesus takes that shame from us; the guilty become guiltless and the unpardonable, pardoned. We become faultless to stand before His glory (Jude 1:24).

We humans are all guilty, and that is exactly why Jesus died on the cross for us. Once we are His children, we should try to live right, but understand this: we will still make mistakes sometimes and choose sin over Him. At these times, the Spirit will convict us of our wrongdoings. So, when we have those pricks in our consciences, we need to stop the activities that caused them and come to God for forgiveness. When we recognize our sinfulness, we need to come to Him with our apologies, ask for His forgiveness, and then we will be completely and totally forgiven. When we come to Jesus, our new verdicts and our new names are: "Forgiven!"

We need to come to God in humility, with respect for Him and respect to our proper positions of servant to the Master, child to the Father, and creation to the Creator. We need to understand that there is unrest in false humility. He sees and knows our hearts, so He knows when we are just pretending and when we are still prideful. He knows when we are coming for show, to keep up appearances and our reputations. We must not lie in our hearts to God. We need to come with a heartfelt approach that is without any pretense. We need not be ashamed to be real. Those people who look perfect and who look like they have it all together are imperfect and in pieces just like we are. When we focus on ourselves and our efforts of trying to look good, or better, or the best, we can lose sight of Him. We can work ourselves up and not even see Him at work. We must be careful not to function in our own strength, pridefully thinking that it is our hands that got us here, our hard work that provided for our needs, and our competence that got us what we wanted. All that we are, and all that we have, is due to the goodness of God in our lives. We need to thank Him and respect Him for what He has done.

God loves all people equally and does not show any favoritism (Acts 10:34). We can come to Him no matter our socioeconomic statuses. We do not need to be ashamed of what we have or do not have. Jesus spent time with the outcasts and the downtrodden, not just with the rich and important people. Those who are exalted on earth in the eyes of others will not receive any special treatment from Him, and those who are bowed down in the dirt will be lifted up at the point of their belief in Him and claimed as His own children (based on 1 Sam. 2:7–9). He is a God of unimaginable love.

We should bring Him our whole hearts even if they are not whole. Hearts can be divided, deceitful, and far from Him, and this is not a good thing. We are capable of pretending to come to Him while in actuality we are keeping our hearts far away. Jesus addressed the hypocrisy of this (see Mark 7:6). People may look at our outward appearances and not see any issues, but God looks at our hearts and knows our pretense. When our hearts are far from Him, we are not in a close relationship with Him and He is being held at a distance. It is more difficult and sometimes even impossible to hear the voice of someone who is far away from us, so when we remove ourselves from God, it will be more difficult to hear Him. So instead of choosing all of these difficulties for ourselves, we should choose to have Him beside us at all times. When God speaks, our hearts have the opportunity and the privilege to respond to Him. If we are near to Him, we will be able to hear Him speak.

3. *Come with salvation.* When we place our faith and trust in God, we will find that He is guiding our paths, directing our steps, holding our hands, and guarding our hearts as we traverse through life. Even when troubles come, He is there doing these things for us. There are some days that we do not think we can run the race—at best, we can only plod along, and at worst, we cannot even make it to the starting line. He knows. On the days when we think that we cannot take another step and winning seems to be an impossibility, He is still God. He has more power than the

circumstances we are succumbing to. He remembers what we are made of, and He remains faithful even when we are faithless (see 2 Tim. 2:13).

We should come to Him in thankfulness. We have so much to be thankful for, even if we cannot see it or have never even thought about it. We can start by being grateful that we were invited to come to Him for salvation and blessings. He is holy, and we are so far from it, but He chose to love us anyway, to the point that Jesus gave His life on the cross for us. Thank you, Jesus, for the grace that has saved a wretch like me!

4. Come with trust. We can come, resolving to trust. There will always be areas where our resolve will be strong and other areas where it will be weak, but this should make no difference or cause any delay in coming to God. We need Him in all areas, and thus, we should make our coming soon, and make it quick. Acting will strengthen our trust, while inaction will weaken it. We can ask Him to increase our faith and to help us with any unbelief that we have. We should be resolved to come to Him for His strength—strength to add to our weakness and more strength to add to our existing strength. We can come even if we are a solitary number. We can stand even if we stand alone. We should be willing to pay the ultimate price for Him because He paid the ultimate price for us. We should come like sheep to the shepherd; they come because they are called by a voice that they know and trust. Resolve to come when you hear Him call. Trust Him with your life, with all that you are.

5. Come with wisdom. It is wise to have a heart that listens for God's voice so that even during times when life seems dead and dark, it will still be able to hear Him. It is also wise to have a responsive heart that is quick to come when God calls it. We need to have the understanding that a delayed response can fill the void with excuses, and before we know it, we might find ourselves disobedient and ignoring His calls. Life and light are there within our grasp; we just need to come forth to receive them. This is wisdom.

We can come to Him whether we know much about Him or little. We can come with whatever amount of spiritual understanding we have. We can come with our searching and ask Him to reveal Himself to us.

We can ask Him to make His will known to us. We can come with our confusion and questioning, our bewilderment and asking "Why me?" He gives wisdom liberally to all who ask for it (James 1:5).

God is a big God who allows us to come to Him no matter what our statuses are. We do not have to be a king to gain the attention of *the* King. We do not have to be perfect to approach the perfect God. We do not have to be a giant of the faith to approach the One who is the source of all faith. We can come no matter the amount of our faith, even if it is as small as a mustard seed. He wants us to be seekers who find Him for the first time. Thereafter, He wants us to be people who continually seek His face. He is there to be found.

When God invited David to seek His face, David decided that his heart would do so (see Ps. 27:8). We can do the same. We do not need to know everything today; we just have to trust that He has our best in mind. We can find a resting place for our bodies, minds, souls, and faith in the safety of His hands. We can place the details of our lives in His capable hands. We can place the recesses of our vulnerable hearts in His loving hands. We can place our trust in Him because of His unfailing hands. He never fails, never breaks His promises, and will never let go of us.

HIS STATUS

We can come to Him whatever our statuses are, because of the status that He holds. He is all these and more:

- Healer—He can minister healing to us in every part of who we are. (Pss. 30:2, 147:3; Isa. 61:1–3; Matt. 12:15, 15:30; Luke 4:40)
- Omnipotent One—He has all the power to do anything that needs to be done. (Matt. 24:30, 28:18; Luke 4:14, 6:19; John 2:11, 17:2)
- Omniscient One—He has all of the knowledge and knows our hearts and our questions. (Pss. 44:21, 139:1–4, 147:5; Isa. 55:8–9; Jer. 33:3; Heb. 4:13)

- Provider—We will find love, grace, and every need supplied in Him. (Prov. 8:21; John 3:16; 2 Cor. 4:7; Eph. 1:18–19, 2:7–9; Phil. 4:19; Col. 1:27)
- Savior—He will save whoever believes in Him. (John 3:16, 6:37; Eph. 3:6; 2 Tim. 1:9–10; 1 John 1:9)
- Shepherd—He will lead, guide, and care for us. (John 10:11, 16:13)
- Teacher—He will teach things that are necessary for living this life and the one beyond. (Matt. 5:2–48, 11:29, 19:16; John 3:2–3, 14:26, 15:1–27)

We should continue to come to God frequently once we belong to Him. He is both our provider and sustainer, and He will give us nourishment and refreshment as we wait on Him. Every day, we should purposely seek renewal and drink deeply from the living water. When we spend time in His presence, we then have time to soak in what He wants to give us. It is important for us to partake of what God has to offer, not only for our own benefit, but also for the benefit of others. We do not exist in a bubble. What God provides for us is life-giving, and when we acquire it, we should then share it with others. We should come and seek out what He wants to give us.

CHAPTER 11
It's Not Me, It's Him

THE "ME" IS NOT ME, THANKFULLY

"Come unto me, all ye that labour and are heavy laden, and I will give you rest" (Matt. 11:28). These are the words of Jesus, calling people to Himself and not to anyone else. I am not saying these words, and it is not me that you are being called to. And you should be very glad that it is not! I can name several reasons why this is so, and after reading the following testimony, you should be able to do so too.

Somehow the phrase "stop and rest" loses the "and" in my life. I am instead left with the phrase "stop rest." I just cannot seem to relax. I sit down to read the Bible, pray, and meditate on God, but my mind goes elsewhere, sometimes very far away. My muscles twitch in anticipation of moving on to something else. My to-do list beckons me. My guilt urges and prods me on relentlessly. I bustle about the house while the rest of the family is relaxing. What am I doing? Why am I doing? If I was even to sit and try to meditate on this thought, I would not succeed at it because I would have to jump up and get busy doing something! My testimony of rest is actually that I have a lack thereof.

People who know me well will tell you that I do not know how to rest or relax. They have told me the same thing over and over, year after year: "You need to rest." And although they tell me this repeatedly, for some reason I do not seem to listen to or heed what I hear. This is not something that I am proud of; nevertheless, it is true. They have told me that I am doing too much, that I make them tired just thinking about how much I do, that I manage time better than anyone else, and that my name appears in the church bulletin for everything (this is an exaggeration because the most I was ever doing at one time was just seven different departments!).

They have stated that they "do not know how I do it." They have queried me about whether I ever have time for myself. Ultimately, they have told me that I have to learn to say no.

My husband once described me to a new acquaintance by saying, "She is a stay-at-home mom who doesn't stay home." Yes, I used to run like mad, and not for the purpose of fun or adventure. And what was the result of so much activity? Well, my health finally crashed. For the second time. It was the year 2011. Two symptoms that surfaced were severe drowsiness and fatigue. These prevented me from staying awake the majority of the day. I only had between four and six waking hours per day, and even during these short intervals, I would often have to take at least one nap. Two subsequent hours of wakefulness was often too much. I underwent some medical tests in an attempt to discover the cause of the problem. One of the doctors assumed I had a more relaxed lifestyle since I was a stay-at-home mom. All I could do in response was think, "Wow, he has no clue who I am." At the time of that appointment, this was the basic rundown of my commitments: weekly school volunteer, church ministry (weekly pianist and Sunday school teacher, once monthly nursery worker), hospice volunteer in two locations, helping to care for an elderly friend, coordinating and participating in an outreach program, volunteering at a charity retail shop, lay counseling two people, teaching a Bible study, traveling to speak at women's events, teaching piano students, playing the piano at special events, driving my kids to and from their schools (which took approximately ninety minutes per day), doing outreach for my personal ministry, praying with people, taking both myself and my daughter to physical therapy appointments (which also involved home exercises), and hosting tea parties for ministry (a multi-day activity). I did not have the time to do the things the doctor thought I was doing while I "stayed home" because when I stayed home it was time for cooking, dishes, laundry, helping kids with homework, and whatever else needed my attention. I think at that time it took me about six months to finish reading a book for pleasure.

In the morning, I often rushed into activities instead of having a time of communion with God. If I did take any time to commune with Him, it was to fall to my knees to offer a sentence of praise, a sentence of confession, a sentence to request help for the day, and a sentence stating my desire to be used by Him; and then came the amen, barely the shortest sentence of my paragraph. All the while I was "sentence praying," my brain was already on its way to the shower so I could get ready to leave, on its way to the kitchen to do the breakfast dishes, or on its way to the laundry room to tackle the ankle-deep mound. What did I really do in that moment of sentence praying? It was like grabbing a crumb from the table and trying to sustain my physical life on that alone. Where was the ingestion of just the right amount for what I needed to sustain me? The balance to maintain my health? The correct intake of sustenance so that there could be an output of useful energy? The intake of what I truly needed to accomplish the tasks of the day? Where was the savoring of the spiritual food? What gain was made in my heart and soul while I made a molehill of laundry into a mountain?

Even after such experiences, I seem to be obsessed with activity. Even in writing this book, I have struggled to take time to stop and rest and meditate. God has been speaking a message to me as I have been preparing the words, but it seems I cannot pause to pray about it or meditate on it because I have to type and print and edit and compile and research, and so on. The cycle of my life seems to be: do, do more, and do more still. I have been dragging chains of pressure, guilt, performance anxiety, fear of failure, and more.

I do, however, stop dragging my chains when I recall something profound that was spoken to me awhile back. Just when my situation seemed hopeless, my dear friend and mentor (who has already walked this road I am currently on) asked me a question as we discussed my overloaded schedule: "We are busy doing all these things, but are we doing what God would have us to do?" That was quite the question. It still is. I have asked myself that question many times since then and have even made course corrections because of it, yet there is a sad fact that remains: I can never get back those moments from the past, and I can never change what has already been done. I did not live right. I did not live well. And I left pain in the people and the path behind me. I have been guilty of neglect with a capital N, guilty of pride with a capital P, and guilty of squandering with a capital S. But I have also been forgiven with a capital F, followed by several exclamation points!

We sometimes do not realize what we are doing to ourselves or others until it is too late and the damage has already been done. Other times we do realize it, but we continue on anyway. Either way, it can come to a point where we stop and start anew. The consequences of the damage remain, but healing can take place and a new path can be forged. We can be better and do better, and both we and others can reap the benefits. We can live with grace, experiencing it in our spiritual lives and letting it exude into our physical lives. God knows that we are not perfect, so He offers us aid to stop our spiritual paths of destruction and proceed differently instead. We may be filled with regret and despair for the time we have lost living outside of His will, but those feelings can be overcome with His mercy and forgiveness. Although painful memories remain, they can serve to remind us of how far we have come—from living for ourselves to living for God. Although we have wasted valuable time, we have the grace of this moment to do something about it. We can never get those moments back that we did not spend with Him, but we can proceed from this moment forward, building and experiencing a wonderful and blossoming relationship. Sorrow can be turned into joy, mourning into laughter, and regret into inspiration. We can ponder the paths of our feet, and take the way that leads us to Jesus (see Prov. 4:26). He has invited us to more.

ME, MYSELF, AND MY ENEMIES

As I am on the path to Jesus, I frequently encounter obstacles; they are known as me, myself, and my enemies. I would imagine that you have heard it said that we can be our own worst enemies. Well, that can be true to an extent, but we also have another real, live enemy who roams the earth: Satan (Job 2:2). Ephesians 6:12 tells us that we "wrestle not against flesh and blood, but against principalities, against powers, against the rulers of the darkness of this world, against spiritual wickedness in high places." All of these things that we wrestle against fall under Satan's command. We have to fight because he wants us to fail. He does not want us to help others come to Jesus, and he does not want us to help others on Jesus's behalf. He wants us to live lives that are displeasing to God. There are things that he tempts us with, encourages us in, and wants to help us excel in. These things distract us, can harm us and others, and can destroy both us and the work that God has given us to do. These temptations and distractions can result in a loss of passion for God and ultimately lead to inactivity in His kingdom. Satan wants to wear out the saints—hurting us, exhausting us, and turning us against God (see Dan. 7:25). He is the accuser of believers and tries to keep us in bondage to our sin and our guilt (see Rev. 12:10). We all have chinks in our armor where our weaknesses are exposed to his attacks. I will give you some examples of the chinks wherein he can thrust his fiery darts. We need to be aware of these areas so we can be on our guard, and better yet, ask for God to be guarding us there. We also need to recognize the obstacles that these chinks can become in our pursuits of God's purposes for us.

THE OBSTACLE OF THE MIND

I don't know about you, but the primary chink for me is my mind. Satan says to me:

1. *"You have to be busy."* I hear this in whispers that seem like yells. I then find myself telling God that I cannot do a particular thing for Him right now because I am too busy. I've got to finish this. I've got to do that. I've got to go there. And while I am there, I've got to do this, that, and the other thing too. I'm a mom, wife, teacher, friend, neighbor, daughter, community member, volunteer, big sister, church member, and so on. I have stuff to do. I am too busy to be busier.

2. *"You have to be self-reliant."* I find myself thinking I can do "it," whatever "it" is. I'm independent. I've got this. I know how to handle that. I know how to do things right and get things done. I can handle the responsibility. I can endure the pressure. Such thoughts cause me to enter into my function mode, relying on myself to get the job done.

3. *"You have to be prideful and concerned regarding your self-image."* I always have to wonder what people will think of me. I cannot allow them to think that I am lazy or that my house is messy. Did I do that right? Did I say the right thing? How did they receive that thing that I just said or did? Do they think I'm antisocial, or pious, or pharisaical, or that they cannot relate to me? Do they think that I am highly capable, or talented, or perfect? I have to keep it all together. I have to conceal my own problems and tears. Never cry; never crack. Smile and nod. Grin and bear it. Be a perfect example, a model citizen, a straight A student all the way.

4. *"You have to be ashamed."* I wrestle with the thoughts in my mind. I tell myself I can't do this because I am afraid. And what about my past, those wretched things that I did? I obsess about and relive my past mistakes and beat myself up over my current ones. I have to be better than this or else the secret is going to come out. I have to keep the calendar packed or else it will be just me and God for the day and then I will have to deal with my "stuff." And inevitably, others will see the stuff too. I think that God will be unable to use me like this, so He may as well give up on me and move on to someone else. I have failed. I have failed Him. After all that He has done for me, look at what I have done wrongly, poorly, belatedly, hurtfully, etc. I have made so many mistakes, too many mistakes.

5. *"You have to be someone you are not."* What will I have to change and give up so that I can be this other person? Where will I have to go? Do I have to let all of my dreams die? Do I have to put my hopes, goals, and plans to death and live unhappily and unfulfilled for the rest of my life? It seems unfair. Why do I have to press on when I just want to quit and go do something for myself for a change?

6. *"You have to be perfectionistic."* Even though I know I can never achieve perfection, I still must try. I try, and try so hard that

I end up driving myself to exhaustion and illness. And then I feel defeated because I just can't be perfect and do things well when I am so tired and ill. Finally, my illness wins out, and I convince myself that I need a break to relax. And then while I am taking my break, I find myself wondering why I even try so hard. Furthermore, if I can't do a good job for God, why even try? I then find that I do not want to bear the guilt of failure, so I do nothing, rather than try something and fail at it. But then there is even more guilt because I have done nothing, and the wedge divides us even further. And because I do not want to bear the guilt of failing or disappointing God, I try harder (to my own detriment), but then I find myself harboring resentment and never returning to full health. It is a vicious cycle. This taskmaster is harsh, cruel, and unrelenting. This is Satan.

How am I doing in life with all of these thoughts leaking in through the chinks in my armor? Sometimes, I listen to this rubbish, and sometimes, I submit to this enemy. My mind has been poisoned. I feel dead. I am numb. I cannot concentrate. I am frazzled. I am forgetting things. I am disappointed. I think that I will never be able to fulfill my dreams. Everything and everyone else comes first—after all, isn't that what serving is all about anyway? These are difficult questions to ask. These are difficult responses to give, yet, they are true. These thoughts are there in the back of my brain, and periodically, they sneak into the forefront. These are the thoughts that I have to reject and disregard. And then, for some reason, I decide I have to chastise myself for having dared to think these thoughts. What kind of person am I? Surely no one else thinks like this! I should just pull myself together, be grateful, and press on. After all, there is work to be done, a reputation to uphold, and a world that is watching me do it. Well, brace yourself, because I have a confession to make: the perfectionist has become perfect at being imperfect! Pray for me, as I pray for you, that we will choose to come under the love, grace, truth, and forgiveness of God rather than under the destruction of our enemies.

THE OBSTACLE OF SIN

Sin is an obstacle that can be giant and glaring or silent and insidious. We need to be aware of it and be willing to do the things necessary to deal with it so that we can move on into all that God has for us. If it is an offense, we need to make it right. If it is an illicit relationship, we need to end it. If we have committed a crime, then we need to confess, pay the consequences, and make restitution. If it is a deception, then we need to put it into the light of truth and confess it. If it is a bad attitude, then we need an adjustment. I could go on and on, as sin has quite a long list. But the good news is that God has a remedy for that long list—a short list with one word on it: *Jesus.*

Shame brings unrest and prevents forward progress because we are running around trying to hide from God and others. If we are not following God's ways, then there is not going to be peace. For example, when Adam and Eve sinned, there was an end to the peace they had known. They could no longer rest in the presence of God and in the bounty that He had given them to enjoy. Now they knew shame and thought that they had to hide from God. I imagine their minds were set on concocting plans of escape from God, blame, and punishment. Perhaps their emotions were in turmoil as they now feared God and had upset their perfect relationship with each other. Their relationship was jeopardized because they had consorted to committing this sin together and then needed someone to blame. Their spirits were no longer at rest because they had broken fellowship with God. Their physical bodies would no longer experience total peace and rest because now they would have to toil, experience pain, and eventually die. They gave up God's best for what *they* thought was best. Rather than resting in His provision and plan, they worked to make one of their own. They thought that they knew better than God and thought that the enemy (Satan) and his lies were better than God and His truth. Sometimes, we are guilty of doing and believing the same, are we not?

The rain falls on the just and on the unjust, so it may seem to us like we can continue on in our waywardness without consequences. The reality, though, is that there are current consequences, whether we recognize them or not, and there will be forthcoming consequences. Not to mention, we are grieving God's heart. He sees and knows all that we do, think, and are. Hiding is pointless. Also, we cannot change our pasts, and the sooner we realize this, stop hiding, and stop listening to the lies of the enemy, the sooner we will find rest. Come. Confess, repent, and move on in victory.

Those days and times when we could have done the right thing are gone, and they are never coming back. Thus, from this point forward, we need to use our current minutes to do things correctly. Our futures can look better than our pasts. We can plan to avoid repeating our mistakes, and we can plan to improve upon what we did poorly in the past. We can be free from the bondage of sin. We can come to Him for forgiveness and seek help for the days ahead. We can learn how to be successful in His eyes and have lives that are filled with joy and peace. His grace and some adjustments to our perspectives will remind us of why we exist and what we need to do to truly live.

Remembering to love Him and love others as we go through our days will make it easier to avoid the obstacles of sin. "Stand fast therefore in the liberty by which Christ has made us free, and do not be entangled again with a yoke of bondage" (Gal. 5:1 NKJV). If we do happen to become re-entangled in the bondage, we do not have to stay that way. Jesus purchased the way of forgiveness so our sins could be blotted out. These sins no longer need to inhibit our approach to God. We can get that clutter moved out of the way and begin to live lives that shape great-looking futures, ones full of freedom and the declaration of God's glory in a dark world. If we live well before Him, there is no shame. If we are forgiven, there is no shame.

THE OBSTACLE OF RESISTANCE

If we fight against God, we are placing distance between the two of us and creating an obstacle of resistance. We may set ourselves at a distance from Him for any number of reasons, such as our anger, attitudes, selfishness, procrastination, unconfessed sins, or simply because we have a misunderstanding of what it means to take up Jesus's yoke. We may have limited understandings of what a yoke is, and thus, see bearing it as an obstacle. We may question how the donning of a yoke is going to alleviate our weariness and ease the weight of the burdens that we bear. This makes no sense to our human minds, so we resist doing it. But the reality is that He can make every part of our lives easier. Yet sometimes, even after we gain an understanding of the concept Jesus taught, we still choose to do things the hard way and learn the hard way. We knowingly and deliberately choose roads that do not include Him. We enter into things without His help. We extract ourselves without His help. We like to be independent, beholden to none. We have stubborn streaks and stubborn pride. In our obstinacy, hard-heartedness, and willfulness, we end up following the ways of the world, but these paths lead us nowhere except further away from God and into more trouble and deeper pain.

Sometimes, we do battle with ourselves—actually, most times. Dare I say all the time? Our flesh wars against the Spirit. The Spirit wars against our flesh. Our wills want to be done. Our roads want to be the ones traveled. There are arguments within our hearts and minds. We know the right things to do, and yet at times, find ourselves resisting doing them. We have to drag our feet back to the right side and the narrow path because sometimes we would rather be doing other things instead—like things on the wrong side and on the wide road. Problems surface when we start buying into the ways of the world instead of into the ways of God. We have heard people say we are supposed to follow our hearts because they are what is true, but the Bible tells us that our hearts are desperately wicked and deceitful (see Jer. 17:9). The world tells us to do whatever feels good and makes us happy, but the Bible tells us that we are sinning when we do the things that we know we are not supposed to do and also when we do not do the things that we know we are supposed to do. Our hearts are dishonest when we are unwillingly doing things out of obligation or when we have impure motives. Our guilt will increase then, not only because we are neglecting what we know to do but also because we are facing the true thoughts and intents of our hearts. The Bible tells us that the way to destruction is wide (Matt. 7:13). This is the easy way, and who in the world doesn't want to do things the easy way? Although He invites us to come and be with Him and learn of Him, we resist. We do so because *here* is fun, and we want to do what we want to do right now. Frankly, we want to enjoy the pleasures of sin for a season. The apostle Paul struggled in this same way (see Rom. 7:14–25). Why did he resist God? More importantly, why do *we* resist? Why do any of us choose to wrestle with God? Why do we fight against His goodness and His holiness?

There are many reasons why we might wrestle with God and resist Him, but they can all be summed up in one word: us. When we are resisting, it is all about us rather than Him. We replace Him with ourselves. The words *me, myself, I, my,* and *mine* fill our hearts, minds, and actions. Life is all about *I* and *my*. It is about what *I* want—my will, my way, my timeline, my glory, my stuff, and my plans. It is *my* resistance, plain and simple.

THE OBSTACLE OF THE "FIX-IT" MENTALITY

Another obstacle that gets in the way of coming to God is a fix-it mentality. Some of us experience difficulty in coming to God "just as we are" because we always want to fix everything, and that includes fixing ourselves first. We have taken on the mentality that we are actually in control of our lives and that we are able to do something about our circumstances in order to achieve desired outcomes. Pop culture tells us: if we believe it, we can achieve it; anything is possible if we put our minds to it; we are the masters of our own destinies; and the power lies within us. I would say the power *lies* within us, all right, and it *lies* outside of us, too. The power of Satan's *lies* has found chinks in the armor of our culture and has moved right on into our unsuspecting and unguarded minds. He leaks in through the media, through curriculum, through people in leadership, through famous icons, and even through religion and churches. We go around trying to be successful at making "it" happen, buying in to the lies that overtly pervade and that subtly creep in. We try and try but get nowhere. We become fraught with exhaustion. Perspiration drips from our brows, gets into our eyes and blinds us, and then we get lost. Being lost distracts us. We stop moving forward so we can try to fix up our messes with whatever is handy, quick, and easy. We turn to empty solutions that deliver painful consequences, and we end up not really fixing anything at all; we instead add to our brokenness.

THE OBSTACLE OF BUSYNESS

So many of us are so busy—*too* busy. It seems like the reply I get now when I ask how people are doing is not the standard "I'm fine," instead it is "I'm busy." Aren't women often frenetic females, weary women, and downtrodden divas? And the men, mincemeat men, hounded hombres, and defeated dudes? Even teens are frequently stressed out and overwhelmed and are often commenting on how tired they are. What are we teaching those around us and passing down to the next generation? Bondage. Restlessness. Pain. Lies. Selfishness. Self-reliance. Why do we allow ourselves to be running for the world rather than resting with God?

It seems like we wear busyness as a badge of honor or view it as a requirement for societal membership. We brag about our busyness, draw sympathy for its excessiveness, discuss it among our peer groups, and try to one-up each other with it. We take pride in how frazzled we look and feel, how sleep deprived we are, and how far behind we've gotten. We drive ourselves to exhaustion and health problems, and drive people away in the process. We become addicted to the adrenaline or the positive attention others give us as we lament.

Somewhere along the way, our brains started thinking that we have to do it all, try it all, and be it all. We have become confused about what God has called us to do. Sometimes we delude ourselves into thinking that all of our busyness pleases God, especially if it is composed of good activities like church work and keeps us from acting in wickedness. We do not seem to know the difference between what things are necessities and priorities and what things are niceties and preferences. His presence goes with us if we are believers, but do we allow it to cover us as we accomplish life, or do we have to make a concerted effort to enter into it because it is buried under all of our busyness?

God has spoken about resting. Some of us are unaware of what He has said, while others of us simply ignore it. One place he addressed the issue was in the Ten Commandments. The fourth commandment says, "Remember the Sabbath day, to keep it holy. Six days you shall labor and do all your work, but the seventh day *is* the Sabbath of the LORD your God" (Exod. 20:8–10 NKJV). Work is to be completed in six days, and the seventh one is to be reserved for rest. However, in my experience, it is rare to find anyone observing and obeying these words. People willfully choose to press on in busyness instead. Human agendas take precedence over God's. Completing tasks becomes more important than keeping His commands. When this is the case, we are going to miss out on some things: time with God, following His plans for us, and His good provision for us through resting.

In all of this busyness, we find a multitude of problems. For example, we can become so busy, focused, driven, and selfish that we become too busy to care about others and assist those who need our help. When my children were young, we viewed a movie that was teaching kids not to be too busy to care for others. Why have we had to resort to teaching *children* to stop amidst their busyness for the sake of others? This makes me wonder where children are learning such busyness. What have we been teaching the younger generation so that we would need to make this course correction? It appears that either they followed our example or we allowed them to get themselves into that condition, perhaps both. Recently, two of my most trusted friends separately said the same thing to me, which confirmed my suspicions. They said that my children have turned out to be just like me and my husband—doing too much. Ouch. The truth hurts, doesn't it? And since I can now answer the question about where my children learned to be like this, I can move on to the next question of what I am going to do about it.

"No" is a simple word, but it seems to be so difficult for us to say when we are presented with new opportunities or asked to take on just one more thing. Reducing our schedules and refusing more activities seems contrary to how people are being taught and how they are being expected to function in the world today. It seems abnormal to slow things down a bit, much less stop them. It is just not what our society is prone to do. I have read several accounts of men, women, teens, and families dealing with the challenges of over-packed schedules. I have seen several book titles that address the topics of the chaos, mayhem, burden, and emptiness of too much busyness. Apparently, busyness is a problem.

All of this busyness impacts us both externally and internally, physically and spiritually. We will become weak, worn down, and worn out in all areas when we go at such a constant and demanding pace. And a strange phenomenon can sometimes occur with busyness: we can just freeze up in the midst of it. Perhaps we will even get to the point that we do not feel like running anymore because there is something else that we would rather be doing—nothing. We will desire a rest, a long rest, maybe even an eternal one. And there it is: we have found burnout. It is important to realize that our faith is not strengthened when we do not spend any time nurturing it or praying for it to be strengthened. Our passion for God will sputter and die when we do not take the time to maintain it. And the equation is: stressed out plus burned out does not equal sold out and poured out for God.

Another problem regarding busyness is that our enemy, Satan, is busy too. He is busy pursuing and attacking us relentlessly. He wants to render us ineffective in our Christian lives so that the kingdom of God does not grow. He wants to steal, kill, and destroy anything good that God may do in and through our lives. Satan has many methods that he custom fits to each of us, but there are definitely some commonalities in his tactics. If he can keep us busy serving him or ourselves rather than serving God, ground is lost for the kingdom. My mentor said to me that we are "burned out, stressed out, stretched out, and not in the will of God." If we spend our days running around doing good but neglect to spend time with Him, we have a problem. We will have neglected an element essential for maintaining relationships and accomplishing tasks: communication. Additionally, we will have neglected to rest and care for our bodies and spirits, which are God's (1 Cor. 6:19–20). Our function modes may be functional, but they are not very practical, nor are they sustainable indefinitely. The five parts of our beings can only remain in states of imbalance for limited amounts of time before damage occurs. We cannot continue at such a pace without pausing for the rest He offers. If we do not stop doing so many things, even good things, eventually we will self-destruct. And it is entirely possible that when we get to this point, we will discover that although we helped others, we did nothing to help God's eternal cause.

Busyness is fraught with danger, so we must be on our guard. It can become a source of bondage and oppression. It can become an idol. It can keep us from developing deep-seated relationships with God. We do not consider God's heart at these times, only our own. I have heard of the word *busy* being used as an acronym—**B**eing **U**nder **S**atan's **Y**oke. I have also heard these words: "If Satan can't make you be bad, he'll make you be busy." I truly believe that there is something to these words. The oppression of tasks suppresses us mentally and spiritually. We are crushed and burdened as someone or something other than God takes the authority over us. We are no longer in control. This entity weighs us down in our bodies, minds, and spirits. During this time of oppression, there is wasting that takes place. Things like joy and peace dissipate. Confidence and passion erode. Relationships weaken. Health declines. Ministry suffers. And most importantly, our testimonies for Christ wane. We can be so busy that we do not come to be filled by God, and thus, we cannot be poured out. What's truly important and what truly matters dwindles away.

Spiritual barrenness comes when we are so busy for God that we are not taking the time to know God. Our service for Him takes priority in our lives instead of Him taking the priority. Our earthly schedules compete with our spiritual ones. Abiding in Jesus is avoided. We press on in our own strength, without taking the time to build our relationships with Him, and thus, we strive without true strength. We run without refreshment. We perform without true peace. We push ourselves beyond our limits in order to achieve perfection, even though achieving perfection will always be beyond possibility. And although rest can be found in knowing that perfection can never be attained, that seems to be knowledge we are not interested in gaining. I ruined my body and some of my relationships while I was pursuing my version of being "busy for God," and those are things that I cannot get back. And now, after everything I have been through and learned, what do I find myself doing on a day when I feel decent? I drive myself to exhaustion trying to make up for lost time. And even though I know the right thing to do, have been told repeatedly the right thing to do, and it is the right thing that I want to do, still, I do not do it. This is pursuing barrenness rather than fruitfulness.

I ignore the promptings from myself, others, and worst of all, from God. The counsel to rest falls on my deaf ears, races through my racing heart, and passes right through my busy hands. My closest circle of friends and prayer partners know that I have this tendency. They speak when I need spoken to. I try to heed them, and occasionally even succeed for a while, but other times, because I have rationalized away sound reasoning, I just do not believe that I can do as they have advised. I just cannot let go of my datebook, address book, teacher's book, record book, and how-to-get-more-done book so that I can pick up *His book*, His Holy Word. I hope everyone enjoys the service that I give them, but deep down I know God wants my heart rather than my service. If I was to make a vertical list of ten yokes that I wear and write my name at the bottom of the stack, this is what it would look like:

***

being a perfectionist
having an endless to-do list
over-extending myself
running myself ragged
not stopping to breathe
not taking time to pray
being crazy-busy
running helter-skelter
having too many irons in the fire and too much on my plate
not taking time to care for my own needs and body
Francee

***

This makes me feel overwhelmed just looking at it on paper. If I do not address this problem, I am going to be crushed beneath the load. As a solution, I need to take up His easy yoke instead of my own overbearing ones. I can take all of these issues and place them onto His shoulders so He can help me bear them. I can put His name in place of my own and then I will be looking at a picture of strength bearing up a huge load instead of a huge load crushing me underneath. The same goes for all of us. When we decide to ask for help in bearing our loads, we can join His name to ours, or better yet, replace our names with His. It will look so much better this way, with His name instead of ours, and it will really take a weight off us too.

I do not embrace much of what philosophers say, but Socrates said something that I can recognize as good advice: "Beware the barrenness of a busy life."[1] If I apply that statement in a spiritual respect, it causes me to ask myself a question that I think we all should be asking ourselves: "Are the things I do eternally significant?" Clean laundry and clean dishes are important, but these are insignificant in comparison to the importance of Christ. And another thing, service *for* Him is different than service *with* Him. If we are yoked to the wrong things, then we are living in bondage and may become entangled. These wrong things may be our schedules, money, people, or careers. This entanglement keeps us from moving in the freedom of Christ. I think, then, that it is advisable not to become entangled in things that are not eternally significant. We do not live and move and have our beings in the calendar, the bank, the friendship, or the workplace; we live and move and have our beings in Jesus, free, the way He meant for us to be free (see Acts 17:28; Gal. 5:1). If we devote ourselves to Him and His intended plans for us, we will have lives that are fruitful. We will be busy bearing fruit rather than trying to glean a harvest from barren fields, wasting our time, energies, and resources on things that are not eternally significant, ending up with empty hands and empty hearts at the end of life.

Maybe you have seen a bit of yourself mirrored in parts of my life. As I think about what a mess I am and what a perfect solution He is, I yearn for His rescue. Feelings of guilt and regret over the time I wasted try to surface, but I will no longer mourn for what is lost because mourning wastes even more time. Beating ourselves up and obsessing with grief is futile. Anxiety about things past does not undo them. What is past is past. Instead, we should celebrate what we have with Him now, and anticipate the great relationships that are going to develop from this moment forward. We can be forgiven and begin to enjoy the sweet fellowship, friendship, kinship, intimacy, security, comfort, joy, and much, much more that God offers to those who choose to become His children and abide in Him. If we learn to say no to jam-packed schedules, we will avoid their negative side effects. This free time will allow us to care for our spirits, affording us the opportunity to find rest and refreshment in God's presence. This free time will also allow us to discover a new way to be busy: Being Under (the) Savior's Yoke.

This alternative type of busyness holds abundant benefits and rewards rather than stress and burnout. There is no bondage in this activity. Being Under the Savior's Yoke means we come to Him with yielded hearts and attitudes. These attitudes will influence the yokes we put on and the ways in which we carry them. Choosing to accept rather than resist His yoke will bring us great and eternal benefits. When we allow Him to place the yoke upon us, He will teach us to be humble and gentle like He is. Which burden will we bear? Will we choose His or ours? Which **B.U.S.Y.** will we be?

THE OBSTACLE OF TOO MUCH

Just as we can have too much physical activity, we can also have too much "spiritual" activity, which really isn't spiritual at all. Too much of a good thing can be an obstacle. Sometimes we feel like we are "churched-out," "Bible studied-out," and "devotioned-out." It seems like the old adage "You can never have too much of a good thing" does not ring true. Some days we simply feel like we have had too much in the spiritual department. How is it even possible to think that we are overloaded, saturated, and buried in "too much" of God? It is because we have something or someone else rather than God. There is too much time with groups of people, too much time spent listening to and reading the words of humans, getting their takes and their slants on things, rather than just having pure, unadulterated time with God. This is the "too much" that we have. We often take God for granted and forget how truly extraordinary He is all by Himself.

This is what we need: time to remember who He truly is, what He has done for us, and what He is yet to do. He is *extraordinary*. Sometimes, we need time with just us and Him, us and His Word, us and His voice in our ears. We need time in our prayer closets and time in individual worship, confession, meditation, and praise. The words of Samuel recorded in 1 Samuel 12:24 (NKJV) beautifully express this thought: "Only fear the LORD, and serve Him in truth with all your heart; for consider what great things He has done for you." He has done extraordinary things for us, and we should take the time to acknowledge them. We can never have too much of *this*!

So, if we are supposed to be focused on spending time with God, whyever did I write this book? My hope is that you do not use this book as a replacement for your time with God. My hope is that reading this book will inspire you to spend more time with God each day. I hope that you can learn from my example and from my mistakes. May this book inspire you to examine your own life and where you stand in relation to God. May this be a time of truly coming to Him and not just to another book. I encourage you to set this book down right now and go spend some time with just the two of you. Listen to Him speak to your heart. Speak your heart to Him. He is calling for you to follow Him; what is your heart doing? Where and when does He want you to go? What does He want you to do? What does He need you to change? To leave behind? To incorporate into your life? What miracle does He want you to experience for yourself or as a part of someone else's life? Whose lives does He want you to affect? What gifts does He want you to put into practice? This, then, is my purpose: to point you to my extraordinary God, who has offered you an invitation that is anything but ordinary.

We need discernment regarding which invitations to accept and which roads to travel. Without discernment, we will enter into things that God has not intended for us to enter. And once we have done something, said something, heard something, or seen something, it cannot be undone. Thus, it is of extreme importance that we are on the correct road. There is a potential for too much busyness in our society today, with the availability of almost any activity you can imagine and special events for just about everything, but just because something is available to us and is a good thing does not mean that it is what God has for us. We are capable of coming up with some pretty good and admirable stuff on our own, but that does not necessarily mean we should be inventing these things. There are also so many great causes and ministries that we can join up with and participate in, but just because we *can* does not mean we *should*. Doing good can actually become an enemy to us because it can distract us from the plans and purposes that God has for our lives. Good things may be accomplished, but while doing them, the better and best things go undone. Trying to do too many things instead of the things that God has called us to do would qualify under this statement. We will not find peace and rest in the wrong hustle and bustle. We will never quite fit or feel quite right when we are in places that we are not supposed to be. All of those other angles we are working are not accomplishing the prescribed tasks God has for us; they are merely distractions. We need to ask God to speak to our hearts and reveal if we are walking in His ways and doing His works or if we are walking in our own ways and doing our own works. May we let nothing be an obstacle to us today.

CHAPTER 12
Yoked to Rest

THE NEED FOR REST

Have you had some difficult things to deal with in your life? Of course you have, you are human. It is probably even highly likely that you are in the midst of something very difficult at this exact moment. Are you? Are you laboring? Are you bearing a heavy burden? Do you need rest? I know I do. I have good news for you, for us: we have been given an invitation to receive some rest. This invitation has come to us straight from the mouth of God. Matthew 11:28 displays the words for us: "Come unto me, all ye that labour and are heavy laden, and I will give you rest."

The words *labor* and *heavy laden* indicate that there will be a need for rest, and Jesus tells us that if we come to Him, we will find that rest. Toil, tiredness, heaviness, and mastery are indicated, but because He is the God of the impossible, He can give us rest. The invitation is open to all who labor and those who are weary, no matter the types of burdens carried or yokes worn. There are so many things in life that can wear us out and wear us down, but His rest is always available to us. Some things weigh on our physical bodies, some on our hearts, some on our minds, and some on our spirits, but He gives peace that is beyond understanding and helps us in our weaknesses. We are not left on our own, nor are we left in hopelessly powerless positions; we can come to Him for help. When we look at our situations and wonder how we are ever going to handle them, we can then look at Him because He knows exactly how. He can give rest to us in all parts of who we are because He is capable of doing so.

We will find help for dealing with every situation imaginable and even the ones we cannot imagine. Even when we are the ones who are bringing the weariness upon ourselves, if we come as Jesus has said, we will find that we are welcomed. If we are trapped in bondage to a habitual sin, He can break it. If we have an addiction or a passion for something that is not what God has desired for us, our desires can be changed. We can choose to come instead of sneaking around in our sin or flagrantly vaunting it. We have been given the opportunity to trade these things in for something wonderful: the way of life that God wants us to follow and the blessings that He will give us if we do. We can put on His yoke and replace the yokes that we have been wearing as we have been wandering and running around. We can lay down our burdens and pick up His grace, laying it across our shoulders to cover us and guide us as we move forward through the fields. We will find love, forgiveness, and fresh starts when we respond to Jesus's invitation. Actually, there are even more things that we will find, but the pages of a book do not provide enough space to tell them all.

THE NEED FOR LABOR

Part of God's plan for us is that we labor. This labor is not a bad thing. God Himself labored for six days when He created the world, and then He rested on the seventh day. He instituted the same process for us: labor and rest. There are benefits to labor, such as profit, sustenance, enjoyment, and good sleep (Ps. 128:2; Prov. 14:23; Eccl. 5:12). However, the time at which the labor is done, the way in which it is done, and the motive with which it is done matters. The Ten Commandments detail a structure for balancing labor and rest: labor for six days, and keep the Sabbath on the seventh day (Exod. 20:8–11). Proverbs 23:4 tells us that labor is not about the money and working for riches. It is not to be done for selfish reasons with a misdirected focus. Labor is to be about doing things that endure unto everlasting life (see John 6:27).

God has called us to serve both Him and others. This will involve effort, but this burden of labor is not meant to be grievous; instead, it is to delight us as we show our love for Him and others. He can help us with the work required in life and with the specific things required of us. We are to work so that we can take care of our needs and also so that we have something to share with others (see Eph. 4:28). We are to labor with love and impact lives (see 1 Thess. 1:3), and when we allow Him to enter into our labors, He can multiply the impact of our efforts. We can labor *with* the grace of God and *within* the grace of God, knowing that our labors in the Lord will not be in vain (see 1 Cor. 15:10, 58).

God labors, and all of His labors are perfect and purposeful. He has given things for His creations to do, as well, but He has also made provision for all of them to rest. People, animals, and even the land itself are given opportunity to rest and be refreshed. For us, though, the rest goes even deeper than the physical realm—it moves into the spiritual. Believers have the privilege of resting in the perfect work of Jesus's redemption. This is no ordinary invitation. Jesus labored on the cross, bleeding and dying, for you, for me, for every one of us. As He labored for His very breath, He labored for our very souls. He was the one doing the work of redeeming us, and His labor was sufficient. There is nothing else we can or need to do to add to it—it is already perfect through Him—all we need to do is believe it.

FREE TO LABOR AND FREE TO REST

We have been given free will to choose whether or not to accept the perfect invitation that Jesus gives, in all of its aspects. We can refuse to come to Him. We can refuse His yoke. We can refuse the weight of His burdens. And we can refuse His rest. But when we say no to the invitation that He gives, in any or all of its parts, we miss an untold number of blessings. I imagine that we all have, at one time or another, refused to accept His help, thinking that we could handle things on our own and in our own strength. How did that go for us? Could it have gone better? Yes, it could have gone better. In hindsight, we are able to see what we missed and what more we needed. But since we cannot go back and change the past, all we can do is learn from it and move forward. We can face our current difficulties, and move forward into those of the future, with the aid of the One who has all the power, ability, and knowledge needed to handle everything that comes our way. This is what we are free to do, but this is also what we are free not to do.

Having free will is an incredible blessing, but our sin natures often misuse that blessing. With our very limited wisdom, we make decisions that are not beneficial to us. We turn aside from what Jesus invites us to do and from what He wants to give us. And sometimes, we turn aside from Him altogether. But turning to anything other than Him is not going to be the best place to receive help. Expecting humans, material goods, organizations, careers, or anything else to bear our burdens is a poorly placed expectation that will only be doomed to failure, disappointment, and heartbreak. It is true that partial support may be found in these things, yet nothing but Jesus will completely remedy our problems or remedy us in all parts of who we are. There is help that only He can give and suffering that only He can alleviate, but we must give Him the opportunity to do so, as He never forces Himself into our lives.

If we are laboring in the midst of difficult situations, there is opportunity for us to seek His help with them. And if the moment of crisis has already passed, He can help us recover from any lingering effects, if only we will turn to Him. Even when situations are not neatly resolved, His help is there. When the consequences of our burdens linger long after the situations pass, His help will remain continually available to us. It is never too late to come to Him, never too late to seek His help, and never too late to continue onward with Him from where we are right now. He always exists, and He is always powerful. He has said that He *will* give us rest; *will* indicates the future, and when we come to Him we are moving into our futures. If we freely will, He surely will.

MATTHEW 11:29

THE YOKE DEFINED

Jesus said, "Take my yoke upon you, and learn of me; for I am meek and lowly in heart: and ye shall find rest unto your souls" (Matt. 11:29). Why was He talking about a yoke, and is that something that even makes sense to many of us in the twenty-first century? Was He even talking to us? Yes, it does make sense, and yes, He was talking to us. He was giving an object lesson through His words, and those words apply to us today since He exists outside of time and His words stand forever.

What is this yoke and what purpose does it have? Simply put, a yoke is a farm implement composed of a wooden frame or bar that is placed on the necks of two or more draft animals so they can work together. The yoke helps them to bear the load or burden that must be borne. The yoke serves as a guide to indicate which direction to go. But Jesus was not talking about farming; there was another meaning indicated in His words. He was referring to circumstances.

Besides being a tool, a yoke can also be viewed as evidence of dominion, as the one in authority places it upon the one in servitude. Literally and figuratively, a yoke can suggest slavery, bondage, hard labor, a burden, or oppression. The Bible discusses yokes in both of these senses. Genesis 27:40 references Esau breaking the yoke of dominion that his brother had over him. Deuteronomy 28:48 tells that the enemy of the Israelites would put a yoke of iron on them and destroy them. Lamentations 1:14 talks about a yoke of transgressions bound together and placed on the neck. In Matthew 23:4, Jesus referenced the religious leaders who were overburdening the people with legalistic rules. So in either a literal or figurative sense, there is a burden that has to be borne.

Based on these descriptions, does a yoke sound appealing to us and like something we would want to wear? Not likely. But yokes are important and helpful when used correctly, worn properly, and employed at the proper time. There is a time to work, and there is a time to work better. Therefore, it is important to don the yoke when it is time to work. There should be no rushing and no dawdling, only moving at the correct time within the proper season. If yokes are not worn at proper times and for proper uses, they are pointless.

Prior to the good and highly anticipated time of harvest, certain things must be accomplished. There is a time of training so that the pair becomes accustomed to wearing the yoke and learns to work together. The yoke must be donned when it is time to plow and prepare the field for seeding. When the task is complete, the yoke is stored in the barn, and the wait for the harvest begins. These various stages affect the end result of the harvest. If any part of the process is done incorrectly, the yield will be affected. Trying to train when it is time to plow will surely result in stress, frustration, and a smaller yield, and both time and energy will be wasted while the focus is on the wrong task. After the planting, the seedlings will be damaged if the pair is allowed to walk through the field while yoked to farm implements. Continuing to wear the yoke after planting will not force change in the timing of the seasons nor encourage the growth process. Trust must be placed in the one who knows the seasons and the proper time to act. Patient waiting must take place as the farmer watches for just the right moment. When the farmer says, "Now," the yoked pair needs to be ready to move and do whatever it is that needs to be done. They also need to be ready to rest when they are told that it is time to do so. And when it is time to harvest, the yoke can be brought out again to aid in hauling the cartful of yield, the precious result of all of the previous labors.

AN UNMATCHED PAIR

Without a yoke, two animals will have the capability to go in two different directions. And if the farmer manages to get the yoke on the two animals but they are unalike, there will still be problems. In Deuteronomy 22:10, the Israelites were commanded not to plow with an ox and donkey together. These animals are mismatched in strength, ability, and temperament. The strong one leads the weak one around, and the strong one may even have to drag the weak one along. The weak one may fight for the control. Things end up lopsided. Rows become crooked. Energy gets wasted. And injury is a possibility.

So, how does a farm implement and a few animals relate to us? When we begin our relationships with Jesus, we are unmatched pairs, yet He wants to be yoked to us. Why would He want to do this when He is strong, righteous, rich, a giver, and the King of all kings, while we are weak, sinful, poor, takers, and peasants? He wants us to come under His yoke because it is better than the ones that we create for ourselves. The yokes we have in our minds, bodies, spirits, and relationships are not the best things for us. We carry yokes such as worry, fear, excessive busyness, independence, discontentment, and disobedience. We waste our breaths and our words speaking things that are vain and harmful. We pursue and maintain some relationships that we should not. We place people before

God and cater to them, spending all of our time and efforts relating to them and none relating to Him. We seek human help rather than His divine help. We place ourselves into the bondage of perfectionism and other obsessive behaviors. We strain our eyes trying to see visions that are not for us to see. We labor without prayer, and thus, labor without God's help and all of the power He could make available to us through His Spirit. Frankly, we make our lives more difficult than they have to be. We simply try to make our own lives rather than allowing God to help us make them according to His perfect plans. Our efforts then result in making life anything but simple or perfect.

When we are yoked to Jesus, we start out being nothing like Him; we are mismatched in strength, ability, and temperament. This can result in all types of issues on our parts. We may find it challenging to humble ourselves and submit to Him and His leadership. Jesus is the strong one, but many of us try to be the strong one in the relationship and try to bend Him to our ways. We try to fit Him into our timetables, wills, and boxes of expected behaviors. We want Him to come out of the vending machine with our answers after we have put in the coins of our requests. We exhibit manipulative behaviors and try to bargain with Him. We try to act certain ways or line up routines of being super-spiritual so that He will come through for us at such a time as we want Him to do so. We think that if we act just right or accomplish certain things in His name, then His timetable for us will be hurried along. Well, it is both foolish and fruitless to assert ourselves, trying to be the ones in control. His strength and our stubbornness do not go well together. God answers to no man.

God's ways and thoughts are higher than our ways and thoughts (Isa. 55:9). So, how can we ever expect to understand them and fit to them if we do not truly know who He is and cannot attain to Him? We need to start with the basics and remember that *He* is God and *we* are not. We should not ever be trying to take away His job. We are the ones that need to be wearing the yoke, not Him. This realization is a good place to begin the relationship and begin developing into a matched pair. Visualize being in a yoke together with Jesus. What does this look like? Are we allowing Him to teach us? Are we willfully pulling the yoke in the direction *we* want it to go or letting *Him* bear the weight and lead us along? What do we see about how we are handling life and the way in which we are allowing God to be a part of it? Do our plans match up with His?

Wearing Jesus's yoke is a method to make us more like Him and a way to develop a deeper relationship with Him. He leads us, teaches us, and guides us. When we wear His yoke, we learn to take on His attributes. When our hearts are beside His heart, we hear truth, receive wisdom, and are covered by His love. When we hear how His heart beats for us, we will be inspired to match our heartbeats to His. His yoke is lovingly placed on us by His own nail-scarred hands, and it will take us in the direction that we need to go, to the depth that we need to go. When we join ourselves to Him, we will gain His strength, His righteousness, His blessings, and His generous heart. We will become children of the King, joint-heirs with Christ (see Rom. 8:17).

THE PROPER FIT

It is important for us to understand Jesus's yoke and how it fits into our lives. When Jesus lived on the earth, people would have understood His words "Take my yoke upon you" from a rabbinical standpoint. Essentially, the teaching was that people must come to God first; after that, they were to obey what He had laid out in the Law.[1] So, to take up Jesus's yoke means that we need to first accept the salvation that He offers, and then accept His plans after that. Accepting His salvation is accepting *eternal* life, and accepting His plans is accepting *abundant* life. In order to attain abundant life, there are particular ways that He prescribes for us to live. We are not earning our salvation, we are just living lives that please God and bring His abundant blessings upon us. His yoke is not about keeping rules—it is about accomplishing His will and His work in the world by advancing the kingdom, fulfilling His purposes for our lives, and leading others to His love and salvation. We need to remember the broader purpose, the totality of God's plan, the eternity after the now. Once we have taken on His salvation, we can take on His mind and His manners. We can take on His work ethic and His love for all humanity. We can take on His strength and His grace. As children of God, we have the opportunity to bring honor to God our Father through Christ-like behavior and obedience. And after we acquire and practice these things, our lives will be abundant.

A matched pair under the yoke is the best situation to have. The unified pair become yokefellows. Because they are such close companions, they can serve together as a powerful team rather than operating in individual and conflicting strength. A yoke enables the pair to share the load and keeps them on a straight path. We can be a part of a pair, matched up with the Holy Spirit. Jesus left the Holy Spirit to live with believers. He is known as the Helper and the Comforter. We were not created to go through life alone, so it is best if we resist trying to do so. It is better to come into fellowship and unity with the One who knows all things, to become Jesus's yokefellow, working alongside the presence of the Holy Spirit. The Spirit knows the paths that we should take, so it is beneficial to listen to Him. He will guide us into all truth (John 16:13). He will also fill us with His power so that we are enabled to do the work.

Being Jesus's yokefellows indicates that we can be His co-laborers. Developing into these co-laborers begins in the heart and remains all about the heart. First, our hearts need to be prepared to wear the yokes. If we are not His children, we cannot fit into the yokes in the first place. If we are His children, we should not have defiant hearts that are trying to change the yokes; instead, we should have willing hearts that submit to His authority and leadership. The yokes are already fashioned to work just right, but the results are left to be decided by our hearts. The attitudes of our hearts will either cause things to go well or to go poorly. Harboring sin in our hearts will affect the ability to communicate with Him. The amount of desire in our hearts will affect the strength of the relationship, and ultimately, the harvest.

Jesus offers yokes that are custom-made for each of us, but at times our hearts resist wearing them. We may try to wear yokes that belong to others, attempting to fit into their places by forcing ourselves to be something that we are not. Other times, we try to add something to the yokes we have been given to wear, but that only makes them ill-fitting, more cumbersome, and improperly functioning. We each have a unique role to fill in God's kingdom and it is best to keep to that role, nothing more and nothing less. Some prepare the fields, some plant, some water, and some bring in the harvest. We need to wear the yokes that Jesus has specifically designed for us so we can complete the process correctly. The best way to co-labor with Him is to be who He made us to be, each and every day.

It is good to evaluate how well things are working out and what the quality of our co-laboring is. How did our days with Jesus go? Did we move left when He moved left, or right when He moved right? Did we step forward in unison with Him? Did we stop when He stopped? Were we sensitive to His leading, to His every prompting? When the yokes are hanging in the barn at the end of the day, will our backs and necks be shaped to them? Can we lie down and sleep in peace because we have done a good day's work and accomplished what God sent us out to do, or will we be nursing the sores of stubborn necks that tried to turn their own ways? Will our muscles be pleasantly tired because we worked cooperatively, or will they ache because we pulled in the wrong directions with resistance, stubbornness, or prideful ignorance? Will our muscles develop fully and equally because we worked well with our partner, or will some parts of us be lopsided and poorly conditioned? Whether our answers are ones of success or failure matters not, because the day is gone. We must now ask ourselves if our bodies will be willing and ready to accept the yokes tomorrow.

Sometimes, it is so difficult to want to put on His yoke because we are looking at it with the wrong perspectives. We see His yoke as heavy bondage when we look at our lives through the eyes of pride. If He asks us to do a small thing, we resist, because we imagine that we should be doing something huge and on display for all to see. We sometimes do not want to go into the fields where He wants us to work because we believe that we need to be heading off somewhere else in order to be great for God. Well, it does not matter how good our lives appear from the outside, because if our hearts are not right and we are not following His plans, we are going nowhere. But with the proper hearts offered up to God, we will go great places, do great things, and have an impact on the world around us even if we never travel far from home or do anything that is seen by another person. Small is big when God is in it, five-loaves-and-two-fish big (see Luke 9:12–17)! Let us set aside our limited thoughts and plans and be a part of the miracles that can happen anywhere. May we let our eyes look on Him, and may we let Him get the glory.

"Give yourself first to the Lord." These were the words that I wanted to type as I began this paragraph, but originally I made a typo that read, "Give yourself first to the Load." As I mistakenly typed "Load" instead of "Lord," it caused me to wonder how often this "slip" actually proves to be true in our lives. Sometimes, we do not monitor ourselves very well, and we allow our loads to take over instead of the Lord. And if we give ourselves first to the loads instead of to the Lord, we will not be at rest. The things to which we surrender become the things which shape us. Our choices have consequences, and we will become someone in particular based on those choices. Choices have cumulative effects, and before we know it, our poor choices will cause us to become people who are different from what we had originally envisioned ourselves becoming—and all because we did not guard our behaviors. Thus, we cannot live carelessly and expect to have great outcomes. We need to give ourselves first to the Lord Jesus and take on the loads that He has for us, exchanging our own for what He offers instead. We can master the loads by giving the loads to the Master. This choice will lead to great things, and we will become who we were meant to become.

Each day, each moment, makes a difference in who we are and who we are becoming. The choices we make affect us outwardly and inwardly, from our behaviors to our spirits. Our shapes will not resemble Jesus if we have not spent time with Him, because we will not know what He is like, nor know how He desires us to live our lives. If we give ourselves first to the loads, then the loads are going to be what shape us. The thoughts and emotions that the loads stir will influence the behaviors that we display, and they likely will not align with behaviors that Jesus would display. Difficult circumstances sometimes showcase how difficult we can be as individuals. If we are not shaped to Jesus's likeness, then our trials will showcase our sinful natures rather than bringing out the good that we could have had in us through Him. We need to choose wisely what shape we want to be.

THE TEACHER AND THE LEARNER

Jesus taught in many locations, and people came to Him there. He taught from boats, mountainsides, roadsides, synagogues, homes, and the supper table, among other places. Wherever we come to learn from Him, we can have Him near to us through His presence and His Word. We can have Him so close, in fact, that He will be a part of us if we invite His Spirit and His Word into our innermost beings. We have a wonderful opportunity to sit at His feet while He is on the throne of our hearts. Concentrated time spent this way will allow us to learn who He is and also who we are.

When Jesus said to take up His yoke and learn from Him, He was inviting us to be taught. He said His yoke is easy and His burden is light. We now get to make the choice about whether to take it on. He does not force us to obey; instead, He lovingly gives us the choice to join Him or not. Forced obedience is far from being easy and light, rather, it is a heavy burden. But this is not the way of Jesus. And since we will not find forced obedience, there is no reason to be unwilling to wear the yoke that He offers. It is a yoke that can be trusted. It is placed on us with love and with a great purpose in mind. We can be transformed into His image when we know what His image consists of and what we need to do to become like Him. We gain this knowledge by studying His characteristics. We will learn to give, love, serve, and obey as He did. His words will set us free—*if* we take them to heart and *heed* them.

In order to properly prepare to move through the fields of life, we need to be willing to learn from Jesus. In order to begin our learning, we need to move ourselves out of the way and off the throne and place Him there instead. Putting on His yoke is essentially saying that we are putting Him on the thrones of our lives, that we are making Him the Lord and Master of our lives. And how beautiful it is that He does not stand off to the side cracking a whip and yelling commands at us. He is instead in the muck and the mire with us and is wearing the yoke along with us, helping us to shoulder the loads that we must carry through life. Thank you, Jesus!

We should let Jesus be our guide through life because He knows the ways to take. Learning His commands, ways, and plans, and following the roads He travels, is how we take His yoke upon us and learn from Him. By following His plans, we will not make wrong turns, get lost, and end up on the wrong roads. There is trouble and misery that we can be spared, if only we will heed and positively respond to what He is inviting us to do. Racing around distractedly does not allow us to sit at His feet to learn how He would have us accomplish the tasks we need to accomplish. We will, however, be able to fulfill our tasks once we have held still to be yoked with Him and paused to learn from Him. A student should be present in the classroom so the teacher can begin the lesson.

Here are some tips for effective learning:

- Learn from Him foremost. Read His teachings, recorded on the pages of the Bible. Listen to His voice.
- Be teachable. Do not be stubborn and rebellious or hold a preconceived idea of what needs to be learned; actually receive what He wants to teach.
- Be still long enough to hear what He is saying. Do not force your hand and your timeline. Do not cut Him off before He is done speaking to you or when He says something that you do not want to hear. Be still as long as it takes.
- Open your spiritual eyes to look for what He is showing you. You will see Him when you are still and purposely focus your attention on Him.

When we are ready to learn, there is great subject matter to study: the life of Jesus. First Peter 2:21–24 tells us that Jesus is our example and we are called to follow in His steps. First John 2:6 tells us that we ought to walk even as He walked. One aspect to examine, learn from, and apply is His thought process. Philippians 2:5 says, "Let this mind be in you, which was also in Christ Jesus." Other aspects to learn about and apply are His character traits and behaviors. We can observe how He acted, responded, and served humanity; then we can imitate His behaviors. He was humble, holy, and selfless, which He beautifully demonstrated on the cross. Philippians 2:7–8 tells us that Jesus made Himself of no reputation but took upon Himself the form of a servant. He was made in the likeness of men, humbled Himself, and became obedient to death on a cross. Once we die to each part of our selves and become sacrificial like Jesus, we become free to live.

Once we have learned this information, we are to properly apply it to living. The key to proper application is seen in Matthew 11:29 where

Jesus tells us about His character. Jesus was "meek and lowly in heart" and because He was, we need to be too. To be meek is to have a manner that is kind, patient, and gentle. To be lowly is to have a humble manner. Several Bible verses discuss meekness and lowliness. First Peter 3:4 tells us that a meek spirit is of great price in God's sight. Galatians 5:23 tells us that meekness is a fruit of the Spirit, so if we are meek, there will be evidence that Jesus is in our lives. As we serve and try to follow His example, we are to walk meekly and worthily of the vocations to which we are called (Eph. 4:1–2). We are told that the Lord respects the lowly (Ps. 138:6), and "with the lowly is wisdom" (Prov. 11:2). The experiences of life give us a choice of how to behave: with pride or humility, with gentleness or incivility. We get to decide how we are going to act, interact, and react in relation to the world around us. We need to be sure to take the time to acquaint ourselves with the ways of Jesus so that we will know how we *ought* to live. We can fall back on His teachings as we navigate through both the mundane and extraordinary days of life. A great thing, too, would be if we could say as the apostle Paul did, "Imitate me, just as I also *imitate* Christ" (1 Cor. 11:1 NKJV). Incorporating the lessons of Jesus into our characters will result in our abilities to act appropriately in the world around us—and change it by doing so.

The knowledge that we receive from Jesus can change who we are and what we are able to do in life. If we submit to His knowledge, authority, and plans, then we will find that living life is much easier to do. Queen Esther prayed, fasted, and submitted to God's plans for her, even at the risk of her own life. There were benefits to her and those around her when she first took steps toward God—and then again as she took subsequent steps that were God-directed. As a result of her submission to God's plans for her life, the Jewish people were spared from destruction (see Esther 4–9). And if we become God's yokefellows as Esther was, He will do great things through our lives as well. This type of relationship is beneficial, just as the one mentioned in Ecclesiastes 4:9–10: "Two are better than one; because they have a good reward for their labour. For if they fall, the one will lift up his fellow: but woe to him that is alone when he falleth; for he hath not another to help him up." We will be more productive and accomplish what God has given us to do if we allow Him to help us with our labors and pick us up when we fall. And another great reason to join with Him in our labors is that *He never falls.*

Knowing that Jesus is our companion in our labors will bring us rest, but what is more, knowing that the very name of Jesus means "YAHWEH saves" will deepen that rest. We will be able to experience this deeper level of rest because we will have the security of the knowledge that intense help is available for any times of difficulty. Salvation through Jesus is the reason that we can begin to rest in our souls, and this is also where we can learn how to rest as we walk through the remaining days of our lives. He has expressly said He will give us rest. His provision of rest manifests as: assured minds because we know we are saved, accepted souls because we are gifted with eternal life at the moment of salvation, and accompanied lives because the Spirit walks with us. Jesus expresses care and concern for us in our troubles. He offers His help and His knowledge. He has proven Himself trustworthy and more than capable because He overcame death and has always kept His promises. In Him and by Him and through Him all things exist (Col. 1:17; Rom. 11:36). What sweet thoughts to dwell on and what comfort to have.

God provides for His children, so there is no need to be anxious about anything; instead, we can rest in all things. Our minds no longer have to fret, rather, they can focus on meaningful things. Psalm 62:6 tells us that God alone is our rock, fortress, and salvation, and we cannot be shaken. We can rest securely in what we know of Him. But the reverse of this is also true. If we do not know Him, then how can we be secure? God is a loving Father who has prescribed ways of living that will bring peace to us, but if we do not take time to learn what those ways are—and then live by them—we will not have peace. He has done great things for us, and we can find rest and security in knowing that everything has been taken care of and we are safe in His hands. What great knowledge to possess!

This knowledge that God wants us to have can be imparted to us as we wear the yoke of Jesus's instruction. We can approach Jesus with trust because He knows our every need and did everything necessary to purchase our redemption. He is asking us to be His disciples, to be teachable and learn from Him. He wants to show us how to live from the point of redemption. If we are wise, we will be instructed and receive knowledge (Prov. 21:11). He tells us about Himself beforehand so we will know what to expect when we come. He says that He is meek and lowly in heart, meaning that He is gentle, humble, and peaceable. Just as someone who is humble makes a better learner than someone who is proud, students are more apt to learn from a teacher who is humble rather than one who is prideful. Jesus is that humble teacher, even though He has all the right in the entire universe—the only right in the entire universe—to be proud of who He is. To Him be all the honor, glory, majesty, and power, forever and ever. Amen!

Jesus came to show us who His Father is and how much He loves us. He is the only source of salvation and the only place of rest (Ps. 62:1). He has taught us how to live and interact with Him and with one another—all built on a foundation of love. He has taught us how to face difficulties, how to face enemies, and how to change the world. He wants to go with us and help us, wherever our paths may lead.

Jesus said that He came to do God's will (Heb. 10:7). He placed God's desires above His own and accomplished amazing and powerful things in His lifetime. Studying Jesus's life will teach us how we can do the same. We will learn about proper priorities, humble servanthood, submission to God's plans, the importance of eternity as it relates to the present, how to care for others, how to increase our faith, how to work and what work to do, how to pray, how to know God and commune with Him, and how to love and be loved. This is just a small sampling of what we can learn from Jesus! John 21:25 tells us that the world cannot contain all of the books that could be written about all of the things Jesus did. The Bible is a treasure trove of knowledge. We can hold His teachings in our hands and in our hearts. We can allow the life in His words to be integrated into our souls, and then allow it to be lived out through our lives.

RESTED SOULS

Sometimes our paths do not seem to lead to rest. We find ourselves in seasons of busyness that seem like they will go on forever and prevent us from ever resting again. People even joke about not resting until they are dead. But we do not have to wait until death or the passing of busy seasons in order to find rest; we can find it now. One way in which we can find rest is to realize that we will never accomplish everything that we think needs to be accomplished. We will, however, be able to accomplish what God wants us to accomplish when we do things in His way and His timing. Just as a field is left to lie fallow so that nutrients can be replenished in the soil for a future planting, so a time of rest for our souls will replenish us and later lead to greater harvests because our souls have been enriched by God. The book of Ecclesiastes tells us that God has a time for all purposes and that He is making things beautiful in His timing (3:1, 11). He is laboring for those who love Him and preparing great things that have never previously been seen, heard, or imagined. Because of this, we should be content to rest in Him until He rests from His labors.

What rests within us can either be beneficial or detrimental to us, and this, in turn, will determine whether we are able to rest. Our rest can be threatened or disrupted by things such as anger, disregarding God, and allowing Satan to gain a foothold. Alternatively, filling our minds, bodies, and spirits with the things of God and conducting ourselves in godly ways will bring life and rest to us. The choice is ours: we can break God's yoke off us and have problems, or we can wear it and have rest. If we go forward without God, we will be lost and misdirected. We will writhe and struggle and wander and weep. But if we do something to move toward God, rest will come. If we are moldable and teachable, we can stop some of our present heartache. We can also stop some future heartache by choosing to discontinue along our own paths so we can follow God's paths instead. We can abandon our ruts, our highways to trouble, our paths to the pigpen, and our dead-end roads. We can begin traveling on the road that leads to life, peace, and Him. It involves a decision and then an action: not to rebel and not to run but instead to receive what God wants to give and teach. Think. Do. Rest. This is how to be on the right path and how to obtain rest for our souls.

MATTHEW 11:30

EASY YOKES

In Matthew 11:30, Jesus said, "For my yoke is easy, and my burden is light." The Greek word for *easy* that is used in this verse can be translated as useful, gentle, pleasant, and kind.[2] Additional words that can be used to define *easy* are serviceable, productive, well-fitted, well-resourced, beneficial, and benevolent.[3] This is the type of yoke that Jesus offers us. How amazing! But He goes even further than offering an easy yoke, He also offers a light burden.

Jesus's original audience had a good understanding of yokes as farm implements, but they also knew about the yoke of living under Roman oppression. The Jewish people were longing for deliverance and freedom—for a lifetime of ease and blessing that did not include the Romans or their heavy taxes. They were thinking about how to be rid of their problems rather than thinking about how to continue on in an easier way, remaining right where they were, living among the same people and circumstances that were causing them so much grief and heartache. I imagine some of us think much the same way today as the oppression and persecution of Christians increases all around the world. "Even so, come, Lord Jesus" (Rev. 22:20) is a phrase probably uttered more now than ever before. But what can we do in the meantime while we wait for the fulfillment of these words? The answer is to do the same thing people did during Jesus's earthly lifetime: come to Him, take up His yoke, and allow Him to ease the burdens. He can show us a better and easier way. Nothing is too hard for Him (Jer. 32:17).

LIGHT BURDENS

A burden is a physical or figurative load that must be borne. Burdens weigh on us, but the force of the loads will depend on what the burdens are and if there is anyone who is helping us to bear them. There are many types of burdens that we bear in life, and we bear them in each part of who we are. Physically, work can be a burden. Relationally, people can be a burden. Spiritually, we can be burdened with sin. Mentally and emotionally, negative things can weigh us down. I am certain we understand what burdens are and how they can take many shapes or forms, but do we realize how often we bring the burdens on ourselves and how often we make them heavier than they have to be? And furthermore, do we realize how to lighten them? Instead of managing all of the details and bearing the loads by ourselves, we can ask God to intervene and have a grand impact upon our situations.

It is in our power to effect change both through human means and through God's power. Our yokes can be lightened or made more grievous depending upon which means we choose to utilize. Sadly, even though we can access God's help and bring change to our lives, some of us choose to remain exactly where we are, comfortable in our human solutions. We choose to simply remain independent. When we proceed in such a manner, we continuously make our lives heavier and harder, heaping up multiple and heavy yokes upon ourselves instead of casting our burdens on the Lord. We proudly wear these heavy yokes and even invent our own labors, thus adding more weight to our loads. We try to restore broken things by using ineffective means. We try to fix our own problems and make things better by expending our own efforts. We try to succeed in our own human strength, but this is not going to bring complete success. It is God's power that will bring full success, and this is what He desires for us.

We can bury ourselves under so many heavy things, and then instead of ridding ourselves of the burdens, we add labor on top of them. There are costs involved when we live like this and do not rest and move in God's power. Things then become even more difficult and weighted with this added exertion. We expend mental and physical effort: we worry, we pace, we toss and turn. We attempt to achieve a real or perceived effect, as if our thoughts and actions will make the burden disappear: we yell, we deny, we tell ourselves this cannot be happening. We labor over minor and meaningless details and cause ourselves great distress. We overthink things and invent hypothetical scenarios that most likely will never come to pass. We tax our brains and expend our energy on solutions that are not the best answers. We give up sleep that our bodies need to restore themselves, while we continue to dwell on our problems and useless solutions. We while away the hours and continue trudging through our misery even though the Bible tells us that it is vain to be up early and stay up late eating the bread of sorrows (Ps. 127:2). Yes, we add more weight to our burdens, and before we know it, things are anything but easy. Our strong efforts to make our burdens lighter through these or other methods will prove to be fruitless.

At other times, we burden ourselves not by trying to make things disappear, but by continuing on with the way things are. We bring heavy burdens upon ourselves when we live in worldly ways. We become self-centered and occupied with our own lives and desires. We become preoccupied—and even consumed—with seeking wealth, prestige, and sensual pleasures. We wholly become slaves to sin and Satan as we try to satiate our lusts. This does not sound like an attractive image does it? Yet, it is an accurate portrayal of us at times. Conversely, sometimes we labor to establish our own righteousness. As we make this attempt, we become slaves to our pride. Ultimately, the burden of sin destroys, and so does the one of self-righteousness. Neither of these burdens directs focus onto Jesus. The burdens become our yokes and our taskmasters all rolled into one. They are heavy and hard, full of rough splinters, and they cause us great discomfort.

When we are fighting against His yoke, it is not going to lead to good ends for us. Furthermore, our choices grieve Him, and they also impact others. Grieving and God do not belong together. Believers are not to grieve the Holy Spirit (see Eph. 4:30), and He does not want to grieve us either (see Lam. 3:33). God wants us to wear His easy yoke, and He wants us to have the best things because we are His beloved children. The best things for us are what *He* has in mind, and He will help us to bear them whatever they happen to be.

Psalm 78 tells how the Israelites grieved God for forty years while they wandered in the wilderness trying to make their own way, disregarding His while they did so. They heaped sins upon themselves, grumbled about His ways, were often discontented and covetous, and provoked Him often. He was offering them rest and great blessings, but they did not want them. They thought they knew a better way. Their hearts were not right with Him, so they lived in iniquity—turning from Him, testing Him, limiting Him, forgetting the miraculous things that He had done for them, and forgetting how He had guided them. And surpassing all of these things: they worshiped idols. They placed all of these yokes upon themselves—none of which were necessary to bear and none of which were part of His plans for their lives. They did not follow His ways, and as a result, they brought great misery on themselves. These behaviors are great examples of what *not* to do.

We need to be sure not to misuse our free will and remain independent of God. We are prone to extend our independence into efforts that create paths for ourselves, sometimes even paths of self-righteousness. We simultaneously act like the Pharisees and also like the people which they treated so poorly. The Pharisees bound heavy and grievous burdens onto the people's shoulders (Matt. 23:4), and today, we bind heavy and grievous burdens onto our own shoulders. We add narrow parameters to things that Jesus gave us the freedom to do. We place regulations and restrictions on ourselves that He never asked us to keep. We end up looking like one of the Pharisees named Nicodemus. He did religious things. He said intellectual things. But he did not know about the life found in spiritual things. He did not have a personal relationship with the Savior of the world, at least not until he chose to take on the yoke of Jesus and gave his life to Him in exchange (see John 3, 19:39). Freely accepting what Jesus freely gives will change everything.

Jesus did not come so that He could lade our shoulders with piles of rules and throw our minds into turmoil wondering how we could ever obey them all. He is not calling us to religiosity—He is calling us to belief and repentance. He is not demanding that we achieve perfection before He agrees to love us. He came to give us life, *new* life, through a spiritual transformation from the states He found us in. Jesus told Nicodemus that spiritual rebirth is necessary (John 3:3). He is not standing over us with a whip and the glare of an angry taskmaster. He longs for us to choose what is best, and it saddens Him when we do not. He wants to heal us from all of our sin: past, present, and future. He took our offenses and nailed them to the cross, yet we keep taking them down and living them out, again and again. He offers us boundless grace, mercy, and forgiveness; may we learn how to accept them.

When we are solely focused on Jesus and allow His mind-set to become our own, we will find that His yoke truly is easy and His burden light. He deserves our full attention since He is to be our role model and our motivation. He was meek, humble, and lowly in heart, and He obediently submitted to God. Observing His commands, following His ways, and setting our own ways aside will bring us the most benefit. We will have a strength that we have never known before as we journey with Him by our sides. With the presence of His Spirit in us, we will be moving in supernatural strength and power while we work. We will be able to do all things, even impossible things—even when we are worn out and worn down—because He will be our strength and He will make our ways perfect. We can rest our minds and our striving on this comforting knowledge.

Burdens become light because He helps to carry them. The things that come into our lives will not always be easy or light, but we will always be able to bear them with His help. We can rely on the strength of His effort rather than depend on our inadequate amounts. We will never be left alone to struggle under the weight; instead, strength beyond strength will arrive to help us in our distresses. Jesus gave us the Spirit to help us in our weaknesses (Rom. 8:26). Allowing His presence and His help will remove stress and give rest and peace. We will discover that He is lifting us at the same time He is lifting our burdens. He will also be shaping us and our burdens into beautiful masterpieces. We are and will be more than conquerors through Him who loved us (Rom. 8:37).

When we come to the ends of our lives, will our life maps look anything like the ones that God had designed and desired for us to follow? I hope and pray that mine will. I pray that the detours and the travels down the wrong roads will be minimal and that my life will look like it is supposed to when it is complete. Actually, after giving this statement some more thought, I would like to be able to say these words on a daily basis and not just hope to be able to say them when I reach the end of my life. Being intentional about wearing the yoke of Jesus will allow me to match His map.

"Come unto me." This invitation is for you. It is for me. It is for all. We all have a choice to make, an RSVP to give. It is up to us to take action. What will our answers be? Will we come to Him to receive help and rest? No matter how many times we have come to Him in the past or even if we have never come to Him previously, now is our opportunity. He is calling for us. Right now. This very moment. He is our only help. He is our only hope. His yoke is easy and His burden is light.

CHAPTER 13

The Rest and the Restless

THE RESTLESSNESS OF LIFE

Choices. Decisions. They are important because they have consequences and make impacts. All day long, day in and day out, we make them; and at the same time, they make us. One of the choices that Jesus sets before us is to choose rest, but we can use our free will and choose unrest. We can lay down our burdens and restlessness, or we can pick them up and heft them higher. We can choose to come to Him for help and peace, or we can continue on in our own ways and on our own paths. We get to choose to be rested or restless.

So many things in life can cause us to be restless, but the biggest underlying cause is when we decide not to involve God in our lives and proceed through them unaccompanied by Him. This independent method for living manifests in many ways, shapes, and forms. Let's examine two categories.

1. THE WAY WE THINK

Restlessness comes from not knowing who God is. People may *think* that they know God, but in reality, do not. The problem arises because of false information being perpetuated that we are all the children of God. It is true that we are all *creations* of God, but we are not all His children. We do not become His child until we make a conscious decision to do so. He created us to know Him, but until we pursue that relationship with Him and accept Jesus's sacrifice, we will not truly know Him and will remain restless and discontent. Know God and know He loves you. Know Jesus and Him crucified. Know you believe in His sacrifice and have become His child. Know these things, and then you will find rest for your soul.

Many people are crying out for peace, but if they do not know God and are not crying out to Him, they are crying out in vain. Some believe that they know how to find peace and that it is something they can achieve on their own. People turn to religion, good works, atheism, polytheism, morality, simple lifestyles, and so on, but these are not the answers to peace. God is the only answer to peace. He is the storehouse of peace and gives peace that is true and lasting, but this cannot be understood until one knows God. As it says in 1 Corinthians 2:14 (NKJV), "But the natural man does not receive the things of the Spirit of God, for they are foolishness to him; nor can he know *them*, because they are spiritually discerned." Minds and hearts are blinded to this knowledge until the key of Jesus's salvation unlocks the door. Jesus came to be peace. He came to be peace between us and God, to be peace in securing our futures and helping us in the present. Despite what goes on around us and the circumstances that we find ourselves in, we can have His true and lasting peace. This does not mean that we will be untouchable and never have bad things surround us, but it does mean that there is a supernatural ability to deal with these circumstances. This is something that only the children of God can understand and experience. He will give us a heart to know Him (Jer. 24:7). And when we know Him, we will know peace.

Restlessness results from our spiritual amnesia. There is a danger in spiritual amnesia because if we do not stand for something, we will fall for anything. And when we are not standing for God, we are busy chasing after something that is not of Him. When we lose focus and forget His purposes, we wander aimlessly. We exist and subsist instead of living and thriving. We wander around trying to stay alive instead of purposefully going through an abundantly blessed life. Jeremiah 50:6 talks about people as lost sheep who have forgotten their resting place and left the mountain for the hill. But God does not want us to strive without knowledge; He wants us to rest with an understanding of Him and His ways. If we will be His people, then He will be our God and will guide us until death. He will remember that we are His children and will lead us beside still waters and through green pastures. He will always be watching over us. We need to remember this. We need to remember Him.

2. THE WAY WE CONDUCT OURSELVES

Restlessness pervades our entire beings when we are looking for something other than God to fulfill us. Our spirits are restless when they are not filled with the things of God as they were created to be. Hearts feel empty when they go searching for temporal things to fill the emptiness. Restlessness comes to relationships as we move from one to another trying to get fulfilled. Our physical bodies are restless, so we fill up our calendars and schedules. Our emotions are restless, so we are moody and unpredictable. Our minds are restless, and we cannot stay focused on one thing for too long. We plan and scheme and try to figure out how to do something else, be something else, and have something else—and that is exactly what happens: we have something else, something other than God. We end up in states of heartbreak, pandemonium, unrest, discontentment, and disappointment, and we remain unfilled and unfulfilled. Our entire beings need God. He is the all in all. He is the only one who perfectly fits with every part of who we are.

We keep ourselves from knowing God because we are seeking other things. We can name more characters from television than we can from the Bible. We spend more time reading novels and magazines than we spend reading the Bible. We spend more money on self-enhancement products than on missions. We spend more time at the gym working on our physical bodies than we do in a Bible study working on our spiritual bodies. We spend more time entertaining ourselves than we spend entertaining angels. We spend more time buying and consuming for our own interests rather than giving to and rescuing lost souls. These are difficult things to have to say and admit, yet they are true.

Restlessness emanates from a life that is not living, walking, working, or resting in God. Sometimes, we are doing too much or doing things that are not what He has conditioned and equipped our bodies to do. When we live like this, we stray off the path of His lush provision and find dryness. We end up wandering around in deserts and wastelands rather than coming to where He is. When we stray, we do not find Him where we arrive; instead, we find barrenness. While we traipse around, we fill up our days and nights with activities and relationships that are fruitless and pointless. We squander our time and our efforts on the wrong things, in the wrong places. We busy ourselves chasing after the things of this world, such as education, fashion, money, power, success, reputations, careers, and entertainment. Our consumer-driven and materialistic society does not give us much time to rest because we are busy accumulating, keeping up, and upgrading. Rather than living abundant lives with our abundance of stuff, we are living shallow lives in the deep end. There is a lot to life—a lot to have in life, be in life, bring to life, and take from life—but not all of these things are expedient. We are restless because these things that we are participating in are not eternally significant. The energy that we are expending is being wasted, since only what we do for His kingdom will last. We will, however, find rest when we are busy chasing the things that He wants us to do and have for the kingdom. When we are pursuing Him, a divine, true, and lasting peace will come over us in the midst of our work and relationships. It is the faithful servants who do things well, and it is they who truly get to rest.

Restlessness derives from being in the wrong type of relationship with God. Playing pretend does not stop the restlessness. In Ezekiel 33:31 (NKJV), God spoke to Ezekiel saying, "So they come to you as people do, they sit before you *as* My people, and they hear your words, but they do not do them; for with their mouth they show much love, *but* their hearts pursue their *own* gain." These people claimed to be for God but lived for themselves. They flattered Him with their lips while keeping their hearts far from Him. Matthew 15:8 tells of Jesus encountering the same thing: people were drawing near with their mouths, but their hearts were far from Him. The people said they were seeking God, but their actions did not prove their words. I am sensing a trend here, and it is not a good one! It is not a good idea to be disingenuous with the One who knows the thoughts and intents of our hearts. It is so easy to say things, but it is quite another to practice them. Rest will not be realized until we realize that life is not all about us. *It is all about Him.* May this not be just the most popular cliché of the day in Christian circles, but may it be a truth that we all sincerely grasp.

Restlessness is inevitable when we turn our backs on God, and it is then perpetuated by our attempts to replace Him with something else that will never satisfy us. He gave to us so that we can give back to Him and others. He does not take from us, and we are not to be taking from others in substitution of Him. Yet in spite of His goodness to us, we choose not to believe in Him, and by doing this, we have then chosen to deny Him and to wander aimlessly. In Jeremiah 2:13, God said, "For my people have committed two evils; they have forsaken me the fountain of living waters, and hewed them out cisterns, broken cisterns, that can hold no water." God broke the yoke off His people, but rather than remaining with Him in gratitude and ceasing the transgression that brought the yoke upon them in the first place, they broke their word and transgressed yet again (Jer. 2:20). He was forsaken, and they did not fear Him. It is a bad idea to not just turn our backs on God but to set our faces against Him, too.

We bring restlessness upon ourselves when we are stubborn and choose our own ways over God's ways. He invites us to come to Him, but we do the opposite—we run away from Him and refuse His teaching. We travel decisively in the opposite direction of what would give us rest and peace. And sometimes, in our pride and rebellion, we even think that *we* will teach *Him* a thing or two. We think that we can take revenge on Him for not giving us what we wanted or for not acting in a way that we expected Him to. We act out in anger and temper tantrums or else give Him the silent treatment, and this definitely does not bring us rest.

Restlessness presents itself when we desire disobedience rather than obedience. We do not want to labor; instead, we want to play. Rather than being laden, we want to be carefree. We try to run around and get free of the burden of obedience, but in reality, all we do is make our burdens heavier. When we are in the wrong, there is no ultimate good that comes of it. While we are busy with our wrongdoing, it may seem pleasurable for a moment because that is how sin is, but ultimately, it leads to destruction and death. The best and safest place to be is within the will of God.

When we carry the wrong things in life or carry too many things, restlessness will manifest in our lives. We carry around things on our minds, hearts, and shoulders that He never designed for us to carry. We keep adding to our piles of burdens, heaping them up and shouldering them, and then find ourselves falling and stumbling beneath the loads. Will we eventually cry out for relief and say, "Enough is enough"? How badly do we want to be freed from all of this? There are actually times when God endeavors to rescue us out of the rut, the ditch, or the pit, but we resist. Why do we, and why would we want to? Are we trying to put on a good show and a happy face, to make it appear that we can take on more than it is possible for us to handle? Whom are we trying to impress? Do we think that we are doing penance? Are we playing the victim, thinking that God will be impressed with all that we are doing to keep the incredible schedules we keep, manage all of the acts we possibly can, and fill all of the roles we take on? What is He looking at? What are His priorities? What are His plans? How is He planning to work the fields and bring the crop in? Is He a cruel taskmaster who will drive us relentlessly until we break and crumble, falling bruised and bleeding to our deaths? No! He is a gentle shepherd who longs to carry us in His arms—so why do we refuse to be carried? He is not driving us away; He is beckoning us to come. He does not want to hurt us; He wants to help us. Coming is a benefit to us. Being rescued will bring us freedom and rest.

Restlessness emerges victorious when we fight our way through life: fighting battles, fighting people, fighting illness, fighting debt, fighting God. Restlessness rises up when we wage battles that we are not meant to be fighting, when we engage the wrong enemies, or when we enter appropriate battles unprepared. So, how are we fighting? Do we fight like gladiators because we think that the lions have been sent in and we have no one to protect us? Being on high alert in our own power is exhausting, but we do not have to live like this; we do not have to fight alone. Rest will come when we pray for discernment over which battles we need to enter and then seek God's help for those necessary battles. We can dwell in God's shelter, finding rest in the shadow of the Most High, the Almighty (Ps. 91:1). We can dwell in the shadow of His wings and find safety and refuge there. God has a history of fighting for His people, so we can trust Him to fight for us (see Exod. 14:14; Deut. 3:22, 20:4). We can let Him be our sword, shield, buckler, rereward, horn of salvation, high tower, fortress, and deliverer (Ps. 18:2, 30; Isa. 52:12; Eph. 6:10–18). Remember that He is the ultimate victor. He is the God of peace who will crush Satan under our feet (see Rom. 16:20). Jesus has overcome and we can rest in that (John 16:33).

When we do not allow God to heal us, we will be restless. We all have scars from self-inflicted wounds and scars from wounds inflicted upon us by others. The scars can be in our bodies, minds, and emotions. But no matter where the scars are or where they came from, God can heal them and turn them into strength, giving us rest in the process. How does He do these things for us? How can we carry on after traumas, disappointments, or the shattering of our lives and dreams? Obsession, compulsion, independence, denial, and self-determination are not what complete the task; these things do not heal scars. The job of healing is accomplished when we surrender our pain into the good hands of God Almighty, who will bring divine healing. He can change our perspectives, and He can change our scars into powerful testimonies. His salvation will deliver us from our pasts, and He will continue to deliver us from the wounds that have marked us. Our lives can be transformed into beautiful pictures of spiritual peace and wholeness. He is able to redeem, and He is able to restore. He is able to repair, and He is able to resurrect. He is able to bring beauty from ashes and joy from mourning (see Isa. 61:3). He can do *all* things.

RESTLESSNESS PUT TO REST

My husband and I both have chronic health problems and he may go blind from a degenerative eye disease. Perhaps soon, neither one of us will be able to work, barring a miracle from God. These are things that could easily cause anxiety and fretting. How will we care for our children, have a house to live in, or put food on the table? The questions swirl and lurk and threaten, but we can set all of them aside and come under His easy yoke. We trust and know that there will be provision for our every need. God is helping us carry this load. "Fear not" are some of my husband's favorite words from the Bible.

When my son is bullied repeatedly at school, I cry and lose sleep and imagine all of the things I want to say and do to those people that are hurting my baby, but then I set all of that aside and come under His easy yoke. I trust that He will protect my child. I realize that I must love and pray for my enemies and that I must take on the mind of Christ, bringing every thought into captivity. When the load is placed on His shoulders, my mind and heart are placed at ease. I sleep sweetly and soundly as I rest in God's arms.

When I look at the behavior of teenagers today and the things that they are exposed to as they go about their daily lives, the fear creeps in that I am going to lose my children to the world once they leave home, or maybe even sooner. My children have a solid spiritual grounding, but how will they stand strong when they go out from under their current godly influences? There is no way to know where they will go in life and what they will do. I do not know the types of people they will become, what types of people they will befriend, and what types of people they will marry. I can fret and worry and what-if myself into a tizzy, or I can choose to set all of that aside and come under His easy yoke. I can trust that He will guide them. He is their Savior and He will teach and convict them. He will go before them and walk beside them because He has promised them that He will. He has promised never to leave them, nor forsake them, just as He has promised me. The load is not mine to carry—it is His. And He will not fail us.

I can set aside the fear because He loves each one in our family perfectly. Am I human and freak out? Yes. Do I fall off the bandwagon of trust and end up back in the classroom, taking "Learning to Trust 101" all over again? Yes. But knowing the Word of God and being in a constant state of prayer will sustain me and keep me heading in the correct direction. Becoming like Jesus will ensure the proper outcome in any situation. And if God is for me, who can be against me? *No one!* There needs to be no wearying of my mind, "for when I am weak, then am I strong" (2 Cor. 12:10), because *He* is strong in my weakness. Furthermore, I can use the trials that I go through to comfort others the way God has comforted me. When we go through difficult times, we learn about a special type of comfort that only He can give. We then have the opportunity to share that comfort with others (see 2 Cor. 1:4). Yes, all of these trials are miniscule and impotent when viewed in the light of His power, and thus, I can put my restlessness to rest.

In the same way that a mother hen gathers her chicks under her wings to protect them from danger, the Bible tells us that God covers us with His wings and shelters us from the calamities of life (Pss. 57:1; 91:4). Just as baby birds are found alive after fires, protected under the wings of their self-sacrificing mothers, so too are God's children found, safe from the firestorms of life that raged around them. We do not have to fight and struggle on our own; we just need to come under His protection. We can say: "Our soul waits for the LORD; He *is* our help and our shield" (Ps. 33:20 NKJV). We can be found alive in the aftermath when no other thing remains standing. He goes before us into battle, and He goes with us into battle; He surrounds us on all sides. And no matter how a specific battle concludes, we can be victorious in Him overall. Our spirits can triumph over all the brokenness of life. The ugly, shattered pieces can be reworked by His hand into mosaics more beautiful than our minds' eyes can ever envision. In Psalm 116:7–9, David said that his soul could return to its rest because the Lord had dealt bountifully with him. His soul was delivered from death, his eyes from tears, and his feet from falling. We can say the same. Regardless of the pain, we are still alive and can continue on with Him. He gives grace to help us in our times of need (Heb. 4:16). He is our light and our salvation, so we do not need to fear (Ps. 27:1). When we give up the fight and let *Him* fight for us instead, we will find a peace and rest that we have never previously known. He gave His life to cover us. Restlessness will be stilled.

In Psalm 66:12, King David talked about going through fires and floods. Some of us have literally been through those things and have had to learn how to trust God and how to get to the other side after experiencing something like that. Others of us know what those words mean figuratively. So, in a sense, all of us know the fires and the floods because trials and difficulties are a part of life. How will we handle them? How will we get through them? The answer is the same, regardless of what the fire or the flood is. The answer for how to get through is: Him. When we are yoked to Him, we can be assured that even as we go through the fires and floods, He is going through them with us. We can take these times of unrest and learn how to know Him in a new way, learning to trust differently and deeper. Sometimes, we enter into difficult areas, but remember, they are just places that we are passing through as we are headed on to somewhere else. While we pass through these fires and floods, He wants us to have effective lives that shine His light and show His love. Only *we* can choose to take the yoke He offers us and become all that He can teach us to be. May we trust and learn as the apostle Paul did: it is God who has delivered us, is delivering us, and will deliver us (see 2 Cor. 1:10). Consider this: if God did such a great thing for us in delivering us from eternal death and has promised such a great thing to us that He will deliver us in life, what do we have to fear? We can be strong and courageous, for God goes with us and He will neither fail nor forsake us.

How do we apply this rest in a life full of chaos? How do we find even a moment to rest? How do we find the freedom to rest? The ability to truly rest? A place to rest? Rest can be found in a concept beyond us, yet it is a concept that can be grasped—it is the supernatural rest of God. This is how we can carry on when rest is elusive: we do it by His power. We can be at rest even when we are running twenty minutes late, are in the middle of eight lanes of traffic with tears streaming down our faces, have torn our jackets, have left kitchens filled with burned-bacon smoke, have the hateful words of family members replaying through our minds, and all the while know we are not going to meet our project deadlines even as we begin our fifty-third hours of work for the week. There is a place that our hearts, minds, and spirits can go, even when our bodies cannot get there themselves. When we cannot get away from all of it, or even any of it, we can go to the All in All: God Almighty. In the midst of it all, He is in our midst.

As Jesus hung on the cross bruised and bleeding, mocked and despised, rejected and ridiculed, He could be at peace because He knew that He had done the work the Father had given Him to do. Although the commute was awful, His clothes were a mess, He likely had not had breakfast, hateful words were filling His ears, and a deadline was fast-approaching, He was exhibiting peace and grace. He controlled His emotions, spoke words of love, gave to those around Him, and comforted His hurting mother. He pressed on through the pain and toward even more pain. All of this because He chose to walk God's way rather than another. He knew that He had a great purpose in life. He knew that He had fulfilled His responsibilities up to this point. He knew that He was redeeming the souls of all mankind by His current actions. He knew that He would be returning to His Father. He knew that someday all things would be right. He *knew*. He knew deep down in His heart, His mind, and His soul. He was at rest even as He suffered. He was at rest even though He was laboring harder than He ever had previously. He had the supernatural rest and peace that came from God His Father, the same rest and peace that can come to us if we have asked God to be *our* Father. This is how we carry on. We "go in the strength of the Lord GOD" (Ps. 71:16). This strength will allow us to rest in the midst of the difficult circumstances that continue on around us. There is no longer a need to be restless, for we have found the source of all peace and rest—His name is Jesus.

So no matter what causes our restlessness, God wants us to come to Him with it. We can come when we are worn out, overwhelmed, and a mess. We can come when we cannot think or cannot think straight. We can come when our mind is weighed down with the problems of life and the new problems of the day. We can come with our dissatisfaction, our disappointment, and our distraction. We can come to Him so heavy laden that we cannot even lift up our heads or lift up our hearts to Him. He will then reach down and lift us up in our entirety: our heads, our hearts, and our souls. He will strengthen us with might in our inner beings and will settle and establish us (Eph. 3:16; 1 Pet. 5:10). He will dwell in us and walk with us (2 Cor. 6:16), and we will know an abundance of peace and rest in His presence.

CHAPTER 14

The Bearing, the Breaking, and the Better

Do we always have to wear a yoke? Do we always have to be bearing a burden? Do we always have to be learning? If we are living and breathing, then yes, this is the case. There are a variety of yokes, though, some of which are custom-made for us to wear and others which are not for us to bear. We need to learn and discern which yokes we need to wear and which burdens we need to carry.

Two burdens that we do not have to bear are our sin and our shame, because Jesus bore them for us upon the cross. He bore the yoke of these burdens completely on His own in order to do the work necessary to purchase redemption for us. The yoke was then broken when He burst forth from the tomb! We can now move on to bearing the yokes that help us live from the points of our salvation until we draw our final breaths.

As we travel through life, do we find ourselves coming to Him for rest when things get serious? Do we long for rest? Do we cry out for it from the bottom of our souls? Are we waiting and hoping that someday there will be a time when we can actually rest? We may find ourselves in just such a circumstance because we are bearing the wrong yokes. Let's examine several yokes that we wear and the impacts of them.

There are yokes that are correct for each of us to wear and there are those that are incorrect. A yoke is a tool, and we need the correct one for the job. If we don a yoke that is ill-fitting or in disrepair, it will not effectively allow for the work to go forward or the burden to be borne. But if we follow the words of Jesus found in Matthew 11:28–30, we will have the right tool for the job. The work will be done, the burden will be borne, and progress will be made. So, if we are feeling overburdened in any part of our lives, we should examine it to see why. Perhaps we are adding something to His yoke, or perhaps we are disallowing something from it. Whatever the case, we are carrying a different yoke than we should be. These wrong tools will not help us live our lives rightly, nor will they help us achieve the harvests He desires for us.

Sometimes, a wrong yoke that we wear is resistance to the yoke that we are supposed to wear. When we try to wear a yoke that is different from what God desires for us, that in itself becomes a yoke. Why do we do this? Do we think we know better than God what yokes we should wear? There is absolutely no way that we can know better than God, so why do we even try? Fighting against God is counterproductive and even destructive, while rest is found in accepting the places in life that God has for us. God draws us by His Spirit. He draws us with loving-kindness. He gives us the right of adoption, but sometimes we scorn that right and turn our backs on Him. We fight and contend with Him like trees fighting and contending with the wind. Fighting results in brokenness and destruction, while bending prevents breakage and adds to the strengthening process. God does not want us to be broken and useless—He wants us to be strengthened for when the storms come. But when we refuse the help that He offers and the blessings that He desires to give us, we will weaken and break. On the other hand, if we seek His help, we will find that He is the way to get through the howling storms and to come out unbroken and stronger than before.

At times, following God's calls and wearing His yokes will mean that change is necessary, but sometimes, we do not want to change. We choose, rather, to don yokes that are ill-fitting, ones that were not custom-designed for us by the creator of the universe. But fighting to have our own ways is not a good thing, because if we are outside of God's will, we are not in good places. Some examples of donning ill-fitting yokes would be the pursuits of things that He does not have in mind for us right now or maybe even ever. We may be trying to keep certain dreams alive while instead we need to let them die. We may be searching for spouses when He wants us to remain single. We may be trying to bear children, yet He wants us to adopt. We may be trying to get ahead in our careers, whereas He wants us to remain in place, change to different careers, or stay home instead. We may refuse to move to new locales. We choose our own positions and fight against His plans because *we* know what we want and *we* know when we want it. We dig in, stiffen our necks, and harden our hearts. I have done some of these same things and a whole host of others.

I will share an example of a time when I was trying to wear a yoke that was not designed for me. At one point, God gave me a vision to form a new ministry. I was to speak, write, teach, counsel, and encourage people to become all that God had designed for them to be. Things began to happen fairly quickly, and the ministry unfolded just as He had designed. I was busily and happily working in this ministry and watching it take shape, but I was also doing so much in other ministries and life in general that I was on the verge of a breakdown. Not only was I heading toward burnout, I was going toward it at full speed—a crash was inevitable. Then, suddenly, things began to slow down, and some aspects of the ministry even seemed to come to a stop.

Shortly after this slowdown, I attended a women's retreat where we were asked to write on a note card what God had spoken to us that day. This is what I wrote: "Hold on to the vision, but rest for now." After I left the retreat, I held on to the vision, but I did not rest. I did not heed those words that God had spoken to me that day. I continued to push on, doing it all and trying to make it all happen. But then, in God's divine wisdom and mercy, some rest was forced upon me by some debilitating health problems. Did I fully rest then? Did I follow the words on my note card when the health problems forced rest upon me? No! I persisted. I pushed myself harder and harder, trying to push on through the pain and illness. I even wavered in my mind and wondered and questioned if I had truly heard God in the first place when He told me to rest.

When I realized that these doubts were springing up, I redoubled my efforts to make sure I was in prayer, in the Word, and sanctifying myself, but seemingly nothing was happening. I did not recover from my illnesses. Then, I began to sense in my spirit that God had placed me into a time of preparation, into a type of holding pattern. It was a time to ready myself for the work ahead. *What!* I was confused and wondered what work could possibly be ahead for me because I thought I *already was* in the midst of the work. What was He saying? Besides, didn't I already know how to do the work and get the work done? Isn't that what I had been doing? And so, despite what I sensed in my spirit about a holding pattern and a preparation time, I grew restless and frustrated. I thought I was already fully prepared to go, yet nothing new was surfacing for me to go and do. The activities that I had been involved in made me feel like I was doing what I was created to do, so I was eager and excited and wanted more than anything to do this "new thing" for Him, whatever it would turn out to be. I was ready to dive into the deep end. Or was I ready to dive *off* the deep end? Whatever was I thinking? I was trying to force my hand and force the timing. I was about to abandon my present and force my future. Wow! Can you imagine? Well, my imagination was off-kilter. How things looked in my mind's eye were different from how they looked in God's, and the truth was, they only needed to look as He pictured them. I only needed to be doing what He imagined for my life. More of the holding pattern was necessary so that my heart and brain could get onto His timeline, but I was fighting it every step of the way.

My yoke was not Jesus's yoke; instead, I wore multiples of my own creation. I had a yoke of misapplied restlessness, a yoke of a season worn too soon, a yoke of self-reliance, and a yoke of a discontented heart—just to name a few. I was prematurely going to task. I got things out of order and put myself before my mission. In my fervor for what was to be *someday,* I almost threw away what was *that day.* I should have been attending to particular current issues while God prepared me for someday. I should have been paying attention to where my first mission field was and been plowing and working there. I needed to be working in the place where God would be at my side (in the field where He was at, not in the one I was trying to enter). One of my primary mission fields at that time was in my own home, the place I rarely was except to lay my head for a few rushed hours of sleep. It was the time to be in the sink with the dishes and the sippy cups, and swirling around with the clothes in the laundering machines, and thinking I should have been a trucker for as many miles as I put on each day for things related to my children's lives. These are the things that I should have been doing, resting while I was at them, but I was not resting in any sense of the word. I was fighting passionately for a different season of life, for what I thought was *supposed* to be, rather than resting in contentment with what God had given me for that moment.

There were several things that I learned during my forced time of rest, some of which are these: rest comes from contentment, from rejoicing, from trusting, from humble service, from sacrificial giving, from surrendering in obedience to God's calling, from growing in faith, and from accepting the "what" and the "when" of what God has for me. I also learned that my vision was for an appointed time. Even though the Lord had spoken to me, for years it would seem that the vision had failed. Now, however, I am confident that the days are at hand when the vision will be fulfilled. One way I know this is that I am sitting here typing this book right now! Writing a book was one of the tasks He called me to fourteen years ago, but only recently has He burdened me that now is the time to actively write and very actively prepare for the future tasks ahead. And one last thing I learned from the rest that was imposed upon me: hold on to the vision, but rest for now, until God's later timing.

The word that God speaks will come to pass. No visions are given in vain. When it is the day for the vision to unfold, He will perform it, regardless of how cooperative or rebellious we have been in the interim. Even if the vision is given for a day a long time from now, there will come a day when He decides that it is time for it to be accomplished. When this time comes, there will be no more waiting—there will only be watching in wonder. What He says, He will do, and the word that He sends forth will accomplish what He pleases. We always need to remain aware of His teaching, and discover what He wants us to do as we encounter each new situation in life on our way to the end goal. Our jobs are to do as He asks at each step in the process and leave the end results up to Him. Life is not static; it is progressive. So even though it may seem we are not making progress, we are getting somewhere—we are getting closer to the fulfillment of the visions and hopefully closer to Him in the process.

God does not want us to struggle and muddle through life. He does not want us to live lives inferior to His visions for us. He does not want us to walk around with wounded and bleeding hearts, yet that is what we give to ourselves when we deny Him and His offerings to us. And once we have done this to ourselves, we go around blaming Him and maligning Him. There can be no respite with behaviors like this. He does not have plans to harm us. He is good and He does what is good; why can we not see and accept that? There will rarely be victories when we fight alone in life, and there will never be any if we fight against God.

We need to gain a proper perspective of what it is to walk with God, rather than in opposition to Him, rather than running on ahead without Him. We need to understand that God is not *a* way to get through life, He is *the* way. We cannot make a new or better way because there is no other way that exists. Jesus even said of Himself that He is "the way, the truth, and the life" (John 14:6). He is the only way to life and peace. We need to walk at His pace with trust and peace in our hearts. And on another note, it works out for the best if we follow Him rather than try to lead the way ourselves.

Stubborn independence is a wrong yoke that we might wear. Sometimes, we are guilty of refusing God just as the Israelites of Jeremiah's day were. We mimic the same words they spoke when God told them to walk in His path: "We will not walk *in it*" (Jer. 6:16 NKJV). Our willful natures break the yoke of Jesus right off our shoulders and take on other yokes instead, yokes like selfishness, stubbornness, and pride. He offers us freedom, but we willfully choose not to walk in it. We willfully speak these words of resistance, think these words, hold these words as the intents of our hearts, and exhibit these words in our attitudes and behaviors. At times, we shrug off God's hand from our lives, and at other times, we throw it off, but unless it is God who is building our lives, they are being built in vain (see Ps. 127:1). He labors and builds for a different kingdom and a different harvest, and He desires that we wear the yokes which will join us to these purposes.

Another yoke that we bear unnecessarily is the one of forcing our hand. We choose to be the ones in control, the pilots and navigators all rolled into one. We sit in the driver's seats and choose our own roads, yet we are not supposed to be driving the carts—we are supposed to be wearing the yokes. We are not the ones who are supposed to be teaching Jesus, He is the one who is supposed to be teaching us. We need to turn the control over to Him and trust Him with our faith. Turning over control means to turn over all parts of who we are; otherwise, we have not truly turned over control. If there is anything that we refuse to surrender, then we are keeping it under our own control. And if there is any area that we refuse to let Him access, then we are still partially in the driver's seat and have not truly surrendered. Trying to retain control in even one area does not allow Him to give us the easiest and lightest load. That "one thing" actually becomes a yoke of bondage if we refuse to let Him have it. And we cannot honestly call Him Lord if we refuse to give Him all that we are, because when we hold onto control, it means we are tied to something else rather than being completely His. There is freedom to be found in letting go of the reins and donning His yoke. When we take our hands off the steering wheels, off the reins, and off the control switches, we will be able to go places we never imagined but which are places He has imagined for us.

Detours in life and the ways in which we handle the detours can become yokes. Things, people, Satan, and self all get in the way of where we are supposed to be heading. We get railroaded, blindsided, broadsided, and dispatched to the ditch. Construction cones pop up everywhere and our itineraries have to be changed. We have to learn how to handle the alternate yokes that want to come down upon our shoulders and keep us from our ultimate destinations. Life is not safe since we live in this fallen world, so how can we pass through it into the places that God has imagined for us? The first place to start is to choose to let Jesus navigate for us rather than trying to navigate through life on our own. At times, the realities of this fallen world will cause us to pass through places that we never wanted to go. Pain, loss, suffering, and temptation will be yokes that end up on our shoulders. It is important at these times to turn to God as He knows exactly how to remedy the things that cause us to call for roadside assistance. He can make the exchange of yokes and affect the amount of weight we must bear. His help and guidance can get us out of the ditches and into the correct furrows to work or into the correct pastures to rest.

Another wrong yoke that we might place upon ourselves is a yoke of aimlessness. Sometimes, we do things just for the sake of doing them. We do something just to be doing something rather than nothing. We labor, and we do it in vain. We labor toward the wrong goals, and we labor ineffectively on our way to achieving those goals. We waste our efforts on useless and fruitless pursuits instead of chasing after God with our whole hearts. This is not a good use of our time, energies, or lives. Life is not an accident—God has designed it with meaning and purpose. So when we hear Him call, we ought to align our thoughts, desires, hopes, goals, and dreams with His.

Destruction that we experience in our lives can become a yoke. We are capable of bringing destruction upon ourselves as we become obsessed and possessed by the wrong things, but at other times, it can come upon us in a moment by Satan's hand. Satan is actively trying to destroy us, but take heart, he can only touch what is temporal. God, on the other hand, is building us up and making us strong so that we can withstand and survive the destructive forces and storms that come upon us. What God builds into our lives and gives us is eternal. It is life, and it is peace. No one can touch what God has for us. No one—including ourselves—can ever pluck us out of God's hand (see John 10:28)!

When Satan derails us, God can put us back on track. We can see this evidenced clearly in the account of Jesus freeing a possessed man from a legion of demons (see Mark 5:1-20). This man could not save himself, and no human being could help him. No one could stop the torment and suffering he experienced. No one person could stand up to this army of Satan. No one, that is, but Jesus. When Jesus showed up nearby, the man ran to Him for help and was then delivered from the demon possession. The man was restored to his right mind and wanted to become a follower of Jesus. The news of this man's healing experience was then shared with family and friends and the townspeople were amazed to hear it. He experienced rest from his suffering as he took Jesus into his life. The yoke of destruction and loss was gone. And just like this man, no matter what we have lost and what armies we have encountered, if we come to Jesus for help, we too will gain rest and will have miraculous stories to share with others.

WEARING THE YOKE BETTER

Instead of wearing just the yoke that Jesus specifically designed for us, there are so many additional yokes that we wear, such that I could write another book on just this one topic. But no matter what the yokes are or how many of them there are, it is possible to bear up under these yokes and to break them entirely. When our yokes are too heavy to bear, or even when we think that they are fairly light and we can handle them, Jesus offers us His easy yoke and light burden. This does not even seem humanly possible. We are so worn out and worn down that we cannot even muster up any hope of change. Days of routine and days of chaos alike cause us to become weary, exhausted, and even hopeless. There is so much on our plates, on our minds, and on our shoulders. We feel pressured from every side: from ourselves, from others, and even from God. We add more and more onto ourselves as we hopelessly try to measure up. We try to prove to everyone that we are worthy. Life becomes duty rather than life. Joy, hope, peace, and patience disappear. How will we ever measure up to everyone's expectations of us? How will we meet the demands upon us? We need a hero, a rescuer, a savior. Good news! Great news! There is one—His name is Jesus!

The amount of rest we experience will correlate with what types of yokes we are carrying and the methods in which we are carrying them. There are burden-bearing techniques that are correct and those that are incorrect, and which ones we choose will make all the difference in our ability to rest. We need to examine the techniques that we are using and make sure they are God's techniques. His ways result in victory and rest. One way that we can always be sure we are bearing our burdens correctly is if we have cast them on the Lord so that He can sustain us (Ps. 55:22). The reverse is also true: a sure way to know that we are carrying our burdens incorrectly is if we have not cast them on the Lord. We are not to carry the weight of the whole world. We are not to carry things alone. Abundant life is at stake when we do not stake our lives in Jesus. Things may be heavy and falling apart all around us, but we can be moving along in peace and rest if we allow Him into our lives in just the correct-fitting way. His shoulders are there beside us to aid in the bearing. His teaching is there to alter our techniques. Following His ways will lead to rest, all the way to our souls.

Trying to be independent of His help as we fulfill His callings on our lives is not only unwise and impractical, it is impossible. We need to stay connected with Him so that we can serve Him in the capacities that He has asked us to, with full spiritual strength. There are many things that we put at risk if we try to proceed without the help of His Holy Spirit, one of which is lost souls. Burdens borne without God's help will downsize the impacts that we could have upon the world. We will grow weary in doing good things and will faint before it is time to bring in the harvest if we are doing all of the work in our pitiable human strength. Attempting to do things in our own strength will cause us to know overwhelming defeats rather than overwhelming victories. All of our good intentions will come to naught without the hand of God orchestrating our actions. May we allow Him to prepare us adequately to do the work, and then allow Him to help us bear the workloads. He can give us rest even as we work because true rest does not come from serving ourselves but from serving Him. With the proper preparations and the proper implementations, we will be able to bring in a greater harvest than we ever could on our own, a harvest of souls for Him.

I want God to be the graphic designer, the fashion designer, the artist, the planner, and the architect of all that I am. I do not want to carry this responsibility because this is not a task I am equipped to handle. I probably would not even enjoy it, given that I cannot draw a straight line with a ruler and do not even enjoy coloring in coloring books. I do not even know how I made it through kindergarten! I do not have the patience to fill in all of the details. Take my flower bed, for example. I have plants coming up that I started from seed. They are growing larger day by day. They are surviving and thriving (which is no small feat under my hand). I am tending them, watering them, and weeding near them. All of these procedures are taking place to aid in the growth process, but can you guess where my focus is? On the flowers that are still to come. Where are the flowers? I want to see the flowers now! I want to know what these plants are going to produce. I want to circumvent the growth process and just have the beauty. So besides not being able to have a career as a colorer of books, I could never be a farmer, either! I am just going to leave it all up to God. He has all things well in hand. I will just agree to rest in the yoke of His timing. He knows what attention the plants need and when they need it. He knows what I need too. And when He is finished with the process, the end result is going to be stunning!

Our life circumstances may be utterly horrible. We may live with poverty, depression, disease, and more. We may go to bed hungry or bruised, may not have a bed to go to, or may not even go to bed because we are so brokenhearted that we cannot sleep. May these circumstances that affect us so negatively be the exact things that cause us to come to Jesus. May our spirits find rest in Him and also a power to sustain us as we move on to tomorrow. May we say, "I lay down and slept; I awoke, for the LORD sustained me" (Ps. 3:5 NKJV).

We should not allow our difficulties to destroy us; instead, we should let them define us as people of strong faith. We need to wear the hope of God and allow its weight to affect our hearts so that we can be joyous in our life's journeys despite their realities. We can break the bondage of suffering, and bear the love and hope of Jesus to those around us, even in our darkest days. We will be able to press on through life with strength and resolve when we are sensitive to His words and His leading and when we exhibit trust, patience, and attentiveness. We will see amazing things when we look up from the loads, and we will be able to accomplish things that we never could on our own. And although we are under these loads, we can feel as if we are on top of them and that they are bearing us upward to God. He knows the times and the seasons, and we can know that He loves us through all of those times and seasons. Let's bear hope in our hearts! May the loads not break us, may they instead yoke us to Jesus. May we not let our trials have the mastery over us, but instead let them be mastered by Jesus. May we allow Him to set us free.

There are multiple cares we have, and there are multiple loads we carry, but we can bear these loads and rest in Him simultaneously. Our burdens do not have to overpower us, and they will not, if we take the time to be led by God in the midst of them. These are not platitudes but truths. I have seen proof in countless lives, including my own. We do not have to wait until we get to the end of the tunnels to see the light; we can see it now, even though it is dark all around us. We can see the light of God's glory shining through the darkest of clouds and the darkest of nights, radiating brightly through the darkness of hopelessness and the darkness of despair. God gives strength beyond strength and peace beyond peace. He is there with us through His Spirit, and He is there with us in love. He does all things well and will be there with us every moment of every day.

He is for us, and He has eternal purpose in each day. He is the fountain of life, and in His light we will see light (Ps. 36:9).

Something can be done with these heavy yokes that we wear: we can be breaking them—or bearing them and bearing them better. We can exchange the hard, oppressive, and worrisome yokes for the easy ones of Jesus. We can seek His help to release us from our wrong yokes, and we can have His assistance in bearing our necessary yokes and bearing them better. It is possible to decrease the weight of the burdens and also decrease the amount of labor that must be expended in carrying them by asking Jesus to share our loads or even take them from us altogether. This is a great exchange! The power of heaviness over us can be broken by His strength. He can give us the ability to carry on with the things we must. We can learn efficiency because of His sufficiency. We are able because *He* is able. He makes everything better. This is the breaking, the bearing, and the better.

God has been giving rest to His people in countless ways and for thousands of years. He has been breaking their yokes and setting them free. Leviticus 26 tells us of when He brought the Israelites out of Egypt, broke the bands of their yoke, and made them go upright. Isaiah 14 tells us He broke the yoke of the Assyrians off His people. The Gospels record how He sent His only Son to break the yoke of sin and death and pay for our opportunity to have eternal rest. In all of these instances, the breakage of the yokes was not dependent upon human strength—it was dependent on God's strength. He is the omnipotent God of the impossible. He gave rest to His people in their minds, emotions, bodies, and souls. He delivered them from fear, sorrow, and hard bondage. He delivered them from the power of their enemies. He delivered them from themselves. He delivered them from death. And He will still deliver!

Let's break some yokes of independence, people! We have created a yoke that says we have to do all and be all, but this yoke can be replaced by Jesus, the One who *is* all and has done all. He offers us rest from trying to be good in our own strength. The yoke of self-righteousness can be broken as we take on His righteousness. We can never do enough to measure up to a righteous standard so that is why He did it for us. It seems an almost unbelievable thing, but I very much believe it! Our sufficiency is in Christ, not ourselves. He came to our world to set us free from the bondage of sin and self. We do not have to sacrifice ourselves—He was the perfect sacrifice. Our efforts can be set aside since He has completed all of the work through His death, burial, and resurrection. Love won the day, and love has won my heart.

"There remains therefore a rest for the people of God. For he who has entered His rest has himself also ceased from his works as God *did* from His" (Heb. 4:9–10 NKJV). There is an opportunity for rest in this current life and then again during eternity. Will we rest now while we wait for the later? Whether we have just become one of His children or are remembering how to be one, the following exercises can help us:

1. *Look to God's Word for rest each day.* We can allow His words to rest upon us and rest within us. Some of my favorite thoughts are derived from Psalm 71:16 (I can go in His strength), Hebrews 13:5 (He will never leave me), and 2 Samuel 22:33 (He is my strength and power, and He makes my way perfect). Using a topical reference of verses is helpful in searching for words that address our current situations. We can find topics regarding ways to be at peace with one another, how God gives His beloved sleep, and how to rejoice in the day. We can allow Him to speak rest into our lives.

2. *Journal ways to achieve rest each day.* We can record the words of the verses that we research and the ways in which we will apply them. For example, if the words I focus on are from Psalm 71:16 (about going in God's strength), I might write a prayer to ask God to strengthen me in my inner being. If the words I focus on are about how to live at peace with all men, my notation might list the names of those I need to reconcile with and the ways in which I will accomplish this. If I choose a verse about not being anxious, my application might be to write out a plan of action such as this: "I will pray repeatedly not to worry about the meeting with my boss on Friday." If the words are about always rejoicing, I might

make a list of things to rejoice about. We can invite His rest into all of our circumstances.

God's children can rest securely in the knowledge that He loves them and is always there for them. He wants to be in relationship with His children every day and in every way so that He can pour out His love into their lives, both now and for all eternity. If we are trusting in God as our Father, then the evidence will be that we are at rest. Whatever the seasons of our lives bring us, if we allow Him to give us His rest, then we will exhibit our trust in Him to a watching world. In normal, everyday, mundane life, we should be at rest. In seasons of great busyness, we should be at rest. In times of great trial, we should be at rest. Does this happen for us? Do we always go from mountaintop experience to mountaintop experience without ever walking through the valley? Not likely. Actually, I am quite certain I have never heard of anyone who has. Why is this the case? Because such experiences do not exist. But in spite of this glaring reality, we can be at rest because the love and security of God never change. He is present to help us in each circumstance of life.

So many people are walking through the valley, crawling through the valley, languishing in the valley, and sadly, there are some who are even dying in the valley. How can we rest in all of life's circumstances: the normal, the busy, and the difficult? We do it by realizing that the rest is not dependent on us—it is dependent on God. We do not have to succumb to the battle that is life. We can have true joy in Him even though the things around us bring no cause for happiness. We can also have true rest by having faith in Him and placing our trust in Him. He will allow us to endure and allow us to rest. Faith places our good times and bad times in His hands and invites Him to work in the midst of them. He can miraculously reverse our circumstances, but even if that is not His plan, He can miraculously reverse us—from a state of unrest to a state of rest, from the valley floor to the mountaintop. His Spirit will do the work if we invite Him to do the work.

At any time, storms can come up, and we can suddenly find ourselves being blown off the mountaintop. Other times, the storms are unrelenting and we are drowning in the valley as the waters rise. Sometimes, it just does not quit. But one thing remains true and certain: God does not quit, either. No matter how things look, no matter how impossible it seems, no matter if we can see or perceive God's presence, He fights for us. Even when the torrents have blinded our eyes of faith, we can trust in His goodness and His plans. Whether we can see a thing in the middle of our life storms or not, there are several things that our hearts can know: what we are facing is temporary, what we are facing is insignificant when compared with His power, the burdens of these life storms can become easier by putting the yokes over onto His shoulders, and we will triumph when we give our burdens to Him. The power of the strong yokes and heavy burdens of life can be broken by the One who is stronger than anything or anyone, and He can make our passages through the valley easier. Yes, yokes can be borne, borne better, or even be broken through His all-sufficient power.

His will is being worked out in our circumstances even when we cannot see it, and it is because of this that we can give thanks in all of them (1 Thess. 5:18). The difficulties that we have encountered and are now encountering are producing something in us that can lead to greatness and fruitfulness in the future. God is not blind to anything that is going on in our lives, and He is not going to waste any of it. He will use even our griefs and afflictions for good, whether for our good or for someone else's. Not all circumstances are good, but the miracles that He is capable of bringing out of them *are* good. It is in difficult times that we can come to know Him in a way we never have previously, and as a result, our yokes can become lighter than they ever were before. We simply need to let Him shoulder the loads with us as He desires to do.

How manifold are His works (Ps. 104:24), and we should give thanks for them. In *everything*, we should thank Him. How are we even able to consider doing this? Rather than focusing on what we do not have, we can focus on how He has dealt bountifully with us. This focus will lighten our loads and help us to bear our yokes better. In fact, moving through life with grateful hearts and also holding perspectives of just how truly blessed we are will make all of our days easier to bear. He *deserves* thanks for the sun *and* for the rain.

CHAPTER 15
A Mind to Rest

At times, we talk about the paradoxes of the Bible. We find that many of the things Jesus asks us to do are not what our culture has taught us to do. He tells us that it is more blessed to give than receive (Acts 20:35), that the greatest will be servants (Matt. 23:11), that the humble will be exalted (Luke 18:14), and that we are to love our enemies (Matt. 5:44; Luke 6:27, 35). We find another paradox in Matthew 11:29 as Jesus tells us that wearing His yoke will give rest to our souls. Doesn't a yoke mean hard work, and doesn't working mean not resting? What He calls us to do sounds impossible, the very concept of a paradox.

What could possibly motivate us to come to Him to take up yokes and work? And what about when and if we just want to take breaks—would coming to Him for yokes sound like something we would want to do? Probably not. I know there are times when I cannot get motivated and just want to rest. It seems absolutely exhausting to don a yoke. The mere thought is overwhelming. I cannot imagine taking on anything else and putting more on my plate (unless it is cookies!). I am just going to have to trust Him on this. He must know something that I do not know in order for Him to speak such words and for them to be proven true in my life. This calls for an investigation. Why would Jesus offer rest? Why do we need it? How does a yoke work out to be a benefit? Why would Jesus invite us to join Him as co-laborers and yokefellows? So many questions. So many answers.

So to answer our biggest question of *why*, we look at His heart. Jesus invites us to do things because He cares about us, wants us to have good lives, and wants us to be part of His life. He loves us with an everlasting love. We, on the other hand, take issue with what He desires for us and even take issue with His love. We want to have our own renditions of good lives and sometimes do not care whether or not He is part of them. We may not even care to have the best type of life possible—the type that He wants us to have—but this is what is available to us. We can have infinitely more than we do. We can have Him—His love, His presence, His power, and His perfect provision. Will we pursue the path to make it so?

He can help to share the loads, bear the loads, and reduce the loads on us. There is supernatural, inexplicable power available to us and a rest like we have never known, right in the midst of work and burdens. Serving can be a joy rather than drudgery. We can allow Him to teach us and guide us, bringing meaning and direction into our lives. We will not need to run off seeking anything else because in Him we will find everything necessary for life. He can give us rest, both inside and out. The choice is ours. The choice to RSVP is ours.

TRANQUIL THOUGHTS

There is much that goes on in the human mind, and those thoughts can make huge impacts on our behaviors. Our minds can either be Christ's or our minds can be our own. A mind left in the hands of a sinful nature is a dangerous place. There are battlefields filled with mines in there. There are ugly, twisted, hateful things we devise. There are schemes we concoct. There are words we plan to say if we ever get the chance. We can think ourselves right out of communing with God and right into the camp of the enemy. We wonder what happened to the gentle and quiet spirits we used to have. We wonder where we went wrong. We wonder what to do now, where to turn, and where to go next. Chaos and confusion can reign supreme. When we finally look up and look around, we wonder where we are and how we ever got here. There is no need to despair, however, because we can take a one-step journey to get back to the safe place of peace and rest. When we draw near to Him, He draws near to us. We can bring our minds to rest in God, and He will bring rest to our minds.

We need rest from the torment of our minds, from our obsessive thoughts—the ones about ourselves and the ones about others. We need rest from the thoughts regarding what took place: if only I had or hadn't done this or that, or said this or that; I messed up; I failed; I denied Him. We need rest from the thoughts of who we think we are not: I am not good enough, talented enough, pretty enough, capable enough, important enough. We need rest from the questions of what to do with the wounds from family members, friends, coworkers, acquaintances, and victimizers. *Why* is the question of the moment, the hour, the day, and the lifetime. All of these thoughts and all of the remembrances of our sins, too, fill our minds to overflowing. Our sins become too much for us to bear. We are troubled and greatly burdened. We are weak and groaning. But it is all there in front of God; nothing is hidden from Him. He sees every pain that we are going through, every anxiety that we have. Even when our hearts pound, our strength fails, the light goes out of our eyes, everyone abandons us, and we have enemies, God hears and we can hope in Him (see Ps. 38:4–15). The torment can stop.

Some basic knowledge and understanding of human nature and divine nature will aid in the process of finding rest for our minds. We need to come to terms with the fact that we are fallen people in a fallen world. We need to realize that not everyone will love us, and no person on earth can meet all of our needs. We need to prepare ourselves for when (not if) we will be cheated, deceived, and wounded deeply by those who supposedly love us and those who are our friends. People will fail us, but God never will. He is perfect, and He is love. If we think like He thinks, and do like He does, we will find our minds filled with joy and peace, even in the darkest of circumstances. This joy and peace will be supernatural, beyond human comprehension, and poured into us by God's Spirit.

What do we do, then, when our minds wander into worry and prevent us from resting? We find rest by changing where we focus. We can be still, and know that He is God (Ps. 46:10). We can seek His kingdom first and not worry about tomorrow (Matt. 6:33–34). Worrying will not add anything to our lives, so we may as well stop doing it. We are told that we should not be anxious about anything but instead pray with supplication and thanksgiving, letting our requests be made known to God. Once we do this, the incomprehensible peace of God will guard our hearts and minds through Christ Jesus (see Phil. 4:6–7). We can ask for help in resting our minds. We can ask for reassurance that our futures are securely in His hands. We are able to cry out to Him, and He is able to deliver us (see Ps. 34:17). Read it and rest: instead of worrying, *rest*!

When our brains are overworked and we are too exhausted to think, somehow we manage to think that we can continue on. This is not healthy. God did not design us to steel our minds so we can get through life. Our minds should not be so taxed. There is no need for them to be incessantly working, but this seems to be the way of the world. However, we are not going to be able to rest when we are thinking like the world thinks and believing that we have to drive hard like the world does. God wants us to renew our minds instead of allowing them to be transformed by the ways of the world (see Rom 12:2), but if we never take time to stop and deliberately focus on what He wants us to think about, renewal is not going to happen.

It is important that we give our minds time to rest. We need to let them have downtime, just as we allow our bodies to have downtime. Our minds can be refreshed by allowing them to think on pleasant things rather than on troublesome or obsessive things. It is important to take time for reflection and gratitude, to think about who we are and why we are here. But we should not just stop to smell the roses—we should take time to think about them and their magnificent beauty. If we allow our thoughts to continue on to who created the roses, we will enter into thoughts of wonder and praise. Little coffee breaks for the mind, little time-outs, and little mental vacations will do much for us, because it is in these moments that we will meet Him there. Note the magnificence of His manifold works, which were made in His wisdom (see Pss. 104, 147). He made the sun, moon, and stars and calls them by name. He also made *us* and knows *our* names! He created the earth and everything in it. He maintains His creation for all of His creatures—on land, in the sea, and in the air. He is great and is clothed with honor and majesty. His glory endures forever. Truly, He is too wonderful to comprehend, but we should surely try!

So here is what we do now, where we turn, and where we go next: we surrender our minds to God. We allow His ways to become our ways and His mind to become our minds. We make sure to think on the things we should. Every thought matters, and so does the manner in which we think it. We need to remove the mines of the mind and fill in the pits so that we are not affected by them later. We need to replace the old thinking with the new, replacing hate with love and evil with good—ultimately, we need to replace all things that are not of God, replacing them with things that are of Him. Oh, the treasure that we will obtain: God's ways and thoughts will bring supreme, divine, and lasting peace.

And here are some amazing thoughts to treasure: He thought of us with so much love that He gave His life for us. He paid off the debt of our sin. The work of redemption has been done once and for all; we do not have to strive to do it. Jesus made the way for us to have peace with God by dying on the cross in our place.

TIMELY THOUGHTS

Rest will come to our minds when we understand that we do not have to depend on ourselves and our limited wisdom but instead can trust in God and His infinite wisdom. We can trust that He knows what He is doing, sees the end from the beginning, and has all things well in hand. Such great knowledge of this great God can calm the anxious thoughts that are prone to fill our minds. And this calm can extend even further, reaching deep into our hearts and spirits. He has conquered some extreme obstacles to make a way for us to have rest and peace in our lives. He gave ultimate rest from our sin and condemnation, so this leaves no doubt in my mind that He can give us rest in other ways. We can trust Him and trust His promises, and therefore know that the promise of Matthew 11:29 will be fulfilled. We *will* find rest (not we *might* find rest). Thank you, Jesus! We sure could use some rest! We need to be in prime condition so that we can accomplish the tasks You call us to do—the ones that take more energy than we have, the ones that are more demanding than we can handle in our own human strength, and the ones that are so amazing that people will know that You have shown up. Actually, we need You in all things!

When crises come, we may be more prone to think about God, but we do not have to wait until then to find God and know God—He is available to know every day, and we can be in relationship with Him at all times. We can build relationships with Him now so that when the crises do arrive, we will be better prepared to handle them because we will already know His truths and know how to navigate through difficulties. We will have good life-coping habits that include walking in step with Him. Rather than expending valuable energy in the crises trying to find God and get Him figured out, we will already know who He is and have His power at work in our lives. We will already have built our trust in Him and will know in our hearts that we will get through these times, even though our eyes cannot see how. Our hearts will know what our minds cannot even begin to process: He is bigger than it all, and He has all things in His sovereign control. We can know it now, and live it later.

Psalm 46:10 says, "Be still, and know that I am God." There is rest required to know God as we actually have to stop long enough to have an encounter with Him. There is a time to cease our striving and watch what He can do. This cessation of activity should go beyond spending an hour at church or even a whole day resting—it should transfer into every day of our lives. If we do not take the time, we will not recognize the time. When we are still, we can gather knowledge about who He is and learn of His character. We can then find rest in the truth of who He is. The more time we invest in gaining knowledge of Him, the more of Him we will know and the more we will be able to rest.

When we take the time to be still, we will discover how things in life *can* work because we will learn what He is capable of accomplishing in us, through us, and for us. We will each come to know what our place is and what His place is. He rules the universe, is sovereign, and sustains all things. He is God over everything, all day, every day, and it is good for us to see that and to know it in our spirits. We should not compartmentalize God, keeping Him in a small window of our lives, only allowing Him to be a portion, a segment, a Christmas-and-Easter type of God. He holds all things in His hands and holds all things together; thus, we do not need to concern ourselves with trying to do those things that are His responsibility. There are things that we simply are not supposed to be carrying in life, and there are other things that we are not supposed to be carrying at this time. If we pick up the ones we are never to carry, or if we pick up the others too early, we will end up hurting ourselves and possibly others. There is peace in knowing the boundaries that He has established for us in time and space. He has set us here for this time and His purposes, and they are going to be accomplished. He is working and waiting for the plans to completely unfold, resting in the knowledge of what is and is to come. He is where we should place our trust. There is rest in knowing *He is God.*

Rest will come to our minds through the assurance that God is with us. In Exodus 33:14, God assured Moses that His presence would go with the Israelites and that He would give them rest. Knowing that He does the same for us allows us to lay down the burdens that cause worrying and striving. He gave good things to the children of Israel, and He gives good things to His children today as well. He can give us rest from our enemies, whether they are seen or unseen, real or imagined. He can give us rest from our labors, both physical and spiritual. He can give rest from wandering and traveling, either in the journeys of life or in our minds. He can give rest from the bondage of difficult physical circumstances or mental, emotional, or spiritual strongholds. God protects, provides, and preserves. He did all of these things to give the Israelites rest, and rest was the result of accepting what He gave. There were times of peace with their enemies, a land flowing with milk and honey, the fulfillment of promises, and rescues from utter destruction. There were times that their hearts were happy and content, as they followed the instructions and the timelines that He had given. But it was when they began to mutter, complain, and covet that they ran into problems and unrest. When their minds left God, they left His path. Their story can be an example for us, both in what to do and in what not to do.

The Israelites were being led by God's presence, but they chose to forsake it. As a consequence of their sin and disbelief, the timeline for their entrance into the Promised Land was delayed by forty years. It was only after a disciplinary period and the deaths of the rebellious ones that they as a people ended up in the place God had in mind for them. He was merciful and remained faithful to His promise to bring them there. We can avoid the heartache they suffered if we will remain faithful to Him and follow Him always—regardless of the circumstances—for as long as it takes, through whatever it is that we must pass through. His presence can change our lives and give us rest, from now until the end of time, if we will but accept it. Jesus said in Matthew 28:20: "I am with you always, even unto the end of the world." We have been promised that the presence of God will remain with us—may we remain with Him.

THANKFUL THOUGHTS

We have most likely learned that although it may not be raining now, one day it will be. Even though we may be living in relative ease right now, we know to anticipate the "rain" of struggles. Part of being human is facing the difficult times that will be forthcoming someday. On the other hand, we may already be living in the "someday" and be in the midst of those struggles right now. Our lives may be in states of chaos, with one crisis after another, and we can barely think straight. How can we rest amid our suffering? How can we praise God anyway? One place to find answers is to look at the life of Job.

There was a way that Job was able to find peace and rest. He said, "In whose hand is the soul of every living thing, and the breath of all mankind. ... With him is wisdom and strength, he hath counsel and understanding" (Job 12:10, 13). Job's burdens were lightened because he placed his trust in God's character. When we meditate on who God is in relation to who we are, our thoughts will become peaceful as we recognize His sovereignty and omnipotence. When we read these verses and see that He has understanding, it can bring relief to our minds to know that at least *He* has things figured out even if *we* do not. God is wise and strong, and He has been around so much longer than we have. He knows how things work—*He* made them! If He created the earth and He created us, then He definitely knows what to do with our lives. Our minds can be calmed by understanding that He holds our lives in His hands and gives us every breath. So when the rains of life come, we can rest safely in His shelter, knowing He is going to bring growth from this downpour.

God can also be our shelter from the fires of life. Daniel 3:1–30 gives the account of three men named Shadrach, Meshach, and Abednego. Their king had them thrown into a fiery furnace—heated seven times hotter than usual—to be executed for their faith in God. They had chosen to serve and obey God only, and God chose to deliver them. While they were in the midst of the furnace, He was there too, miraculously protecting them. The king even saw God there and commented about a fourth being in the furnace that looked like the Son of God. The king called for the servants of the Most High God to come out of the furnace. They miraculously did so, exiting with no injuries and not even smelling of smoke. The only way this was possible was because of God. The fire had been much too hot for them on their own and would have destroyed them, but God was with them in the midst of their fiery trial. He will be with us in ours, too. Spiritually, we will be able to triumph, even if the circumstances around us do not change. And like these three servants of the Most High God, we can resolve that no matter what comes to us or what threatens us, the Lord our God will we serve, and Him only will we obey.

There is an even better example that we can look to for how to handle the fire of suffering: Jesus. We can see that He rested amid His suffering. How could He do it? How could He choose rest rather than escape, rather than choosing not to go through with this plan? He was able to do what He did because He trusted that His Father's plan was right and good. In John 6:38, Jesus explained that He had come down from heaven not to do His own will but the will of God who had sent Him. He spent time in communion with God and allowed God to help Him carry His burden. He processed His thoughts and presented them in humble prayer: "O My Father, if it is possible, let this cup pass from Me; nevertheless, not as I will, but as You *will*" (Matt. 26:39 NKJV). And although He strongly cried and expressed His fear to His Father, He still chose to learn obedience through His suffering (see Heb. 5:7–8). He was open and honest with God and expressed His desires, yet He still chose to submit to God's plan. Suffering in such a way was undesirable to His human body, yet He laid down His life for the greater good of following God's perfect plan. The deep and honest conversations with God resulted in being able to put the issue to rest in His own mind. When He surrendered His will to God's plan, He found peace. As He agonized in a turbulent and clamorous situation, His heart did not have to be troubled. He suffered for us so that

God could bring many sons to glory (Heb. 2:10). To Him, that was worth it. *We* were worth it.

How can *we* rest amid suffering? How do we rest when our children languish in illness, are wasting away, are dying? How do we rest when our spouses leave us for others or turn out to be unlike the persons we married? How do we rest when our businesses are sued, the companies take our jobs, the banks take our homes, and people take our dignities? How do we rest when our children are wounded physically, mentally, or emotionally? How do we rest when we have prodigal children who throw our words away or back at us? How do we rest when we are tortured and imprisoned for our faith, and all that we cherish is taken from us? How do we rest when we are given the choices of fleeing, denying Christ, or dying for our faith? The answer to all of these questions is to stay our minds on Christ (Isa. 26:3). We can follow the examples of Job, Shadrach, Meshach, Abednego, and most of all, Jesus. They walked the earth experiencing the yokes of suffering and trials, but they allowed God to help them shoulder the loads. They learned from God and found that they were capable of completing their journeys by surrendering to His leadership. God knows what we are facing at this moment, and He also knows what is up ahead for us. He equips us to deal with the trials and helps us to bear up under them. Even when the whole world is against us, God remains for us.

We cannot effectively live in a fake faith, oblivious to real pain, real suffering, and real faith. We have to be real, and we have to find real help. During times of affliction, when it seems that rest is impossible, we can cling to these words: "Therefore we do not lose heart. Even though our outward *man* is perishing, yet the inward man is being renewed day by day. For our light affliction, which is but for a moment, is working for us a far more exceeding *and* eternal weight of glory, while we do not look at the things which are seen, but at the things which are not seen. For the things which are seen *are* temporary, but the things which *are* not seen are eternal" (2 Cor. 4:16–18 NKJV). Remember God loves us and is *for* us (see Rom. 8:31). He can heal our broken hearts and bind up our wounds (Ps. 147:3). We can come to Him so that He can be our refuge "until these calamities be overpast" (Ps. 57:1). We can be at rest in God alone, for salvation comes from Him (Ps. 62:1).

When we walk in God's ways, He walks in our lives. I am so thankful to have this knowledge since without it I would be ill from the many anxious thoughts whirling through my mind. With the way things are in the world today, especially in regard to dangers to my children, there is much cause for worry. Every once in a while, I feel horribly guilty that I ever had children to begin with when I see what they are going through and will still have to face in the future, but then I remember that God has a plan for their lives. He will guide them through the dark days ahead. It is because He gave me these children that I have them, and all of us, together and individually, are to be salt and light. We are to make the world a better place with His love, and show people the difference that He can make in their lives. We can do all things through Him because He is our strength—with Him, nothing is impossible. He is making our ways perfect, and the knowledge of His perfect ways will give great rest.

Rest can come from knowing that God's will is being accomplished in our lives. Will we like everything that happens to us? No. But we can trust that He is working. There are steps in our journeys that will be awful, but God can bring good out of anything because He *is* good and He does what is good. Right now we can quote Romans 8:28: "And we know that all things work together for good to them that love God, to them who are the called according to his purpose." Another verse that is helpful is Psalm 94:19 (NKJV), which says, "In the multitude of my anxieties within me, Your comforts delight my soul." Pondering the things that God can do for us will bring rest to our minds. We can know that God works on behalf of His children. He rises up against evil, stands against evil, helps us, and upholds us (see Ps. 94). No anxiety is necessary on our parts, just knowledge and rest. He is a good God of purpose.

Rest can come from changing the things we can change. There are some things, however, that we will never be able to change, so we just need to let those things go. We can obsess and orchestrate and relive and redo in our minds, but we cannot change these things. As it says in Matthew 6:27, none of us can add to our statures by worrying. We just need to remind ourselves of what is true about God, and release the things that we cannot figure out or fix.

During a time of infertility, I was counseled to speak God's truth even when I did not feel it. I could not change the circumstances, but I knew the One who could. I knew He was omnipotent. I knew that His timing was not my own. I had to trust that if He wanted the situation to change, He would change it, and I just had to stop trying to force my hand. Speaking truth took the worry from my mind and redirected my thoughts to who God is and what He is capable of doing. I could look at the undesirable circumstances and search for the good in them—the good that would come out of them and how they could be used to make me better and stronger with God's strength. When we know that God is on our side, we can be changed, we can change others, and we can change the world.

The dark does not have to stay dark; remember, light can be found before the trials are over. If we open our eyes and look around, we will see God and His light surrounding us. Now. We can ask Him to send His light and His truth to lead us (Ps. 43:3). There is light at the entrance of His words (Ps. 119:130). When we sit in darkness, He will be a light to us, and when we fall, we will arise (Mic. 7:8). He will be a lamp to our feet and a light to our paths (Ps. 119:105). He is the all-powerful and ever-present God. Even when we fall into times of helplessness and powerlessness and our days become dark, He does not change. He can never be rendered powerless, and He will never break His promise of staying by our sides. His eyes are upon us, and He knows what we are going through. He has already rescued us from the kingdom of darkness (Col. 1:12–14), and He is able to rescue us even now. In the end, we will be overcomers (1 John 5:4–5) who will no longer walk in the shadows of the kingdom of darkness because we will have entered into His glorious light. Nations will come to His light and kings to the brightness of His dawn (Isa. 60:3).

Rest and unrest are inextricably linked to how much we allow God into our lives. I can see this relationship when I examine how He has impacted my own life. How would my life be different without Him? Well, there would be great cause for distress, and there would be no place to truly find rest. I would be bearing heavy things like anger, bitterness, guilt, an unrealistic schedule, perfectionism, compulsion, competitiveness, covetousness, frustration, discouragement, disappointment, and more. And I would be doing it all on my own. How would my life be different with more of Him? It would be richer and fuller because a life with Him in it is a blessed life. Psalm 103 is a wonderful chapter that can help us meditate on the goodness of God. In His goodness there is mercy, forgiveness, loving-kindness, healing, redemption, satisfaction, renewal, and more. Other chapters that can give great perspective are Job 38–41. The words found there can draw our minds to how incredible and powerful God is. And what's more, we have access to this amazing God! The terrible things in life can be allowed to break us, or with God's help, they can be allowed to make us, and make us into people who are better and stronger than we ever were previously. He has brought me from a mighty long way, and I need to take some time to think about that. How far has He brought you? Think about it and then praise His glorious name!

Perspective can bring rest to our minds or it can bring unrest. We often weary ourselves thinking, "Woe is me. I've got it so bad." But what if we were to change how we think about things? We all suffer in some way as part of being human and living in a fallen world. Suffering is real to us, and it is difficult. There can be rest, however, in realizing just how good we actually have it, even though our circumstances are terrible. We can focus on the benefits that we have instead of focusing on the things that we lack. For example, if we look at the life of a persecuted Christian in a country hostile to Christianity, we can see the reality that we are barely persecuted. We really do not even know what suffering is. Look at the apostle Paul. He was beaten, stoned, imprisoned, and whipped for the sake of Christ. Today, some Christians are losing their homes, jobs, families, and even their lives because they refuse to renounce Christ. Have we suffered like that? Likely not. Instead, here we sit with restless pocketbooks and anxieties over what our neighbors have and we do not. Have we even yet borne in our bodies the marks for the Lord as Paul and these others have done? We have cause to give thanks.

I am not suggesting that we be Pollyannas, pretending there is nothing wrong in life and claiming that everything is awesome. Life is most definitely real, and it most definitely hurts—*a lot*—but God is real, too, and He helps and heals. He restores broken hearts. He catches falling tears. He hears every cry. We have cause to give thanks.

I have heard this statement many times: "Life is what you make it." This is a futile human attempt to make life look pretty. The underlying principle is that there is something that can be done about the lives we live. But sometimes, we just cannot change our lives no matter how much we try. What we *can* do is ask God to change them and change our perspectives of them. When we look at things through God's eyes, with an eternal perspective, our views will surely change. We will no longer be blinded by what the enemy puts in front of us to keep us from seeing what God wants us to see. For example, Satan does not want us to see our blessings. He does not want us to praise God or serve God but instead wants us to turn our backs on Him in bitterness and anger. Satan also wants us to be so inwardly-focused that we do not help others in the name of Christ. But God wants us to see the blessings that He has made available for our lives and wants us to use them to bless others in turn. So, this is what we are presented with: two perspectives. Satan can blind us from what truly matters, and God can open our eyes to what truly matters. Whose vision are we going to trust?

Regardless of the states of our circumstances, it is here that we can seek out God's joy, peace, and strength—even when we struggle, even when there is loss, even when we are overwhelmed. No matter what happens and no matter the trials and sorrows that we find ourselves involved in, our minds can be at ease and our hearts can be at rest. Even when we are rendered nearly helpless, we are never truly helpless, because we have the Helper. We can rest contentedly, knowing that we rest in His hands. We have cause to give thanks.

In addition to health issues, I deal with the normal things of life that everyone else does: financial issues, vehicle breakdowns, runaway dogs, complicated family relationships, the loss of loved ones, etc. There are also undesirable realities of life that I have to face. Things have not gone as I had planned. Things have not turned out the way I had envisioned. People have not treated me as I had hoped. There have been devastations and limitations. Essentially, my dreams are gone. I have been in the depths of despair—hurting, suffering, lonely, broken, disappointed, frustrated, angry, and dissatisfied. Yes, I have been all of these things and more. But even as much as I am limited in my life, I have cause to give thanks. God's dreams for my life are so much better, and they are in the process of unfolding.

Over the years, I have had a perspective adjustment. I have come to the conclusion that if this is the road that God desires for me to walk—because through me He is achieving a great and eternal purpose—then I most definitely want to walk it, and walk it with gratitude. I have experiences, circumstances, and even a physical body that I never signed up for, but despite all this, I have a boundless treasure because I have God as my Father, Jesus Christ as my Savior, and the Holy Spirit as my Helper. God Almighty is on my side! And if He is for me, then absolutely no one can be against me! I have cause to give *much* thanks.

Who can help me? Who can understand me? *Jesus.* He offers help, hope, rest, peace, joy, and so much more. He is all-sufficient. Second Corinthians 12:9 (NKJV) tells us what the Lord said to Paul, who suffered greatly: "My grace is sufficient for you, for My strength is made perfect in weakness." I have taken these words and applied them to my own situation. They have healed my heart and have given me the strength and courage to continue the race. God is omnipotent, omnipresent, and omniscient. We can come to Him for help to bear up under the loads. We can learn from Him, ascertaining how to do life so that the weight of our yokes shifts onto His shoulders. He *can* make a way out of no way. He can make the fields fertile. He can help us to be meek and gentle under the hard taskmasters of our lives. He can teach us how to love, how to forgive, and how to endure. He can do all of these things and more; I know because He has done them for me. How can I not give thanks! Will you come to know, and will you come to give thanks?

Rest comes from holding to our faith, even when circumstances make it difficult to believe. We can determine in our minds and hearts that we are going to rest, we are going to trust, and we are going to believe. Because He owns our hearts and sees all with His eyes, we can know with our hearts things that our eyes cannot see. This is faith. And faith, even faith the size of a mustard seed, can grow into something great, just as an actual mustard seed does. When the plant is fully grown, the birds of the air can rest under the shadow of its branches (Mark 4:30–32). That tiny faith will grow, and beauty will come to rest in it. There can be songs of joy sung from grateful hearts and lips. We can honor and praise Him because in all circumstances and at all times, He is worthy to be praised.

Whatever the future brings, whether bad or good, we can determine to glorify His name. Like Job, we can exercise faith and praise God anyway. Job's trials were unbelievably huge, and yet, he had faith in the God who was bigger. We can say in the same vein as Job that whether God gives or takes away, we will bless His name (see Job 1:21). Our souls can be still because God is on our side when we are on His side. He is for us when we are for Him. Not all circumstances will be good, but *He* will always be good. He is the Lord, and He does not change. Let us patiently endure the trials of life, for the rewards on the other side will be sweeter than we can even imagine. Keep the faith. He will always remain, and He will always remain faithful.

Knowing that His plans and purposes for us are good can do much to bring us peace. Despite our pain, despite the anguish that we are going through, we can be encouraged if we think about how He may use this in the future. There can be hope and even excitement to think about what is on the other side of these difficult times in our lives. God can use and redeem these awful circumstances and restore us to health and wholeness in our minds, hearts, and spirits. Even in the physical realm, good can be brought forth of evil when God intervenes and restores what the locusts have eaten. We should not lose hope in our circumstances but instead remember His redemption draws nigh (Luke 21:28). May we let these temporary trials turn our eyes toward our eternal rescue. Let us place our hope in God and wait expectantly for His arrival. And while we are waiting, let us give thanks. And let us continue to thank Him as long as we draw breath.

CHAPTER 16
The Rest of My Relationships

We have been invited to relationships. We have been created for relationships. We have been designed for relationships. But if we expect human relationships to fulfill us and complete us, we will be left empty and disappointed. Furthermore, inventing our own rules in relationships rather than following what God has laid out for them will bring us nothing but trouble. Imagine, then, how things will transpire when we try to set up guidelines and parameters for how we will relate with God. We tend to do life how we want to do it and then ask Him to bless it. The reality, though, is that when we are not following His ways and His plans, things are not going to go well for us. If we are holding iniquity in our hearts, He will not hear us (Ps. 66:18). If we do not forgive others, then He cannot forgive us (Matt. 6:15). There will be a gap in communication and a divide stretched between us. And in the case of a relationship with God, absence does not make the heart grow fonder. When we allow our hearts to drift further and further away by not spending time with Him, or by spending time on the pursuit of things that are not what He has for us at this stage of our lives (or ever, for that matter), we will become more and more unfulfilled, restless, and dissatisfied. We are all longing for love, and because God is love, what we are longing for is God.

Our human condition and the angst we carry as we search for peace and rest can only be satisfied in a right relationship with God. But sometimes, we are not in right relationships with God. Our priorities get out of order, and we forget how to treat Him and interact with Him. We become restless because we are in want or in need. We become discontent with what we have, where we are, and what we are doing. We wonder how long before God will give us what we want. We convince ourselves that if He would just give us something in particular, then we would be happy. We try to fill up our lives with things that we think will make them right and satisfy those feelings. We try to live morally and generously and respectfully of others. We try to be self-sacrificing, pleasant, and productive. We try to do more, be more, and have more—but if we leave God out of the equation, really all we do is become less. We become less of who God wants us to be and less of who He made us to be.

Since the time God created Adam, He designed that people would be in relationships with others, beginning with Himself. Occasionally, however, things do not go so well. Sometimes, there is unrest. To combat this problem and find rest in our relationships, we need to get ourselves in order first. We often allow ourselves, our families, and our friends to come before God, yet they are not supposed to be our first priority—God is. The greatest commandment tells us that we are to love the Lord our God with all of our hearts, minds, souls, and strength. Our goal should be Him before all else (see Matt. 22:37–39). And once we have placed Him first, and then move on to loving others, it is important that we do it well. It is important to Him that we are in unity with other believers and that we "love one another with a pure heart fervently" (1 Pet. 1:22). We are even to love our enemies (Matt. 5:43–48). If we are in step with God, then we will be acting properly toward others. If we focus on being godly examples to others, we will bring peace to our relationships. Fewer negative things will arise to pull our hearts and minds away from a restful time. Thus, loving others adequately, correctly, and wholeheartedly will bring rest to ourselves and rest to our relationships with God. When God is the foundation of our relationships, they will be blessed and will also be a blessing.

How does this actually happen, though? How can we feel blessed and rested when there are so many people vying for our attention, some of whom ask nicely for it and some of whom demand it? It seems like the needs are never-ending, and sometimes, the more that we do, the more that is required of us the next time because we appear capable of handling things. We can become so entangled in all of the relationships and projects our lives demand that we stir ourselves up into frenzies and tizzies until we make ourselves dizzy. Our hearts race while our minds whirl and our feet hurry. We are not looking for rest at this point, nor are we even thinking about it, because we just need to get things done and move on to the next thing that needs to be done. We put our priorities in line behind everyone else's. Life seems to speed by in a blur, and at times, the days become indistinguishable from one another. For example, when someone asks me what I did last week, I often find that I cannot recall what I did yesterday, let alone a week ago. The pressure mounts. I feel rushed and unsettled. I feel simultaneously pushed and pulled in many directions. When asked if I ever take a break, I laugh tritely. Rest is a luxury—who has time for that? Well, it is time for a reality check!

We can strain relationships and find ourselves growing resentful if our priorities get out of order. We can become prideful by thinking that we are the only ones capable of doing something and that everyone needs us and will never be able to get along without us. We sometimes think that we are the only ones who can care for our children properly, meet the needs of our spouses, be the kinds of friends our friends need, and keep the committees running. We drive ourselves to exhaustion by trying to meet everyone's needs completely and perfectly. If we continue on in this fashion, we will never find freedom in body, mind, or spirit. Furthermore, the effects of our bondage will eventually spill out onto others in forms such as bitterness, resentment, and impatience. God has a calling for us to be in relationships, but we need to be in the correct ones, in the correct ways. The relationships are not meant to place us in bondage but exist so that we may love and serve the people He places in our paths. We are not called to be all things to all people—He takes care of that aspect. We should be taking care of each one as God directs us to but also be pointing them in His direction so that they know it is Him they truly need.

It is not humanly possible to be all things to all people at all times, so we need to stop trying to be it. In order to find rest in our relationships, we need to examine what is taking place within them and what is taking place within us. Where does the pressure come from and why? Sometimes, we need to let some things go and just do what is reasonable and rational. We are only one person, and if we want to be able to give to the people in our lives, we need to have something to be able to give. We acquire the "something" by resting in God. When we rest, we have time to process what is happening and discover what is important and necessary. Once we do this, we can then apply the new knowledge to how we live and how we interact with people. If our relationships with God are foremost, then we will be able to give the most to others because we have gone to the greatest source to obtain something to give.

We need to make sure that the people around us know they are loved, by us and by God. We need to look at them and interact with them the way that God does: with love, mercy, and compassion. We can show them that they are valuable to us and to Him by giving them our time and attention and cheering them along on the good paths in life. We can speak life and pour love into their lives, just as God has done for us. He loved us so much that He gave us His Son, and He loved them so much that He gave them the same. We need to look at people with an eternal perspective.

The things that seem like a great deal of work in maintaining relationships actually bring us rest: things like forgiving and forgiving repeatedly (Matt. 6:14, 18:22; Mark 11:26), loving our enemies and praying for them (Matt. 5:43–48), restoring what was wrongly taken or damaged (Exod. 22; Lev. 6), turning the other cheek (Matt. 5:39), and rising at midnight to help feed our neighbor's company (Luke 11:5–8). It is important to do these things, and as much as lies within us, to live at peace with everyone (Rom. 12:18). We can mend relationships, right wrongs, and go above and beyond normal human behavior when God's Spirit rests in us and is allowed to enter into our relationships. We are responsible for our own selves, and we are accountable to God for our own actions. May we live well in the sight of all men, but most importantly, in the sight of God.

Well, what do we do when things go wrong? What do we do when life is not perfect and our relationships get downright messy, are difficult to maintain, and sometimes even dissipate? Can we rest when we lose relationships, even the ones we thought were permanent but turned out not to be? Yes. Even when we lose the people most important to us through the separations of abandonment, betrayal, or death, God is still there—and He is at work. And at these times when we are left behind in the most serious of ways, we can know God in deeper ways than we ever have previously. Although we will no longer be our former selves due to these changes in our lives, and maybe even will question who we are now, we can know Him more and better and discover our identities in Him. Even when we can do nothing to fix the situations or make them better, God can give us peace and rest. His comfort is boundless. He is a father to the fatherless, a husband to the widows (Ps. 68:5), and a friend to those who walk in His ways (John 15:14). He will never leave us, and we will never lose Him.

RETREAT: NO CABINS NECESSARY

How can we contain ourselves or maintain any semblance of peace when the world around us is unraveling and we are busy running helter-skelter? The way to accomplish this is by taking the time to think on God, connecting our spirits to His. He compasses our ways and our lying down, He besets us before and behind, He lays His hand upon us, and He has plans for us that were formulated even before we were formed in the womb (Ps. 139:3, 5, 16). He cares for us and loves us deeply, and this should bring great peace and rest to our souls.

Because He cares so much about our lives, we should be cognizant of what we are doing with them. Our lifestyles should not interfere in our relationships with God, and yet they so often do. Too often in my case, I might add. How often do we proceed merrily on our own ways, with our own agendas, never giving Him a second thought, or even a first one? Well, it sure is difficult to abide in Jesus if we never actually stay with Him. And if we are not abiding in Him, then we will not know how to be His disciples. Also, if we neglect our relationships with Him, the tasks we work at will lack the fullness and richness they could potentially have if we were taking the time to be with Him, learning everything He wants to teach us. We need to hold still and not pass by Him yet again. We need to stop neglecting His heart for us. Time with Him will remind us of who He is, who we are, and who we can be through Him. When we do things His way, there is rest and the work gets done; this is the miracle of a yielded life.

Life is difficult, but not having a relationship with God makes it all the more so. We can know *about* God, but that is quite different from having a personal relationship *with* Him. Even as a believer, trying to live for God without spending time with Him is hard. If I do not truly know God, then I cannot be a disciple. And if I know God but do not spend time with Him, then I will not be an effective disciple. It is difficult to follow something you know little or nothing of. God desires that we spend time with Him, not because it benefits Him, but because it benefits us and others. Only He can give us what we truly need to live and to live well. It is important to have time alone with Him so that He can hold us together and keep us from unraveling under all of the pressures of life. He cares for us in our bodies, minds, and spirits and can bring wholeness to our fragmented lives. The difficult will not seem as difficult when the good hand of our God is upon us!

Taking time to connect with God is a conscious coming to His side. Choices will have to be made to give up some good things in order to have the best thing: Him. When we come, we will be like branches that are connecting to the vine for strength and nourishment. If we are wise, we will stay there, but if not, then it will be like we have cut ourselves off from Him—and we all know that cut branches do not thrive very long without their life-support systems. Thus, maintaining our relationships with God will make us stronger and result in spiritual health for us. A connection to Him will give us access to knowledge and power that will have strong and lasting effects upon our lives. When we abide, we are part of Him, and His life flowing through us will cause us to flourish.

I think back to a time many years ago when our region experienced an ice storm. The mayor declared a state of emergency as over 100,000 people lost power. Some people were without power for nearly two weeks. During this time, a friend told me about a sign posted in a store window that read: "Plug in to Jesus. His power never fails." What a wonderful and true statement: "His power never fails." Power is part of His character. In fact, He is omnipotent—He is not just powerful, but all-powerful. And when we plug in to Him, we have access to that power. Moreover, we do not have to wait for storms to come in order to access this power; we can do it right now.

We also do not have to wait for times of calm in order to access God's power. We do not need to run away to cabins in the woods or attend special events in order to find Him. It would be great if we could pour one hundred percent of ourselves into pursuing God and spending time with Him in such ways, but realistically, the world in which we live does not afford such luxury. How do we handle this truth? We find another way. When obligations prevent us from being able to completely escape for rest, we can at least learn how to rest in the midst of them. Anywhere, and at any time, even if just in our thoughts, we can access Him. We simply retreat from the connectedness to our surroundings and connect to Him instead. Once we access God's power, we will begin to experience abundant lives. And coming to Him and resting in Him are the means by which we will maintain them.

Maintaining abundant lives will consist of maintaining balance in the five parts of our beings. We need to be sure that these parts are balanced according to God's scale and that care is not lacking for any part. We have the opportunity to give up the good and the bad so that we can have the best, His best. We can choose to do things His way rather than ours, and with His strength rather than ours. Our inner and outer lives can be influenced by Him, and they, in turn, can be an influence on the entire world around us. If we abide in Him in all parts of who we are, we will be able to go and bear fruit that will remain. His strong presence in us will make us strong out in the world, all for His glory.

God is a Spirit, and those who worship Him must worship Him in spirit and in truth (John 4:24); therefore, we need to take time to nurture our spirits and keep them in healthy conditions. We need to ensure that we are not hindering the work of the Holy Spirit within us by cluttering up our hearts and minds with things that are not of eternal significance. Ultimately, it is not about us, but sometimes, it has to be. We need to periodically have times of introspection in order to understand what is going on in these heads and hearts of ours. We need to take assessments of how we are living, thinking, feeling, and relating so that we can determine whether we are living in godly ways and following God's will. We need to ask God what areas of our lives need improvement, what changes need to be made, what things need to be released, and what unnecessary burdens are being carried. We must ask whether we are on track and moving forward, or whether we are stuck on ourselves, our hang-ups, our desires, and our obsessions. We need to stop. Breathe. Think. Reflect. Who are we, and what are we all about? Are we about ourselves, or are we about Him? Are we about making a name for ourselves or making His name great? We need answers to these questions because these questions are what determine the courses of our lives. The answers will explain where we are now and where we can go from here. If we are off track, then we will find ourselves in detours. We will be unable to focus on nurturing our spirits because we will be too busy being lost, focused on trying to find the way back to the right path. However, if we are on track, the path will be easier, and our spirits will be able to rest and remain healthy. And healthy spirits will worship God.

Time alone with God is not about being fancy—it is about being together with Him. It is not about finding the perfect formula; it is about finding Him. Occasionally, we set up special times (e.g., retreats and vacations) to get away from it all and have focused time with Him, but spending money for lavish events and deluxe gadgets is not necessary in order to have special time with God. The time will be special simply because we are in His presence—He has blessed us with the privilege of approaching Him. So instead of periodic fancy retreats, there are small things that we can do on a daily basis that will make huge differences.

Consistently spending time in His presence will give us great benefits. Some days, the realities of life crowd our hours, but every small thing that we do to enter His presence can have a tremendous impact on us and on our levels of peace and rest. A small step toward God is still a step toward God, and one that brings Him toward us. If we are only able to escape in our minds and our spirits, we can still name it for what it is: time with God. We can pray, praise, quote verses, meditate on Him, and count our blessings. All of this can take place even as we go about our daily activities and required duties. It can be done from the comfort of our own homes, the desks in our cubicles, the driver's seats of our cars, or anywhere else that we happen to be. When He becomes the theme of our activities and of our stillness, we become the focus of His blessings.

During the times we rest in His presence, we can learn about His plans for humanity and His specific plans for us. We can examine whether or not we are truly doing God's will and whether or not we are allowing Him to affect our priorities. His ways are better than our ways. What He deems as important is all-important. We need to surrender to His agenda and give Him first priority in our lives, placing Him in the position of sovereignty. As we do this, we will fill the roles He has created us to fill rather than having a role reversal. He will be God and we will be human—instead of us trying to be God and treating Him as if He is human.

Spending time in God's Word and also speaking with Him in prayer will give us the answers and knowledge that we need to live the most fulfilling lives possible. His words bring us salvation, hope, grace, love, comfort, wisdom, prophecy, and so much more. We are told that the holy scriptures are able to make us "wise unto salvation through faith which is in Christ Jesus," and because they are also profitable for doctrine, reproof, correction, and instruction in righteousness, they will perfect (complete) us and thoroughly equip us for all good works (2 Tim. 3:15–17). His words are valuable and inspiring. They will teach, guide, and direct us until the time that Jesus comes again. First Peter 1:13 says to "hope to the end for the grace that is to be brought unto you at the revelation of Jesus Christ." These words will tide us over until we see the Word Himself.

Spending time in prayer is an amazing opportunity to communicate with God before we see Him face-to-face. As we pray, we get to receive fresh communication from Him that is specifically fashioned for our individual lives. Taking time to listen to and talk to God will affect everything about us and the lives we live. First and foremost, prayer serves to center us onto who we are and why we exist: life is all about Him. Prayer can take place anytime and anywhere, but having specific places to pray that we name our "prayer closets" can encourage us to engage in prayer more frequently. When we pass by these designated spaces, we will remember our past times with Him and will feel called to join Him there again. But even if we have no physical spaces to specifically go to for prayer and communion with Him, there are places from whence He calls to us: He calls from our spirits. The important thing to remember is that today we have the opportunity to be alone with God in our spirits, no matter our physical locations. We need to remove the distractions from ourselves (or remove ourselves from the distractions) and come to the place where His presence is, to rest under the sound of His voice. For this moment, we do not need to attend to anything else or focus on anything else except Him and what we will say to each other.

One thing I have recently begun to do is keep a "praise journal." This activity brings great peace to my heart and mind. In this journal, I record things that are so magnificent and miraculous and awe-inspiring that I never want to forget them. I can read the pages and tell my human mind not to forget who God is, nor forget His great acts and great goodness to me. I will share one entry with you:

> June 17, 2016: I stood looking at a magnificent sunset from the hand of my magnificent Creator. I was so overwhelmed I began to tear up, so amazed that I was beholding such beauty. And then a lark sang (my favorite bird)! Then I really started to cry, and thought, "What is man, that thou art mindful of him? and the son of man, that thou visitest him?"[1] Nine o'clock p.m. and I was hearing many bird calls and watching the beauty change, anticipating what would come next. The temperature was perfect. There was a wonderful smell. Thank you God for my senses to experience You and Your Spirit communing with my spirit. I am overwhelmed by Your goodness to me.

I was grateful to be outside, witnessing such beauty. I was enraptured as He captured my heart that day, pouring out His goodness upon me. I thank Him for blessing me in this way! I thank Him for allowing me to be in His presence and tangibly feel His love.

Although not every day holds the experience I wrote about in my journal—or at least I do not notice it every day—every day holds God. He is doing amazing things to reveal Himself to us; we just need to stop and take notice. We can take notice of Him when we sit at the dining room table to journal, do Bible study, pray, or meditate on Him. We can sense Him when we get facedown on the floor with fervent pleas and offers of deep gratitude. We can commune with Him through heart songs or voiced praise as we commute from point A to point B, whether walking down the hall from room to room or driving through traffic. We can hear Him speak through worship music, sermons, or devotional

CDs that we listen to while we drive or do our household chores. As we pile another load into the washing machine, we can thank Him for the people whose clothes we are washing and for the modern conveniences of electricity, running water, and appliances. We can put our Bibles on top of our alarm clocks so that we remember to spend time with Him before our feet hit the floor, or we can pull our Bibles down from the shelves or out from under the coffee table clutter, open them, and intake His words. We can get out of bed and go to His house even though we are tired and have a million things to do at home. We can place telephone calls to give encouragement, to pray, to engage in spiritual conversations, and to share observations of how God is at work in our lives. Normal everyday activities can be intertwined with God's presence, and when they are, they become extraordinary.

REPOSE: NO CALENDARS NECESSARY

No discussion of rest would be complete without examining what God says about it. Remember that He desires for us to rest. He designed it that way thousands of years ago, before lifestyles were lived at such a frenetic pace. He instituted the Sabbath to specifically give us the opportunity to rest and to enter into a deliberate time of relating with Him. Working for six days and then resting on the seventh followed the precedent that He had set when He created the world in six days and then rested on the seventh (see Ex. 20:9–11). Jesus also talked about the topic of rest and said that the Sabbath was made for man (Mark 2:27). There is an intent to this observance and specific ways in which to accomplish it. God takes the Sabbath seriously, and He wants us to protect this time for Him and for our rest.

We are supposed to follow this commandment just as we do all of the others, yet it seems we are always putting conditions upon it that accommodate our plans rather than observing it in the way God designed it. We have added to and subtracted from the observance of the Sabbath in many ways, yet the truth still remains: God commanded a day of rest that is to be holy. I am not talking about heedlessly luxuriating and doing whatever we want for a day and calling it "rest." The Sabbath is a time to focus on God and stop focusing on ourselves, our pleasures, and our tasks. It is a time to refresh and renew ourselves with His type of renewal. When we follow His command and His intent, our bodies will be allowed to rest as they need to, our minds will turn to think on Him, and our spirits will enter into His presence. When we are deliberately observing this commandment, we are deliberately entering into His presence, and rest will be a blessing that flows from this time. When our minds are on Him, they will not be on our worries, our problems, our schedules, or our circumstances. When we stop allowing things, people, and other pursuits to overshadow our relationships with God, we will find the things of the world growing dimmer and the light and love of His presence growing brighter. I encourage all of us to let go of the pursuit of material things and selfish pleasures; instead, let's pursue God's character, words, and plans and purposes for our lives. He wants what is best for us—we should stop long enough to receive it from His loving hands. It may seem like time is passing us by or being wasted when we pause to be with Him, but when we change our perspectives to His perspective, we will see eternal time and spiritual movement in the kingdom of God.

The purpose of life, both temporal and eternal, is to spend time in God's presence. Following His command to remember the Sabbath day and make it holy will bring amazing benefits to our lives in all parts of who we are. But imagine what would happen if we were to make time to focus on Him every day! Observing the Sabbath is the perfect opportunity to discover who He is and what a life with Him is all about, but what's more, He has made Himself available to us every day. Spending time getting to know Him each day will amaze us more than just one day will. Yes, it is true, rest can even go beyond one special day of pause and reflection! This means we do not need to do our resting just one day per week while living frenetically the other six. Also, we are not limited to having Him in our full view for only one day while we spend the other six without Him, a forgotten memory or a longed-for presence. Believers have something the Israelites did not have when the command of the Sabbath was instituted: we have the Holy Spirit dwelling within us. We have the privilege and opportunity to be with God all day, every day—we just need to take advantage of this opportunity and learn how to make Him part of our daily lives. Why does it matter? Because He wants each of us to be in a relationship with Him. Today is the day to be with Him, Sabbath or not.

REMEMBER: COMMUNION IS NECESSARY

We will not have peace or rest in our spirits if we are not following God's ways, and that will translate to our bodies as well. The breakdown brings the breakdown. If we allow our relationships with Him to erode, then everything else will too. We need to be good stewards of the time that He has given us. Times of physical rest will allow us to put Him in His place and us in ours. He is to be our focus—not other things. It is also important to care for our bodies so that we can complete the work He has for us to do.

Downtime is necessary to rejuvenate our spiritual and relational lives. When we are weary in our minds and bodies, our fatigue will likely cause irritability and destructive behaviors, but if we spend time in God's presence, it will prove to be restorative to us. Even Jesus, amid a busy life of ministry, took time to pray and seek rest in the presence of His Father. He had much to do, many places to go, and multitudes of people to see, yet He made rest and prayer a priority. He did not allow Himself to be pulled in countless directions, He allowed Himself to be pulled in one direction: into the way of the Father and into His presence, will, and timing. He allowed His body and spirit to rest. He was filled up so that He could pour out. And because we are to imitate the behaviors of Jesus, we should be communing with God the Father just as He did. If we are working relentlessly, there will be negative impacts on our lives, and these will spread from our lives to the lives of those around us. We have to learn how to seek God's help, staunch the tide of busyness, and sometimes say no. We need to make a point of taking time-outs so that we can talk with God and be infused with peace and rest.

We want our lives to run smoothly and well, but reality will strike, and there will be times of breakdowns, misfirings, misuses, mishaps, and the like. Because of this inevitability, there needs to be routine maintenance, proper usage, time for repairs, and the giving of grace to ourselves. We are human, and we will fail, but we also have the opportunity to conduct

THE REST OF MY RELATIONSHIPS

ourselves in manners that will tend toward success and away from states of failure, disrepair, or stagnancy. Isaiah 40:25–31 tells us that we are not equal to the Holy One. We cannot be strong all the time, nor can we ever be perfect. These truths should prompt us to look to Him for help. He created all things, and He is strong. He does not faint, nor grow weary— as a matter of fact, He empowers the faint and strengthens those who are without might. Our strength will be renewed as we wait upon Him. We will be able to mount up as though we have the wings of eagles. We will be able to walk and run without weariness or fainting. He will help us so that instead of just enduring life, we can thrive while we live it. So, in order to operate in this prime condition, old seasons need to be put to rest and replaced with the new things that God has for us. God will transform us and bring us out of stagnancy, and we will then function better with the updated changes. When we seek Him, He will grow us and raise us up in strength. This is reality. This is life with Him.

We will reap countless and significant benefits when we pursue relationships with God. We can experience His touch in all parts of our beings. Let's examine a few of the ways this can take place:

1. *There is rest for believers.* Rest is attained by faith in the work of Jesus (see Heb. 4:3); thus, we do not have to work to earn God's love and salvation. Jesus is the Lamb of God who takes away the sin of the world (John 1:29). We can come and rest from our pasts, from the memories and regrets, because our sins have been blotted out. His love, grace, and sacrifice paid the price of our debts; His salvation is a free gift (Eph. 2:8–9). Belief in Him gives us the assurance that we will enter heaven and gain eternal rest for our souls.

2. *We will be heard and helped.* When we examine accounts found in the Bible, we see God repeatedly proving Himself. He answers when we pray, and He will be with us in times of trouble to deliver us (see Ps. 91:15). We can rest assured that He will keep His promises. We can hold fast to our faith despite the tests and trials that come. Even though everything around us gives way, God is

constant. He is still God, no matter what happens. We just need to believe—believe that it will be even as He has said. When we cannot wrap our minds around what is happening, we can let God wrap His arms around us. He is faithful to those who belong to Him (see 2 Tim. 2:13). "Therefore know that the LORD your God, He *is* God, the faithful God who keeps covenant and mercy for a thousand generations with those who love Him and keep His commandments" (Deut. 7:9 NKJV).

3. *We will receive provision and be sustained.* God gives us life and gives us all things richly to enjoy (1 Tim. 6:17). In Him, all things live and move and have their being (Acts 17:28), and He fills our empty hands with His good and perfect gifts (see James 1:17). We can rest in the knowledge that He gives us what is best at the time that it is best.

4. *We will be filled.* Time alone with God will fill us with things that do not come naturally or easily to us. The gifts, knowledge, and love that He pours into us will influence our thoughts, emotions, and actions, which will then spill over onto others. Hearts that have been touched by God become new and beautiful creations. We will be able to deliver a report to our boss with a smile, drive considerately in traffic, give of our resources to help others in need, and do things simply for the sake of blessing others. As we interact with those around us, whether we know them well or consider them strangers, we can bless their days with words of prayer, encouragement, and the simple phrase "Jesus loves you." We will find that in focusing our hearts, minds, and words of blessing upon others, we are changed and blessed in the process. We will find refreshment in doing the things that God has called us to do, in the unique manners in which He has called each of us to do them. Our spirits will rest in hope, and we will be able to share that hope with others.

5. *We will find peace in His presence.* God's presence will lead and accompany us. King David said that he could not be shaken

because the Lord was always with him at his right hand (Ps. 16:8). God's presence allowed David to rest with hope (see Acts 2:25–26). We, too, can be strong, secure, and hopeful because God is also right beside us. David said that the Lord was his shepherd who made him to lie down in green pastures, led him beside still waters, restored him, and accompanied him through the valley of the shadow of death. David did not need to fear any evil because God was with him—even in the presence of his enemies—and was giving him abundance, goodness, mercy, and a dwelling place with Him forever (see Ps. 23). David was continually with God, being held by the right hand and being led by God's counsel. God is who he desired. God was his strength and portion, and he knew that it was good to draw near to Him and trust Him (see Ps. 73:23–26, 28). We can have the same peace that David experienced by interacting with God in the same ways he did. Although times may come when we might be jiggled a bit in our faith, we cannot be shaken from our sure foundation.

6. *We will find hope.* God is the source of all hope (see Ps. 62:5) and the source of things that give hope. He is the source of salvation and eternal life. He is our rock and our fortress, our strength and stability, our protection from the enemy. We will not be shaken when we place our hope in Him because He is the unshakable God. We, like others, can have hope by recognizing the truth of who He is.

Second Chronicles 14 gives an account of King Asa leading the Israelites into battle against a multitude of their enemies. They named God as their God and prayed that the enemy would not prevail against them. They placed their hope in God's help and protection because King Asa realized where true help came from. By examining some phrases found within one of his prayers, we can see evidence of his trust in God. Asa cried out saying, "LORD, *it is* nothing for You to help, whether with many or with those who have no power; help us, O LORD our God, for we rest on You, and in Your name we go against this multitude. O LORD, You *are* our God; do not let man prevail against You!" (2 Chron. 14:11 NKJV). When we need help and answers, a perspective like this can stop any fruitless searching. When we place our hope in God, we will be kept from the disappointment and frustration found in seeking help from humans, who truly cannot help us. It is *God* who can quash our hopelessness. It is He who can aid our helplessness. He has the power to help and to save, no matter how large the enemy is that looms in front of us. *He* is hope itself.

It is an amazing thing to be in relationship with God. He ministers to each part of who we are, giving us just what we need for each part. We do not need to strive to obtain these things, and we do not need to hurry Him along. He will be our bread day by day (Matt. 6:11), and He will supply us with the peace that passes all understanding while we wait for the provision to come (see Phil. 4:7). We will find that in His presence there is fullness of joy (Ps. 16:11), rest, hope, healing, and deliverance (Pss. 40, 66). Even when things are difficult and things look bleak, we can be whole and healthy people from an overall perspective—in our bodies, minds, and souls. We can trust God to do what He has said, and we can trust Him to meet every need that we have. We can trust Him to always be there for us because He loves us with an everlasting love.

CHAPTER 17
Journey to Rest

REST IS FOR OVERALL HEALTH

Life is a daily task that can require much of us, sometimes more than we have to give. Life can get ridiculously busy, especially during particular seasons. When it is the season of planning a wedding or a graduation, that event tends to take up the majority of our time, thoughts, energies, and so on. We plan, prepare, shop, spend, compile, order, invite, preview, inspect, craft, decorate, and assemble—day in and day out—all for an event that lasts only a few hours. Do we ever pour that amount of time, thought, and energy into eternity? Do we even give it any thought at all, or are we too caught up in living for the now and focusing on short-term goals and events? Are we fatiguing ourselves with the wrong things so that we are too tired to do the right things? Yes, at times we are. Focus, trajectory, and vision can all get off track.

On occasion, we will need to intentionally take time to cease from our labors; otherwise, it will not happen. Whether we are in seasons of ordinary routine or seasons of extraordinary activity, rest is necessary for health in all parts of who we are: minds, bodies, emotions, spirits, and relational selves. These five parts of our beings are interrelated, so it is important that we care for each part properly in order to be healthy overall. We likely know from experience that when we are not physically healthy, we cannot function at our optimum levels or fulfill our potentials. Likewise, if we are not healthy in the other parts of who we are, then our abilities to function will be hindered and we will be unable to reach our full potentials. It is easier to face life when we have been rejuvenated in any one part of who we are, so imagine what we could do if we were healthy in all five. We could affect lasting change in our lives and in the lives of others. One person can change the world!

Think about the techniques of physical exercise: stretch, warm up, work out, cool down, stretch, rest. I rarely seem to find myself running my life in this way. I seldom enter into that last phase of rest. I flutter around from thing to thing, rarely letting my to-do piles sit idle. If the piles are nearly knocked down for the day, I find myself thinking of all of the other things that I can or should add to them, and then I get busy with the new additions. I do quite a bit of Christmas shopping in January and plan for my children's birthday parties that are nine and eleven months out. I have piles of work all over the house. These piles contain projects that do not need attention for months, along with those that need attention today, but I am too busy to get to them because I am still working on the things from yesterday. It is a vicious cycle. With all of this clutter in my home and in my schedule, how can I find peace? With all of the continual preparation and responsibility, when can my mind and body ever rest? Even when I lie down in bed, my mind is not ready to sleep although my body was ready hours ago. I have lists all over the house: on the calendar, the mirror, the counter, the nightstand, the dining room table, clipped to my purse, etc. My daughter says that I am "freakishly organized." You might not think so if you were to glance around at the piles, but I have a plan, and I am working on it! I am doing so many things and trying to maintain so many relationships that I make myself crazy. It sure would be nice to relax once in a while. I would really like to sit down and read a book. Maybe write one too. I have manuscript-related items in one of those piles!

I gave my mother a beautiful journal a few years ago, but she recently gave it back to me. She stated that since I was a writer and she was not, perhaps I could make better use of it. Guess what? I am more apt to tear pages out of journals and make to-do lists on them rather than write down my thoughts and feelings on them. There you have it, some alternative uses for journals: as gifts, as re-gifts, and as stacks of to-do list papers bound together and just waiting to be written upon! Actually, the best use of them is to write down your praises!

Because of this workload I am attempting to carry, I find that it frequently takes me months to finish reading one book for pleasure. My books become continual cliffhangers! Although I may have gotten to read three sentences today, it may be two weeks before I find out what happens in the next one. It might be so long between readings that I forget what I read last time and have to backtrack. I think you can probably see where this is headed! My son says that I read a lot, but what he does not realize is that the five books on the dining room table are ones that I am using as research for my speaking, teaching, writing, counseling, and whatever academic pursuit I may be involved in at the time. I am doing my devotions and Bible studies. I am figuring out how to help someone. I am looking for just the right scripture verse to drop in the mail. I am reading the paperwork my children bring home from school. I am reading health information for a family member or friend. I am reading my list of what I bought people for Christmas the previous year so as not to duplicate it when I go shopping in the next year (in January!). I am reading my multiple to-do lists. I think you get the point. Yes, that's me. If I could read in the dark, I would. I do not have to go quite that far, though, as I have many mini-flashlights and book lights around the house so as not to disturb anyone who is sleeping. Stove lights and microwave lights work too. And I must mention that our clothes dryer has a light in it, so as long as I prop open the door, I can read in the laundry room! So many words, so little time.

So, do I ever rest or relax? Yes, I occasionally rest, but when I do, I am often loaded with guilt. You know the old adage about all work and no play being an awful way to spend the day? Contrary to these words of wisdom, I find myself thinking that I could always be doing more and becoming more than I am—for myself and for others. When writer's block sets in, I find myself thinking that I really should be working on my book. Presently, it is half past two o'clock in the morning, and I am busily typing. My alarm goes off at half past six so that I can get the kids out the door to school. Is this healthy? Some nights (or should I say mornings?), I have gone to bed after four o'clock, gotten less than two hours of sleep, and then headed right into chores, projects, or writing the moment I arose. And frequently, I have felt guilty because I did not get everything accomplished before my day finally came to an end.

So, what does Jesus want me to learn about Him while I carry on in such a manner? What is He teaching me as I obey His calling to write this book? I must ask myself some difficult questions. Did I rest today like Jesus rested? Did I rest when He called me to rest? Am I being a good example to those around me and to my readers? Am I learning lessons from Him as I go through life and then actually applying them? I must say good night, now. I see the hint that the Lord has laid out for me in black and white. Until next time, dear reader, you get the cliffhanger and I get some sleep!

Jesus told the disciples to come apart and rest for a while because their lives had been, as we would say today, "go, go, go." Jesus's life was like that, too, but there was also another dimension to it. He slept, ate, attended church, celebrated, worked, traveled, and spent time with family and friends; but He also took time to withdraw by Himself so that He could pray and spend time in God's presence. Jesus exhibited the best example of how to live a balanced life. We should imitate His practices, and when doing so, not feel guilty. We should be fine with taking rests from our labors so that we can focus on God and restore our bodies, minds, and souls. We will never accomplish everything that is begging to be accomplished, nor will we meet everyone's expectations. We must realize that the most important thing to be doing is that which God has asked us to do, and to be working at it with all of our might. We should work to the best of our abilities and be satisfied with that. Nothing more. Nothing less. We should not let the myth of "doing it all" deceive us from the truth—the truth that He has already laid the foundation for all that He needs us to do and will be helping us to build on that foundation. We need to be sure not to miss out on real life while we chase an impossible one. We need to seek Him and His paths for our lives, resting and working as He directs.

All-encompassing rest is more than a possibility in life—it is a surety—a result of coming to God. When we come to God, we must decide to stop trying to forcefully produce. We need to release these efforts so that He can bring rest and restoration to each part of our beings. Just as a farmer cannot force his crops to grow, neither can we force growth to happen before the timing of the season. And at times, our fields just need to rest. Farmers leave fields fallow from time to time to allow the soil to regain nutrients for a future planting season. We need to take some time to receive nutrition, too, rather than always be trying to produce a product and take care of the entire growth process by ourselves, all at once. Our health depends upon us resting. When we slow down, God will heal, nourish, and prepare us for future seasons of growth. He will bring rest to our minds, to our bodies, and most of all, to our souls. And while we are resting, we can refocus our eyes and hearts to know that He is God. Our return to seasons of production will then be healthy and fruitful.

Resting in God does not mean that we are doing nothing and idly wasting time. When we are resting, we are doing something that is essential, so it is actually a great use of our time. Work, play, and service can all be done as we rest with Him. Rest is a great lifetime habit in which to participate. We can rest with Him in good times and bad, in sickness and in health, in joy and in sorrow, in plenty and in want. It somewhat sounds like marriage vows, doesn't it? As we live our lives, we will experience these various conditions. Seasons are going to come and go, but if we have pledged our lives to Him, He will always be at our sides. He will be our faithful partner as we go through life. Will we turn to see Him, hear Him, and let Him hold our hands to accompany us on our journeys through life? And will we take the time to rest in Him? It is time for Him to be over all.

REST IN OUR PHYSICAL BODIES

THE DRIVE-THRU LIFE

We live lives that are fast-paced and highly charged. We are on the run and on the go. We are in the express checkouts and in the drive-thru lanes. We scarf the junk calories en route to the next places, the next appointments on our jam-packed schedules. Do we do the same with our spiritual lives? Do we treat them like express lanes for speedy checkouts? Or perhaps like drive-thru lanes, where we can grab a few morsels to tide us over and then make a quick exit? If we are honest, the answer is yes. Sometimes, maybe even frequently, we let other things take priority over our time with God. We might read a short Bible passage or breathe a quick prayer before we run off to do the next thing—if we are on top of things, that is—otherwise, we likely let those things slide. We may organize (or is it disorganize?) our lives in such ways that we have no time to think and feel, to enjoy the beauty of life, to learn of and love God. We find that it is hard to sit still through an hour of church once per week. We focus on what comes next rather than savoring His current presence with us. We are trying to do so many things at once that we cannot be deeply devoted to any one thing. We do this and that; bits and pieces; his, hers, and theirs. But what about us and ours? What about God for us, and us for God?

We often do not nourish ourselves with His daily bread. We are wasting away, all the while thinking we are fat and happy. In reality, things are not pretty, but we think our lives are beautiful, rich, and full. But just as fast food from the drive-thru does not put our bodies into premium shape, neither does fast spiritual food keep us in prime condition. If we are out of shape physically, then we will easily tire; the same is true in our spiritual lives.

Do we meet ourselves coming and going? Do we pass by others without even a glance because there is no time to look? Are there necessary activities on our calendars? Are there unnecessary ones, as well? Are we wearing our busyness like status symbols, as something that gives us significance? Busywork and overflowing plates of obligations can keep us from caring for our bodies properly and can keep us from caring for others. We can be our own worst enemies by penciling in too many things while also putting off physical rest. We can end up ruining our lives and the lives of those around us, bit by bit, day by day. Some overloaded people have eventually gone so far as to collapse under the strain they have put their bodies through—others have lost their lives. I have come dangerously close to this. Frequently, I am utterly exhausted and have literally made myself ill, yet I make excuses for why I cannot rest at these times. There is *something* that needs my attention; I am sure of it! But the damage goes even deeper than the physical. We will find ourselves neglecting God and others, when it is *they* who need our attention.

We seem to be a society of excuses and neglect. Because we are "too busy," we do not do the things that we should in order to care for ourselves or others properly. No time to eat properly, sleep enough, or exercise adequately. No time to rest our minds. No time to rest our emotions. This can be a dangerous path to walk down, leading us into burnout and resentment and also causing serious health problems. Medical experts tell us that stress produces more cortisol than necessary, which in turn leads to weight gain. Poor diets can lead to obesity, diabetes, and malnutrition. Not engaging in exercise can lead to obesity, heart disease, fatigue, and weakness. We could mention many more side effects, many more things that are detrimental to our health. To avoid serious consequences, it is important that we take some time to rest as we journey through life. And resting just long enough to grab some coffee before we race back to our vehicles and hit the traffic lanes again is not enough. Besides, we can only rest until the time and money runs out, the spas close, the vacations end, or the counselors retire. Life is going to continue on. We are going to age, go through cycles of life, and become ill yet again. Thus, it is important to figure out how to rest in the midst of everything. We have to stop. We *need* to stop. Remember the testimony of the time I was not healthy in any area of who I was? My body is still paying for it all these years later. Please rest. Be a good steward of what God has given you. Take care of yourself, and take care of others.

Rest is vital to our bodies in all parts of who we are. We need to relieve the stress. We need to give our bodies time to repair themselves. If we do not rest mentally, we may have nervous breakdowns. If we do not rest emotionally, then we will have more difficulty maintaining self-control. Without downtime, we may drive ourselves to illness and make poor choices. We will be set back in what needs to be accomplished as our bodies struggle through illness and confusion. Our minds may not be able to process things appropriately and this, in turn, may cause us to act inappropriately and impulsively. We need to have some respite in order to reflect and assess where we are in life. We need time to think about where we should be and where we are currently headed. Will we find the two to be in alignment? We need to ascertain whether we are headed in the directions that will accomplish God's plans and purposes for our lives. We do this by asking ourselves some important questions, such as whether or not we are in God's will and if we are fulfilling the callings that He has given to us. Are we stopping long enough so that He can equip and prepare us for what is to come? Are we storing up strength for the journey ahead? Are we committed to accomplishing His will? Rest is important on every level so that we can answer yes to all of these questions.

In the Old Testament account of Elijah (1 Kings 19:1–18), we find Elijah sleeping from exhaustion after defeating the prophets on Mount Carmel. He was then awakened twice by an angel who told him to rise and eat because the journey that lay ahead was going to be difficult. Elijah went in the strength of that food for forty days. Then, God showed up to meet with him. After talking through some things, God gave him his next tasking. Elijah needed rest and strengthening that was both physical and spiritual—because of what he had just experienced and in preparation for what was to come. We, like Elijah, have come through some difficulties and still have tasks ahead of us. Are we resting, restoring, and preparing? Are we nourishing our bodies and our spirits through rest or destroying them through frenetic and fruitless activities, never allowing ourselves to recover and prepare for what is next? I can tell you this from experience: if I am doing too many things, then I am not doing any one thing well. If I am dividing up my efforts into haphazard chunks, then the results will be haphazard displays of inattention, incompletion, and divided loyalties. I will surely not be resting, and I will not have time to prepare for what is coming next because I will be too busy being overwhelmed by what is now.

Some of you may be asking the question, "But isn't the Christian life about going and fulfilling the Great Commission, doing things for God, serving in the church and the community, and rearing children in the correct way?" The answer is definitely yes, but we are to be doing all of these things in the appropriate manners and at the appropriate times. We go through many seasons in life, and different things are required of us at different times, but whatever the season, we are to do our best, and let God do the rest. And let Him give us rest, too. However, this rest does not mean hiding from the work at hand. We should not make plans to withdraw permanently or limit ourselves with any other timelines. There needs to be a balance. At times, we will be in isolation and seclusion, but we are not to be avoiding the work of the ministry; we can still pray and find a way to encourage others and share Jesus. It is important to be willing to go out again whenever God wants our work shifts to begin. Hearts need to be listening for His voice. He is speaking. He is alive and active in the world and active in the lives of people who allow Him to be. Do we ever stop to hear what He is trying to say to us? Do we need to listen more intently? When God prompts us to listen, we should stop and *listen*.

At times, our human schedules do not make it seem feasible to take rests, even so that we can listen to what is being said to us. We are so busy multitasking and trying to surmount and accomplish the to-do piles that we block out the voices and perceived distractions around us, even the voice of God. But it is important that we stop what we are doing and not put off the opportunities to hear God speak. It is of utmost importance to listen to His promptings and then take action. If we do not take immediate action, we may find that something else comes up and interferes with the opportunity. We may get distracted by yet another thing that needs to be done. Furthermore, since we are not guaranteed our next breaths, postponing a meeting with God may prohibit that meeting from ever taking place. Yes, it is true that believers will have an eternity in heaven to spend time listening to God, but while we are here, He has work for us to do and abundant life for us to live—and we need Him to tell us how to accomplish it. We need to be listening for the how-to of God.

It is going to take effort, determination, and intentionality to care for ourselves and allow ourselves to rest, and most importantly, to align our life activities with where God wants us to go. One method that can help us in our efforts is to take inventories and examine our schedules with intent. We can ask the following questions of ourselves: What do I need to do to bring rest in the midst of the schedules I keep? How do I align myself with God's plans for me? These inventories can be eye-opening experiences as we evaluate where we are focusing and on what we are spending our energies and the precious hours of our lives. We can look at the details of our activities and process exactly what is occurring in each situation. For example, are we parents "preparing" drive-thru meals the majority of the week while we commute from activity to activity? Have we put our children into these activities, or have we allowed our children to pull us into them? If these are activities that we are unable to let go of, how can we live abundantly in the midst of them? How can we turn them into something of eternal significance that will actually bring rest to our souls and simultaneously share Jesus with others? We are to move in such ways that we are in step with Him. He is the one who best can lead us and help us to bear the loads that are too heavy for us, the burdens that are too great for us. Let the sufficiency of Jesus turn your labors into labors of efficiency.

PARADOXES OF NECESSITY

Some of the things that we must do to follow Jesus seem paradoxical, but when we do them, they will result in seemingly impossible blessings. They do not make sense to our human minds, but we follow a God of the impossible, so the blessings do come. I will discuss three paradoxes:

1. *We must come before we can go.* Invitations to come will precede our commands to go. God will invite us to come to Him to receive what He wants us to have, and once we have done that, He will have us go. Thus, we should be waiting until it is God's time for us to go, and before that, we should be acting upon the invitations to come. We see this evidenced in the life of Moses. After Moses had lived in Midian for forty years, an angel of the Lord appeared to him in a burning bush. When Moses saw the bush, he went for a closer look. As he approached it, the voice of the Lord came to him. God told Moses that He had seen the affliction of His people in Egypt. He then gave Moses a task. He said, "And now come, I will send thee into Egypt" (Acts 7:34). Moses came, and then God tasked him to go. Moses had lived many ordinary years as a shepherd, but when God was ready, it was time for Moses to go and do something extraordinary. There were things that Moses had learned while he waited those forty years, but when God showed up to talk to him, his learning took a big leap. He learned that he was just a man and would need to come to God for help first in order to be able to go and accomplish the task ahead of him. He learned what to say, what to do, where to go, how to use his equipment, and how to deal with various scenarios that would arise. These waiting years may have seemed like a waste while Moses was

shepherding for his father-in-law, but God was putting things into motion and bringing things to fruition so that when it *was* time for Moses to go, he could accomplish God's plan and purpose perfectly. God will also call us to do things and then He will give us what we need to accomplish what He has asked.

At times, God's invitations will call us for the briefest of moments. They will be those nudges in our spirits, when we know that God is speaking something to us, giving us something to do or say or heed. As we obediently accomplish the tasks, the strength and ability used will actually be His. When we come to get strength, we will be able to go in strength. We need to come to be equipped so that we can go into all the world and preach the gospel to every creature (see Mark 16:15). We need to come to learn what Jesus did so that we can go and do likewise. We need to come and obtain seed before we can go out and sow it. We need to come to be healed so we can go and bring healing to others. Ten lepers came to Jesus for healing. He sent them on their ways to go show themselves to the priest, and as they went, the healing came (Luke 17:14). They became living testimonies to God's amazing power. We can become part of that same testimony. Every need that we have, He can supply. Every weakness that we have can be overcome by His strength. Every fear and every doubt that plagues our minds can be drowned out by the company of His voice. When we come, we *can* go. We will be able to do above and beyond all that we can ask, think, or imagine when we walk according to His plans, because *He* is able (see Eph. 3:20).

2. *Working well lets us rest.* Approaching tasks and routines differently can bring us rest. When we look at our gigantic to-do piles or our lengthy to-do lists, things can seem overwhelmingly hopeless. But if we focus on God's priorities and set our minds to accomplish the tasks that He desires us to accomplish, we will find that our stress levels decrease. If we allow His presence to be active within us, we will be empowered to accomplish our great purposes in life, *His* purposes. And all the while we are working at our tasks, we can pray, meditate, study His Word, and worship. And hope will grow.

Recall the time when Jesus told the disciples to rest for a while. There had to be intentionality in resting. Ministry can get so busy that we neglect both our physical and spiritual bodies. People have great needs, but it is impossible for us to assist with every single one of them—as much as we would like to do so. There is a time to take a break, step back, rest, and refuel. God understands how important this is for us—He created us. He knows that we need time to rejuvenate and be fed because being wound too tight is not good for us in any part of our beings and can lead to dangerous consequences. Another great benefit of this refueling is that He will give us what we need for others, to help the many, or even just the solitary one that He calls us to help.

It is important that we take time away from our work so that we can participate in activities that refresh and renew us. But as we take this time away, we must allow God to minister to our need for renewal rather than improvising something on our own that *we* think will renew us. Spending time in His presence is the best option for renewal. True communion restores weary hearts and minds and enables us to become more resilient. We must have His armor on in order to survive the battles of life. We must help those who fight alongside us. We must snatch the wounded from the clutches of the enemy. Our minds need to understand the plans so that we can carry them out properly. Our hearts need to be strengthened so that we will carry out the plans faithfully. We need physical strength so that we are not laid up when we are supposed to be on the battlefields. God needs to command us as we advance in the kingdom of darkness so that we can help rescue souls and bring them to the kingdom of light.

Life is no longer like it was when we were children, with days of carefree play and no schedules to keep. Now our lives consist of timing our days for thing after thing after thing. We shuttle ourselves and others to work, school, sports, stores, children's events, social obligations, church, and many other places and activities. This packed scheduling and constant movement is not what Jesus demonstrated to us through His life and teachings. He showed how to carry out one's life purpose and calling but also how to escape the cares of the world and seek solitude. He was always focused on God and service to Him, but He did not drive Himself into the ground doing it. He was not distracted from His purpose by all the noise of the world but was instead in tune with His Father's heart. He took time to be with His Father in the midst of work and travel but also withdrew from activity altogether for times of restoration, prayer, and communion. He took time to rest so that His work would be effective when He returned to it. He came to His Father for help and direction and then worked to give Him the glory as He completed His tasks well. God was there to hear Jesus's prayers and provide Him with the strength He needed to do His life's work, when it was time to be at work. He will do the same for us.

3. *We can rest and run at the same time.* We need to get our entire bodies fit for living this life. There is a race to be won, and there is a prize to be obtained. There is a goal, and there is a finish line. It is important to condition ourselves for the race that we are in, and while we are in it, to make sure there is nothing slowing us down, wearing us down, or depleting our strength. If our bodies are properly conditioned, we can run farther before we grow weary. We can learn how to breathe efficiently and transfer our energy as we run each step. It is important that we are progressing through life rather than being stuck on a treadmill; however, we need to be proceeding down the correct paths so that we will arrive at the destinations God desires for us. And throughout all of it, yielding to His plans will enable us to rest and run at the same time.

My son was a long-distance runner in high school. One day I asked him, "What makes running easier?" His reply was, "Do what Coach tells you to do." The coach knows how to get the job done. He knows the strengths and weaknesses of each runner, and it is his job to train and encourage each one to improve upon those strengths while diminishing the weaknesses. I applied my son's statement spiritually and found the implications to be quite profound. If we follow God's designs, for life in general and for our lives in particular, then we are going to find it easier to run our races. We will be stronger runners both because He wanted us to be and because we allowed Him to help us develop into them. We will win the prizes when our races are finished, and we will become champions for Him. The prophet Isaiah said that "*they that wait upon the* LORD *shall renew their strength; they shall mount up with wings as eagles; they shall run, and not be weary; and they shall walk, and not faint*" (Isa. 40:31, emphasis mine). This is how we rest and run at the same time.

STEPS IN A JOURNEY

A journey will begin when we take the first step. That first step will take effort, as will all the ones after it, but hopefully, the determination to finish will lie behind each step. There may be times when we desire to fall back on what is easy and familiar, and there may be other times when that is exactly what we do because we slip into function mode without even realizing it, and thus, neglect to seek His help; but when we realize what we have done, we can switch over into God's mode, and with His help, continue forward. When we wander off the path or start slipping backward, we simply need to get back on the path, steady our footing, and step forward again. Notice I said *when*, not *if*. We are human, and we will fail—but God offers us His mercies, new every morning (Lam. 3:22–23). And remember, we have the help of the Holy Spirit to make any necessary changes as we journey through life. He can help us make habits out of coming to God, spending time with Him, and seeking His help. And when we do not neglect to ask for His help, we will make many forward steps. When we step closer to God, He will step closer to us, and we will have the most wonderful traveling companion we ever could. And once we begin to reap the benefits of completing God's callings, our desire to press on further will increase, and we will find the perseverance worth it.

CHAPTER 18

Strong to the Core

OBTAINING STRENGTH AND REST

There are times when things get so hectic that we just want the world to stop so we can step off for a while. We can become so burdened with busyness and the cares of life that we do not really take care of life. But God has something better for us—something more fulfilling and something more energizing. It will involve developing some disciplines and applying some strategies to help us downsize our lives and upsize them at the same time. We can go deeper into the presence of God where there is real rest. We can get to know Him, perhaps truly for the first time, and emerge as new and stronger people, ready to face any challenges that arise. When we attach our entire selves to Him, we will be healthy and productive in life. When we abide in Him, we will be strong to the core and able to live out our lives as people of strength and faith. At times, we will face struggles, and at times, we will yearn for rest, but when we are connected to God, we can press on.

As a house divided against itself cannot stand, it is also true that our faith cannot stand if it is not coming to Jesus in communion and unity. When we are being strong-willed, we are actually weak, because we are going our own ways rather than God's, and thus, we do not have His power with us. And without His power, we are rendered powerless, because we cannot do anything apart from Him (see John 15). We cannot stand without Him, only fail and fall. We will be weak and easily crushed beneath the loads of life if we do not have His support. To avoid these negative things that come with detachment, we must surrender our wills to His. We must put down our loads and take up His cross. We need to be His in our entireties, and when we are, we will obtain His strength, a strength that can surpass all obstacles and withstand all storms. We will be strong, to our very cores.

Jesus was strong to His very core because He had the strength of the Father in Him. When the time came to battle death and fight for our souls, Jesus prayed and sought God's plan and then became obedient unto death, even death on the cross (Phil. 2:8). He rested in His decision to follow God's will and was strengthened for the journey ahead, the journey to the cross. He rested in the perfect plan that His Father had for Him: the redemption of all humanity. He rested in the knowledge that there was a plan that extended beyond what His physical eyes could see. He rested in the security of the Father's love for Him. He rested in the joy of knowing that God would be glorified and people would be saved. He rested in the knowledge that it was He who was chosen for this task. We have been chosen for tasks as well: we are to live the lives that God has for us. They are lives that reach beyond what our eyes can see. May we rest in His plans for us, me in mine, and you in yours.

God has *you* to live *your* life and *me* to live *mine*. Each of us is capable of living the lives that God has designed for us and in ways that will glorify Him. We are each comprised of a unique mind, body, and spirit. Comparisons, jealousies, and coveting of others serve no purpose and bring no rest to us. Pining over what we do not have will not serve us or others well. We are not called to complain; we are called to be content. We are to set aside our fickleness and be grateful instead. So even though I wanted red hair but ended up with brown (perhaps the red color went to my rosacea, instead), I should be content. Even though I wanted to be taller but am instead shrinking from the effects of car accidents, scoliosis, and several other back problems, I am to be content. We might find ourselves sometimes wanting different marriages, children, spouses, houses, cars, jobs, and extended families, but this is not what we are called to do; instead, we are called to be content. Maybe we want to live in Hawaii but live in Kansas instead. Be content. Maybe we want to live in Victorian mansions but live in studio apartments instead. Be content. Maybe we want to drive shiny red convertibles but cannot even afford car insurance on rusty sedans. Be content.

We need to be content where we are and focusing on the things that truly matter. Instead of being shallow, we should dig down deep into our heart of hearts and be grateful for the many blessings that God has given us, for there *are* many. The apostle Paul, even with all of his suffering and want, said that he had learned to be content whatever his state (Phil. 4:11). May we do the same. We can have peace, rest, and contentment in our spirits, even in the midst of storms, chaos, imperfect circumstances, disappointments, and lengthy to-do lists. God has perfect plans for each of us that will work perfectly.

It is paradoxical, but during times of stillness there are intentional activities that we can be doing in order to become stronger. We can rest and act at the same time. We can minister while God is ministering to us. We can be still and gain the knowledge that He is God (Ps. 46:10). Once we are doing these strengthening activities, we will recover strength and gain more strength. We will then be able to operate within that new strength. This is how (if we have learned what rest really means) we can be both working and resting at the same time. This is how we become more mature and more effective. This is where we move from milk to meat, from toddling around unsteadily to running the race. We are strong and able when we allow Him to establish, strengthen, and settle us. This stillness will clarify and deepen our relationships with God, and it will forge the strength of our identities in Him. We will be equipped to do the things that He calls us to do, and we will be ready when He says that it is time for us to go forth into the fields. Be still and know.

Ultimate strength comes from God as He ministers it to us and infuses us with it through various methods. While His plans are unfolding, we can be active in strengthening ourselves with God's type of strength by seeking Him for it and receiving it from His hand. This strength will give us the abilities to be fervent, be resilient, endure, withstand pressure, and have the mental and emotional qualities necessary to deal with difficulties. There will be times when we are called to work, times when we are called to rest, and times when we are called to do both simultaneously. We need to be sure that we are in the correct modes at the correct times; otherwise, we will impede what God is trying to accomplish in our lives. The acquisition of strength will come from resting in God, in whichever states He has called us to be. As life happens, so will His strength—in us and through us.

YOKED TO STRENGTH

Strength comes from maturing in Christ and remaining teachable. We need to understand that we cannot work effectively unless we have had the proper training. We need to look at our growth and maturation measurements to see if we are still sipping the milk when we should be devouring the meat, and then we have to decide which it is that we want to consume. Are we allowing Him to strengthen us so that someday we will be able to do the work that He has for us to do? A yoke does not imply that half of the team will be doing all of the work while the other just moseys along. There are some things that we are responsible to do, and we need to learn what those things are. We will not be effective in accomplishing the tasks ahead of us if we do not learn how God desires that we do them. God's skills are strong skills.

Further strength will come as we exercise our faith. We need to take action to build muscle. We cannot become stronger by sitting down, ignoring and resisting the processes that stretch and grow us. Also, if we want to shed the unwanted pounds of burdens, we need to take action. We can ask for a personal trainer (the best one is God Himself), but He also provides other believers to mentor and encourage us and keep us on track for Him. With help and accountability, we will find it easier to step toward His love, forgiveness, and assistance.

Sometimes, however, we will get off track because of our human natures. Sin is a burden and a weight that so easily besets us. It gets in the way of running the race that is set before us (see Heb. 12:1). Corrections and adjustments need to be made in order to continue on in our yokes and to become stronger after our mistakes. We need to take the necessary steps to lay our sin burdens aside, and pick up forgiveness instead. We can lay these burdens of sin down, along with their accompanying guilt, and carry only weights that will make us healthy.

Corrections and adjustments will also come from God, and these will make us stronger. Jeremiah 31:18 tells of a bull that was unaccustomed to the yoke. It was chastised if it turned where it was not supposed to go. At times, we need to be chastised, as we resist God's teachings and stubbornly insist on going our own ways. The intent of the chastisement is to restore us to proper states. We need to understand that we are not to force our hand and attempt to command the lead by overpowering the One who is stronger than us. It is best to submit to God's authority and be bulls if that is what He is teaching us to be. If we act like racehorses who just want to finish in a hurry and get the glory of the prize, we will miss the opportunities to walk the paths that the Master has laid out for us. Thus, when we have made mistakes, we need to patiently accept correction and learn from the mistakes. The sooner we submit our stubborn wills, the sooner we will effectively learn and mature and be able to get back into the furrows where the work needs to be accomplished. And wonderfully, there is no condemnation for those who are in Christ Jesus because our sins were forgiven at the cross (see Rom. 8:1). Jesus exercised great love for us. Will we do the same for Him in return? He has a plan, and He wants to use us within it to accomplish great things for His kingdom.

We are to be co-laborers together with God. He put us here in these fields to work, but we cannot do the work effectively unless we have had the proper training to prepare us and the proper rest to rejuvenate us. We also cannot bear the loads unless we have been strengthened. We need to come to Him for rest so we can obtain that strength. Whatever it is that we have to carry in life, it is made more bearable when we allow Him to help us and allow Him to take the weight onto *His* shoulders. He does not stand afar off watching us labor and struggle beneath the loads, rather, if we are following Him, He will fall into step beside us and take on the yoke, making our ways easier. It is His strength through us that allows us to do all the things that need to be done (see Phil. 4:13). Let's come so that we can go and do these things!

I believe that the words of Matthew 11:28–30 imply an extraordinary invitation: we need to come so that we can go. If we were not to go, what then would be the purpose of learning of Him? To hoard the knowledge to ourselves? To do nothing with this knowledge to benefit anyone other than ourselves? No. There is a very important reason why we are supposed to learn of Him: the Great Commission (Matt. 28:19–20). It would behoove us to be still and attend to what is being taught. We will gain eternally important information that we will need to go and share with others.

Do we ever wonder how we can obtain rest from Him if we are going into all the world to preach the gospel to every creature? Strength and rest will come from being properly equipped and prepared for the task. The things that we learn from Jesus will give us strength *for* the work and strength *as* we work. We will be able to fulfill the Great Commission because He will give us exactly what we need to finish the task. We can go into all the world—beyond our own homes, our own families, and our own neighborhoods—because God can equip us to go beyond. He can multiply and magnify our efforts. When there is rest in our spirits and God-given ability in our beings, we can accomplish the work of difficult tasks. We will even be able to add our God-infused strength to the strength of others. When God is on the other side of the yoke, our burdens will be light. Even though there may be much physical toil, emotional pain, and mental anguish, at the same time there can be peace that passes all understanding, supernatural strength, and fire that burns so brightly in our souls that our physical needs will become secondary to the tasks He has called us to do. Let us burn for Him with light and love in this temporary life, doing things that will matter for all eternity.

Supernatural strength will be needed to get through the difficulties of life and donning God's yoke and God's armor will give us that strength. Since we are engaged in a spiritual battle, we need to do all that we can to stand (see Eph. 6:13). We need to be strong in our spiritual walks, strong in our faith, and gain further strength by standing firm. If we keep the faith, hold fast to the faith, and stay true to the faith—despite what others do and what goes on in the world around us—then we will be strong and we will be at rest. Faithfulness to God and encouragement from Him will grow our strength. We will be able to hear the voice of the Spirit guiding us in the ways in which we should go. We will be able to stand in the freedom wherewith Christ has made us free. When we do this, we will not struggle under burdens of guilt and regret, but instead will have peace. There will be a satisfaction we experience when we have done right and done well. When we have done all for Him, we can wait in anticipation of hearing Him say, "Well done, good and faithful servant."

Strength will come as we look up and move forward. Times may get really tough for us and we will need a place to rest, but one place that we should not rest is in the valley of despair because this will stop our forward progress and cause us to be downcast. In the valley, there are mists and shadows and deep crevasses. The valley floor is far away from the sun, and the crevasses are further still. Here it can be like a cold dungeon with stale air. We should not hide in these places, nor give up the fight while we are in these places, rather, we should look to God for help to bear up under these trials and then move onward and upward. God wants us to be close to Him in high places, out of the gloom and shadows, up where the air is clear and His presence is near, warm, and bright. Aspire to rise victoriously over the low points of life and draw near to Him. Determine to leave behind the fears, failures, regrets, sin, and power that the difficulties wield. See that there is a beautiful mountaintop to climb toward that will lead us up and away from our troubles and closer to Him. We can reach the summit when climbing in His strength. We need to lift up our eyes to where our help will come from and then make our way toward it, toward Him. Our help comes from the Lord, the Maker of heaven and earth (Ps. 121:2).

We can have strong hearts when we are filled with God's hope (see Ps. 31:24). Hoping in Him and what He is going to do—rather than fretting, worrying, or being anxious—will bring rest to us. Hope raises us above the despair that tries to drag us down. We can rest and not be moved because God is our rock, Jesus is our cornerstone, and faith is our firm foundation. We can build our hope on Him because He is a strong stay and a mighty fortress. "I have set the LORD always before me: because he is at my right hand, I shall not be moved. Therefore my heart is glad, and my glory rejoiceth: my flesh also shall rest in hope" (Ps. 16:8–9).

As we move through life, we do not need to be hopeless and paralyzed by fear but instead need to be anchored in God, our hope. We can release the fear and place our hope and trust in Him. If we set the Lord always before us and keep Him at our right hands, then we will be stayed and moored in a strong place. He is where our hope, strength, and rest will come from. I imagine looking over at Him beside me in the yoke, sharing and even bearing all the weight, and I am filled with comfort and hope. The Lord will fight for His people, and we will hold our peace (see Ex.

14:14). And because He fights for us, we can have hope. There is hope all the way around. He is the Victor and the conquering King!

Strength comes from inviting God into every waking moment. The plans do not have to be elaborate but just need to include us and God having time together. There are simple ways to make this time together a reality. Upon waking, we can offer gratitude, commit our days to Him, and ask for His help as we face them. We can pray and praise as we commute to work or as we walk from room to room at home. We can breathe out prayers to Him all throughout our days, in every circumstance, as conflicts arise and as decisions have to be made. We can pray over our meals. We can read His Word during our breaks or in place of some other activity. We can gaze upon the beauty of creation around us and also notice the people He has placed in our paths. We will be able to see His light and His love as we go forward, and then we will be able to reflect it back to the world around us. When we close our eyes to sleep, we can count our blessings. Our spirits will be refreshed and renewed as we invite His presence into our every waking moment. Sleep. Repeat.

Strengthening by God will result in the ability to move powerfully in and for the kingdom of God. His rule and authority in our lives will enable us to accomplish feats we never could on our own. We do not need to be scared to fail, we need to fail to be scared. Fear not! We can achieve more if He is on our sides and we are on His. However, we need to give Him our whole hearts and not just the bare minimums we think we can get by with. Partial surrender is not surrender. We need to ask ourselves the hard question of whose we really are. Have we invited God to be our master, or are we trying to be the masters? Does everything we own belong to Him, and have we given Him free access to use it—or do we keep some, or all, under lock and key, reserved for our uses alone? Will we spend our days for Him, or will we spend them for ourselves? May our answers be that we are going to use all that God has given us and all that He has equipped us with to bring glory to Him. Making our lives living sacrifices and acts of worship will strengthen us. May we each be a strong presence for Him in this world because we have the strength of His presence within us, all the way to our very cores.

CHAPTER 19
Waiting Times and Waiting Rooms

WATCH AND WAIT

The Bible talks about waiting for God, but we find ourselves living in a world where it is difficult for us to do any sort of waiting, even when it is necessary or required of us. We are members and products of the infamous microwave society—we want things *now*. And if we are task-oriented people, too, then the waiting is especially difficult. Sometimes, though, our strength will just have to come through times of waiting where it will appear that we are not doing any moving at all. Every part of who we are needs to learn how to wait on God, and sometimes, it will take all of our strength just to be still and wait. Our ways are not His ways, and we often do not want to make His ways our ways, or at least not in the time frames He has in mind. So, how do we reconcile what we are supposed to do with what we are inclined to do? We need to overcome the challenges and develop disciplines that will assist us with this matter. A great first step is to overcome ourselves. We do this by being overcome with God's Spirit instead.

We need to make sure that we are waiting properly by submitting to the Spirit's promptings. Although we may be disciples who are investing time in the Word, prayer, and fellowship, we may find ourselves outside of God's timelines. We are supposed to walk with God, but we often think He walks too slowly. If we allow ourselves to do so, we can actually grow restless in our reading, our prayer lives, and our church participation. If we allow our restlessness to grow and allow negative thoughts and feelings to fill our hearts and minds, we will begin to resent His ways and timing. This negativity will cause us to head down the path of discontentment. And rather than waiting for Him to fit all the pieces of His plans together, we will allow our dissatisfaction to drive us to come up with other plans. We will grow more and more restless until finally, we run on ahead without Him, searching for someone or something else that will get the job done *now*. Problems will arise from this behavior, though. When we interfere, things will not unfold as He wants them to; they may even be completely destroyed. Also, running on ahead without His hand to help us results in tripping, stumbling, falling, and injury. Restless spirits do not stay on course, nor run or pace the race well.

Our discontent and our restlessness skews our vision and causes us to become impatient with what we perceive as God's delays. We can come up with all kinds of reasons as to why we think God needs to get busy working the way that we want Him to work. Now. I can truly testify to this, especially when He has given me a vision for something that will happen sometime in the future. When I know that He has a task ahead for me, I just want to get busy and get it done. I am eager to do and eager to please, but I am also unprepared and arriving ahead of the race day. God's ways and timing are perfect, while my ways are to run off pell-mell with my shoes only halfway on, if they are on at all. Because of this tendency, I have to deliberately force myself to wait during times that are supposed to be waiting periods for me. I have to allow the details of God's plan to unfold according to His tempo rather than exert my will and try to make things happen prematurely. I have to realize that right now I am supposed to be resting and preparing for what is to come, and beyond realizing it, I need to submit to it.

Our inability to wait for God's timing can cause us to step out hastily and recklessly, but it can also cause us to refrain from stepping out at all. We can get ourselves into uncomfortable and troubling situations when we allow ourselves to be impatient and restless—but also when we allow ourselves to be fearful and hesitant. When we are impatient, we try to plant when it is time to plow, or try to harvest before the crop is fully mature. When we are reckless, we sow the wrong seeds in the wrong fields, or we forget to even sow the seeds. And when we are fearful or hesitant, perhaps we do not even attempt to tend the crops, or else by the time we do finally get to the fields, it is too late. Consequently, all of our ill behaviors get the processes out of order, and under conditions like these, things can no longer come to pass the way they were meant to. Detours have to be taken, courses have to be corrected, and sometimes, irreparable damage is done.

We can see a prime example of such behavior when we look at how the Israelites left God's path for their own shortly after they were delivered from Egypt. God wanted them to enter the Promised Land in a specific way and time, but they did not want to go that route and accomplish what He asked them to do along the way to their destination. Their disobedience then resulted in a very long scenic route that was not very vacation-like (see Num. 32). Unpleasant consequences result when we cannot wait and when we cannot leave well enough alone, but they also result when all we do is wait at a time when God wants us to be moving along.

Our striving and rushing do not make things better for us and the situations; they only make it worse. Our inaction does not lead to any good results either. It is impossible to have peace and rest when we fight what God desires; however, when we surrender our agendas to His bigger and better plans, immeasurable peace will enter our hearts and minds. What He has in mind for us is beyond anything we could ever imagine. His plans and purposes are grand and unfathomable. He sees the end from the beginning. Sometimes, however, we become prideful and think that we deserve certain things. But instead of making our lives in our own images, we should be making them in God's image. Rather than trying to pick up in the middle where we think He left off, we should trust Him. We are currently alive within the times and the bounds that He has appointed for us to live (Acts 17:26). He holds our lives and breaths in His hands; thus, we should trust Him with His plans and timing. We are not called to be restless and press on without Him, we are called to rest and wait patiently *with* Him.

It seems counterintuitive, countercultural, and counterproductive to rest. Resting is the opposite of what we are taught and the opposite of what we normally do. We strive and rush and race—against the clock, against the calendar, against others, and against ourselves. We try to accomplish what we are told to do, what we are pressured to do, and what we are obligated to do. It is good to be productive and responsible—if we are being productive and responsible with the things that God has called us to do, that is.

Our perspectives should be plumbed with God's perspective so that we do not miss the blessings of life, the abundance of life, and the true meaning of life. He gave us our lives for this time and for specific reasons, but if we are focusing on our own pursuits, we are not focusing on His. When we are busy looking at ourselves, we will miss seeing where He wants us to go; we will also miss what He has for us along the way and at our destinations. Also, this self-interest will turn our characters into something less than desirable. We might end up becoming snippy, gruff, angry, impatient, prideful, and grouchily exhausted. Thus, in order to find the treasures that God has for us, we need to defy both our selfish natures and the pressures of society that send us searching for our own treasures. Our motives need to be pure. Our efforts should not be for the purpose of vainglory. King David said that the Lord daily loads us with benefits (Ps. 68:19). This is a wonderful "burden" to have, but we have to choose to accept it. We have to set aside the rush hour so we can have the rest hour. The resting period does not even need to be an hour, though, because rest can come to us at any moment in which we focus upon God and accept the peace and endurance He provides to His children. And nothing can counter that.

When we patiently look to see where God is working and find evidence of His efforts, we will be amazed. We must realize, though, that there will be times when we will not seem to see Him at work. He *is* working, though, for His great and glorious purposes, of which He so graciously allows us to be a part. We do not need to fret and wring our hands with impatience—He is getting the job done whether we can see it or not. We do not need to know the details of the future, we just need to know the God of the past, present, and future, who holds every detail in His hands. We are His workmanship and His masterpieces, created with love and time. He is not only doing things around us, He is doing things in us and through us while we wait on Him. And if we yield to His plans, there will be more productivity. Just as allowing an artist to set the pace and mode for completing a masterpiece results in more beauty, so it is with God. It is better that we allow Him to work in *His* way and at *His* pace rather than us trying to force the style and rush the completion. I don't know about you, but I want Him to do great and beautiful things in my life, all for His glory! Remind me to wait on Him, would you, please?

While we take the time to wait on God, we can become better and stronger disciples. We can grow more in our knowledge of Him, be better equipped for the days ahead, and discover a great and lasting peace for the present. Waiting periods provide a great opportunity to better learn how to seek His face, listen for His voice, pray more, and become more like Him. Waiting times can be times of revelation where we not only learn more about God and *His plans* but also more about ourselves and *our plans*. Waiting will teach us what we are made of and the purpose for which He has made us. We will discover our strengths and honestly face our weaknesses. We will learn what it is that we need to steer clear of, what areas of our characters need to be strengthened, and what specific equipping is needed to get the jobs done at the proper times. As we do the things that He calls us to do in the waiting times, and as we learn the things that He teaches us then, we will truly be ready when He says that it is time for us to go.

ROOM FOR WAITING

No matter where we find ourselves in life, rest can come in the waiting times. It can come in those times we call the desert. It can come in those times we find ourselves in a waiting room. Our waiting rooms may be in hospitals, courtrooms, boardrooms, principal's offices, prayer closets, or even on the other end of the telephone lines. Rest can come when we find ourselves in a holding pattern. It can come when we wait on the edges of our seats. Even when we feel all alone, our minds are dry, and we cannot cry any more tears, we can rest. When our minds wander and when our minds scream, we can rest. When our hearts ache and break and all we can do is cry, we can rest. When our castles crumble and our dreams die, we can rest. We may be waiting for God to do something, or we may be past waiting for God to do something, and yet, we can wait on God. These moments of forced stillness and these moments of pain can be the perfect times to wait on Him. We can wait for Him to enter our hurts, our hearts, our minds, our spirits, and our circumstances. We can wait for His healing balm, His words of direction, and His words of love and comfort. He does come near in our expectation. Listening hearts hear Him. Waiting spirits sense Him. Words we have never heard spoken previously and words He has whispered to us a thousand times over can be heard in the waiting. At the moments we set our burdens down in exchange for what He offers, our waits for peace and rest will end. Do we want what He offers? Will we leave room for waiting?

David had to wait for years to fulfill his calling to become king. During that waiting time—filled with joy, triumph, pain, and danger—he grew closer to God. Do we want to grow closer to God while we wait?

Moses had to wait the majority of his life before his calling even came, before it was time to go and lead God's people. While God was putting everything into place, Moses grew up as the adopted son of Pharaoh's daughter, killed a man and fled the country, married and learned the trade of shepherding in his new country, had children, and reached eighty years old. He had committed a grievous sin that could not be rectified, but he continued to live his everyday life rather than be paralyzed with uncertainty about his future. Do we continue to live while we wait for our futures, or are we distracted because we are too busy longing for the days when we will get to do something great for God like other people are doing? Well, we just need to wait and rest according to His timing and not covet the activities that others are involved in. We need to be at peace with His current plans for us and not complain or worry about whatever else is going on around us. God has a time that is just right for each of us, and it is unlike anyone else's time. And besides, we can do great things for Him now, even while we wait.

Jesus had to wait the longest of anyone to fulfill His calling. His calling to save sinners was given from the foundation of the world but was not fulfilled until just the exact moment that God had planned. Galatians 4:4 tells us that "when the fullness of the time was come, God sent forth his Son." To begin the process of fulfilling His calling, Jesus first had to be born as a human baby. When He neared the age of thirty, His miraculous ministry began. Pieces fell into place as He lived out His days, serving God and serving others, all while waiting for the time to walk to the cross. At the cross, He fulfilled His calling to be the Savior of the world, satisfying the debt of our sin and gaining victory over death and hell. He had waited thousands of years to act on His calling, and when it was finally time, He did it very well! Thank you, Jesus, for the great work that you have done for all humanity—the work that you have done for *me*.

I have seen a slogan on various merchandise, "No Jesus, No Peace. Know Jesus, Know Peace." I think waiting and patience are similarly interdependent: no waiting, no patience; know waiting, know patience. We can allow patience to be developed in our lives while we wait for the time of the harvest. Instead of the waiting times becoming hindrances, they can help carry us further on our ways toward God and toward abundant life. Daniel is a good example of this. He was a faithfully and frequently praying man, but even he had to wait for answers to his prayers (see Dan. 10). While Daniel waited, he could rest confidently in the knowledge that God had heard his prayers and would give an answer. He had learned this knowledge by coming to God in the past and was then able to apply it to his future situations. We, like Daniel, have no need to fret about the future; instead, we can rest in the knowledge that God always keeps His promises. What He has for us *will* come to pass. One day, we *will* be delivered from our waiting rooms. Furthermore, when it is time to leave our waiting rooms, we will have His full blessing. What He has said, He will do. *Not one word* of His will fail. In the meantime, we can learn to watch for what He is up to, look for where His hand is leading, and identify which directions He wants to take our lives. We can become more attuned to His movements and His voice, watching and listening for our invitations to arrive.

Although waiting times can be difficult for us, they can teach us patience and endurance. It is possible to learn to wait without restlessness and even gain benefits in the interim. A lifestyle of waiting on God is more effective, productive, and worthwhile than anything we could do on our own. We can invite His Spirit to fill us, live through us, and enable us to do more than is humanly possible. When we let Him take the lead, anything can be accomplished. Waiting is not a waste because with God nothing is wasted. If we allow Him to help us with our yokes, even during the times when we are in the waiting rooms rather than out in the fields working, there will be peace and rest. His yoke is easy and His burden is light; ours can be too. Hurry up and wait! God has great plans for us!

"NOW WHAT?"

Once we have rested and spent time in a waiting room, what comes next? Is it time to leave now? Time to get busy? In specifics, it all depends on God's plans and timing for us as individuals and on how well we surrender and obey. Just because we have rested and spent time in a waiting room, it does not mean that we are finished doing either of these things. We may need further rest, and we may need to spend more time waiting. We may need to rest *and* work while we are in a waiting room. We may need to fulfill a season right where we are at, or we may need to enter into a new one. It may be time to be poured out, or it may be time for further preparation in order to be able to pour out in the future. The answer to "Now what?" is "Now God." Whatever He determines is best is what we should do next.

There are times when God calls us to work, and there are times when He calls us to rest. He calls us "to do," and He calls us "to be." How do we know which we are to be doing? We can gain some ideas by looking at Jesus's involvement in the lives of His followers. He sent some of them out to work. He called some of them aside to rest. When we look at the lives of Mary and Martha (Luke 10:38–42), we see that sometimes the decision remains with us. Mary intentionally set aside the work of entertaining houseguests in order to be taught at the feet of Jesus. Her sister, Martha, busily entertained the guests and expected Mary's help. Mary ignored the expectations and demands of her sister and moved on to something better, something that would benefit her eternally rather than just for that moment. She was acquiring something that was needful and something that could never be taken from her. There are seasons when we need to be like Mary and just sit at Jesus's feet. There are other times when we need to be like Martha, attending to the tasks at hand, up and about serving those around us, busy at that very moment. Dinner does not serve itself, after all. Yet, if it is not time for dinner to go on the table, then we should not be putting it there. So, in order to decipher the difference of whether we should be doing or being, we need to know the season into which God has called us. That day, Jesus said Mary had made the better choice. Whatever time it is for us according to God, that is the schedule we need to be following, all the while abiding in Him.

We can do the work while we are resting in Him, and sometimes the work that He has for us is simply to rest. During our times of rest, God can pour into us, refresh our spirits, and equip us for the things that we will do as servants. There will come a time, however, when we will need to get up and get busy, but we will never have to stop being in His presence, learning at His feet. With pure motives, prayerful attitudes, and the power of the Holy Spirit, we can accomplish the work He gives us to do and yet be present with Him at the same time, finding rest in our spirits.

It is important to get up from His feet to work because if we only rest, then we are not fulfilling the Great Commission. If we were only meant to be sitting at His feet all of the time, then we would be in front of His throne in heaven. We see by Jesus's example and teaching that there is a purpose for which believers are put here on this earth: we are to be salt and light. But if we are at home hiding in our prayer closets or have our noses in our devotional books every waking moment, then we are not helping the lost to come to Him. Jesus was not always in the synagogue listening to and reading the words of God, nor was He always in a quiet place praying—Jesus came to serve. Jesus sent His disciples into the world just as God had sent Him (see Luke 10:1; John 17:18). Furthermore, at the time of His ascension, He let His followers know what they were to continue doing during His absence: they were to go into all the world and serve (see Matt. 28:18–20; Mark 16:15). For those of us who follow Him now, there are things that we need to be doing in His absence. There is work to accomplish until He is once again present. Jesus came to serve and to give His life as a ransom for many, and if we are truly following His example, serving will be what we do too. May we come and go, not as we please, but as He pleases.

The two greatest commandments He has given us are to love Him and to love our neighbors. One way in which we can show our love is to serve both Him and them. One of our acts of service should be to carry the burdens of others, no matter if they live near to us or far away. All people are our neighbors, so our view and focus need to extend beyond the four walls in which we live. Jesus did not live in a microcosm—He lived for the entire world—He died for it, too. He carried the physical and spiritual burdens of people, and as His imitators, we must also do it. We are His yokefellows and are co-laboring with God (1 Cor. 3:9), and part of the work we do is His work of caring for others. And amazingly, when we serve others, we are actually serving Him (see Matt. 25:31–40).

We all carry heavy burdens in life, whether we show them to the world or not. Since this is the case, we need to realize that others need our help. We ought to look intently with both our physical and spiritual eyes to discern what they truly need. We need to look past *our* pain and into *their* pain so that we can bring them hope. We were not put on this earth to serve ourselves—we are here to serve God and others with love. Galatians 6:2 tells us that when we are bearing one another's burdens, we are fulfilling the law of Christ, the law of love. People need us to serve them with God's love and also encourage them on His behalf. We can bring them His comfort as they walk along the difficult roads of life. And because God is laboring with us, the impacts of our efforts will be multiplied. This is what we do while we wait and while we work.

CHAPTER 20

"Yes," for the Win

QUESTIONS AND ANSWERS

What will we do about the questions that fill our hearts and minds? What will we do about the questions that have been presented to us as we have investigated God's extraordinary invitations? We have many questions about God, and we want answers, but the truth is that we will never understand everything because He is God and we are not. Despite this limited human understanding, there are some important questions that can and should be answered:

1. *Why is it important to come to Jesus?* If we want to go to heaven, first we have to come to Jesus. He is the only way to the Father. If we do not accept Him, then we have accepted a death sentence—eternal separation from Him (Matt. 25:41).

2. *Where can we come to Him?* To come to Jesus means that we have to go to where He is. We have to take the path that He has determined we must take. This path leads us to the cross where He sacrificed His life for us. This is where we believe and receive His righteousness to cover our sin.

3. *When can we come to Him?* We do not have to wait for a particular time. We do not have to be well-organized and prepared. We do not have to clean ourselves up first. He will meet us wherever we are at in life when we choose to come to Him. We can come now because "now is the accepted time; behold, now is the day of salvation" (2 Cor. 6:2).

We can take a step toward Jesus from anywhere, at any time. We can come while sitting in church, sitting at our desks at work, sitting in the privacy of our own homes, or from anywhere else we happen to be. The stepping forward can take place as soon as we realize the need to come. In that moment, the surrounding circumstances do not matter. It does not matter what we have or do not have. It does not matter who we are or who we are not. Moses was in the desert shepherding. Some of the disciples were working on their fishing nets. Samuel was in bed for the night. Paul was traveling to another city, intent on bringing harm to Christians. The thief was dying on a cross for his crimes. The man with a sick child came out of his house to find Jesus. The palsied man came down through the roof. All of these people, whoever they were, whatever they were doing, came toward God.

I took my first step toward Jesus and His salvation while sitting in a church pew as an eight-year-old. I heard Him call to my heart, and I came, never moving from the pew but totally moving in my heart and spirit. I took another step toward Jesus for help and rescue while I lay in my sickbed. I took a step into a new calling of ministry while I sat at my dining room table. I took a step into an incredible awareness of His presence while I was walking in a tree nursery. Each of these "steps" led into amazing journeys with Him that continue to impact me today.

I will share a few details with you just to give you an idea of what happened when I came. My salvation changed and influenced my entire life, and I would not be who I am today without it. This became the foundation for how I live my life. I am still alive today because I came to Him for rescue. I am writing this book as a facet of the ministry He gave me. And the walk in the tree nursery was a profound experience that pervaded my being and ingrained a memory in me that still fills me with awe. I was at a women's retreat that was being held at a historic tree nursery in August 2006. It was a beautiful place with a large variety of trees and a creek running through the property. I went out for a walk at the close of the retreat to look around the property, and this led to a time and experience unlike any other I had ever known. It was at this time when I experienced true rest. While my feet walked the earth, I took a step into His throne room to worship, and my heart composed a song. I came to God yet never moved from my place amongst the pines.

It would be wonderful to be able to feel that again, to capture that moment and not let go of it. But that is not how life works in the physical realm. We have to get back to being busy. Time passes, and we can never recreate moments exactly as they were. Despite this reality, however, we can always enter into rest spiritually if we are seeking to find our rest in Him. I have taken many specific steps toward Him over the years, but I have also set my heart to move in His direction each day.

4. *How do we come to Him?* The answer to this question is both simple and easy: all that we do is come. We just need to take the first step and move toward Him; it is as easy as that. Does it sound too good to be true? It is too good, and it is also true! Jesus takes us just as we are, whether we are a mess or whether we have it all together. We may be filled with doubt and ask how it is even possible to come to Jesus when we are so broken. We have sins in our pasts, we have current sins, and we may have already made plans for sin in our futures. But these impossible situations do not keep us from the reality of the possible. We can come with confidence because He will receive us. His invitation is open to all.

When we are weak and wavering, He is strong and sure. When we are blind and lost, He is sight and found. He has everything we need. He *is* everything we need. He will complete us as we complete the simple task of inviting Him into our lives. This is how we come to Him. We are welcome here. We will not be turned away. There is no risk, and there is no pain. This invitation will not hurt us—it will heal us. Come. Take the step toward God. Find love, forgiveness, and the help needed to live life. There are no barriers to coming other than our disbelief and refusals to come. Break down those barriers and step into a relationship with God, for now and for all eternity. Come now, and come quickly, because He came for us and is coming again soon.

GIVING OUR ANSWER

Remember, one small step toward God will cause Him to draw near to us. No matter how long or how short our journeys, they begin when we take the first step. Will we take it? Will we come? Will we say "Yes," and then choose to go? Will we go past the crowds to Him, past the righteous, past the naysayers, past the obligations, past the family expectations, past the physical restrictions, past our pasts, past our lifestyles of sin, go past it all and come to Him? I hope that we will. I hope that we will go past anything that lies between us and Him, not just this once, but every day.

We should each take a moment to look at where we are right now and where we are heading. We can come to Him whether we are on the mountaintop or in the valley. We can come whether we have it all together or it is falling all apart. We can come whether we are experiencing great joy or deep sorrow. We can come whether we have traveling companions or are all alone. Whatever the circumstances, we can come to Him and rest during our journeys, and then continue on, with Him by our sides.

Will it be worth it to respond favorably to God's invitations? Yes! Most definitely, yes! We will not even need to exercise a trial period to find out if it will be worth it because we can know beforehand that it is going to be. He is trustworthy, and His love does not disappoint. This world and this current life are not all there is; there is more to come. There is eternity to come. We need an eternal focus, eyes that see past the reality of now. Jesus offers us an invitation to eternal life so that we may benefit in having a relationship with Him in heaven. There is no pressure or obligation to accept His invitation—all that He does is make the offer. The choice is completely up to us. He will come into our lives if we answer yes when He knocks (Rev. 3:20), and then His answer to us will be admittance into heaven.

The Bible tells us that Jesus is "*the* way, *the* truth, and *the* life" (John 14:6, emphasis mine). He alone is always truthful and reliable. He alone gives abundant life and eternal life. He is life itself. There is knowledge to be gained here, and we simply need to make the decision to follow through with what we have learned. We have to decide where we go from here. I do not presume to have all the answers, but I do have *the* Answer. I know the way that I am going, and I invite you to join me—I am going the way of Jesus.

This is no ordinary invitation that has been extended to you—*Jesus* has invited you! I am inviting you too, so consider yourself doubly invited! This invitation is to your eternal destiny and to eternity itself. The God of the universe, the creator of all things, is asking you to be with Him forever. Great thought, planning, and preparation have gone into this. It is so extremely important that it was planned before the foundation of the world. And as Jesus prayed before His crucifixion, He prayed for those who would believe on His name (see John 17:20). He stretched out His arms in love when He died on the cross, and He still holds them open now, waiting to welcome you into His eternal embrace. All that you have to do is RSVP and say you will come.

At times, invitations can make us feel pressured, but know that this invitation to come to God is completely your decision. There is no pressure upon you to act; you have free will, a free choice. But please understand, the declination of the invitation, the no that you give, will result in quite a loss for you; nevertheless, it is your choice. I urge you to choose life, but the choice is yours. Just as Moses told the Israelites that they could choose between life and death (see Deut. 30:19), so I tell you. God has set these same two choices before you. You can choose to spend eternity with Him forever or else choose to spend it separated from Him. The Bible tells us that whoever believes on Him is not condemned, but he who does not believe on Him is condemned already (John 3:18). Jesus did not come into the world to condemn, He came to save. Please accept that He did this for you; let Him save you. RSVP and let Him know that you want to accept His invitation to eternal life.

This decision is important to take care of because seconds are ticking off of the minutes of our lives. None of us is guaranteed tomorrow or even the next breath. We cannot see into the future and do not know when the time of the invitation will end; thus, it is wise to act now while we have the opportunity. Right now, we can see that the invitation has been going on hour after hour, day after day, year after year, but we are told that one day it will stop. This invitation of a lifetime will only come to us during our lifetimes; thus, we can only respond within our lifetimes. No one else can make the choice for us. Please join those of us who have already sent in our RSVPs. Spend all eternity in the presence of the loving Almighty God, King of the universe.

We make time for all sorts of things, but making time for God is the most important of all. He could have kept a schedule too busy for us, busy being the King of the universe, but instead He stepped down and gave people His time and even His very life. Jesus spent many days toiling on this earth rather than enjoying the glory of heaven and the company of His Father, and then He suffered an agonizing death on the cross in order to purchase our redemption. Do we believe this? Do *you* believe this?

Imagine that you have received a written invitation from God, calling you to a most glorious event. The invitation tells you the who, what, when, where, why, and how, as well as the method of RSVP. The venue is heaven. The host is God Himself. The occasion is eternal life. The time is soon. The dress code is the righteousness of Jesus. Things to bring are praise and thanksgiving as you enter the gates. Oh, one more thing, you do not have to *imagine* that you have received a written invitation from God with all of the aforementioned things listed within it because a *real* invitation has already been given to you in the form of the Word of God, the Bible! He also displayed His invitation to you in the sacrifice of Jesus Christ! How will you respond to this amazing invitation? This is a question that only you can answer. Please do not forget to RSVP.

CHAPTER 21
Awaiting the Big Day

People have asked questions of God in regard to His coming. In Psalm 101:2 (NKJV), King David asked, "Oh, when will You come to me?" What is the answer to this question? Although no one can tell us when He will come, we can rest assured that He has done some coming and is *still going to* do some coming! And it is going to be quite the coming indeed! Psalm 50:3 says, "Our God shall come," and indeed, He will come. God's purpose for time was fulfilled when Jesus came to die for us, and His purpose for eternity will be fulfilled when Jesus comes again. The time of that return is getting closer every day, every moment!

Jesus taught His disciples to pray that His kingdom would come (Matt. 6:10). Which kingdom are you and I praying for today, and in which kingdom are we choosing to live? Are we dwelling in the kingdom of God, where there is rest and peace, where He provides all that we need, or are we dwelling in the kingdom of the world, chasing around after all that glitters and all that we want? Are we living for ourselves or living for Him? There is a banquet coming, and Jesus has invited us to dine with Him. We have all been given the opportunity to come so that the wedding feast in His kingdom will be furnished with guests. Will we choose to join Him in the celebration? Will we be ready when the time of the marriage feast arrives? He will come as a groom to get His bride. Will we join Him in His kingdom or stay behind in our own?

We know He came in the past. We know He is coming in the future. But what do we know about His coming in the interim, in the present? He definitely comes, and we can definitely experience Him! Some of the ways He shows Himself are signs, wonders, miracles, gifts of the Spirit, visions, dreams, creation, His Word, and the moving of the Holy Spirit. Sometimes, He comes to us in subtle ways and other times, in dramatic ways. He comes at times when things are fine and at times when it seems all hope is lost.

Sometimes God will show up during our storms in ways that we do not expect and in ways that we never imagined. In the account given in John 6:15–21, the disciples were in a boat, heading to Capernaum. As they were making their way in the dark, there was a windstorm, and the waves were rising. The disciples were toiling in rowing when suddenly they saw Jesus coming toward them, walking on the waves in the midst of the storm. They were afraid, but as He came, He told them not to be. When they realized it was Him, they happily brought Him into the boat, and immediately they were at the shore of their destination. There are some truths to be gleaned from this story. Jesus came to be with His followers. He came during a storm. He demonstrated His power. He performed miracles. He spoke words of peace. He removed fear from the situation. He took them safely to their destination. The disciples had a choice: to continue being afraid or to receive assurance during a fearful time by willingly receiving Jesus into the boat. They chose to believe it was Him and accepted Him into their circumstance. Because they invited Him in, they were not left on their own to flounder about and drown. They were rescued by His mighty hand and helped onward to their destination.

Mark 4:37–39 tells of another storm that the disciples encountered. While the storm raged, Jesus was sleeping through it, right there in the boat with them. When they woke Him and accusingly asked whether or not He cared that they were perishing, He got up and stilled the storm. When Jesus spoke the words "Peace, be still," there was not just calm, "there was a great calm" (v. 39). He then asked the disciples why they were so fearful and why they had no faith. We find ourselves in the same boat at times, going through storms without our faith, not recognizing or remembering the power of God right there beside us. But He is the same God today as He was then, and He can bring peace and great calm to our storms. He can give incomprehensible peace because He is the Prince of

Peace. He rules over all creation, and He can give us the faith that we need to live in it and survive its storms, whatever types they may be.

We may be in trouble and afraid. We may be in the middle of a raging sea on a dark and stormy night, tossed by waves and blown by wind, but Jesus can come to us on the water, above the storm and unaffected by it, because He has all the power. Other times, He may come to us in subtle ways as He did to the woman at the well, to speak with us and take care of our spiritual needs. But whether His entrance is dramatic or subtle, or in His time frame rather than ours, either way the truth remains: He comes! Regardless of how He enters the scene, He will receive our doubting questions and allow us to rise in the storms and conquer them with faith. And furthermore, He will be with us as we travel to the next place in life and also be there when we stop at the well for rest and a drink of living water.

Jesus's ultimate coming will be His second coming, and it is not going to be subtle! He told people that one day they would see Him coming again (Mark 13:26). Isaiah prophesied about His coming: "And in that day there shall be a root of Jesse, which shall stand for an ensign of the people; to it shall the Gentiles seek: and his rest shall be glorious" (Isa. 11:10). James tells us that the coming of the Lord draws near (James 5:8). We can read many more words from the Bible about His coming, and we can also open our eyes to see the signs happening all around us that Jesus prophesied would happen. There are still some things that need to take place before His arrival, but He told us that when we begin to see these precursory events happen, we should lift up our heads because our redemption draws nigh (Luke 21:28). In Revelation 22:20, Jesus said, "Surely I come quickly," and John replied by saying, "Amen. Even so, come, Lord Jesus." I am repeating John's words with my own lips! How exciting to think that our own eyes will one day look upon the King who has come!

What God purposes *will* come to pass. He has said that He is coming back, so He will. He does not lie and will not go back on His word (see Num. 23:19). He always keeps His promises, and no one can thwart what He purposes. "For yet a little while, and he that shall come will come, and will not tarry" (Heb. 10:37). The Bible tells us that "the day of the Lord will come as a thief in the night" (2 Pet. 3:10). It will be quick and catch many off guard; thus, we should not toss His invitation onto our to-do piles, making plans to get around to it eventually. Because we cannot know if we will live to take our next breaths or if He will suddenly arrive, it is absolutely essential to be ready. Today. Now. As the old adage says, "Do not put off until tomorrow what you can do today." We can apply those words to this instance as very sound advice. We are here today, living and breathing, so we still have the opportunity to act upon our RSVP. Will He see our faith in Him when He comes looking for it (Luke 18:8)? We need to take hold of the opportunity He invites us to and reply with a yes. He is the door to life. Walk through it.

WHILE WE WAIT

I believe that Jesus's words "Come unto me" (Matt. 11:28) carry a message that we need to learn for ourselves and then share with others around us, both believers and unbelievers alike. Believers need to come so that they can be filled and equipped. The lost need to come so that they can be saved. When those of us who have already said yes to the invitation are busy inviting others to accept it, we are helping the Host to get the word out by literally getting *the Word* out. We are laborers sent forth into the field of souls, and we all have stations to occupy: some sow, some water, and then God brings the growth. God reconciled us to Himself through Christ and has now given us the ministry of reconciliation. We are His ambassadors, as though He were pleading through us (see 2 Cor. 5:19–20). We have been tasked to share God's love with a lost and dying world. People need to hear the message of the gospel so they will gain an understanding that Jesus came to die for them. The church must go. *We* must go. Souls are waiting for the good news that we possess, some of whom have heard it previously and some never at all. Hearts need to be prepared for Jesus's return, and while we wait for Him, we have the opportunity to help people prepare.

How many unbelievers know that they need to come to Jesus? They may intellectually know who Jesus is, what He did, and that Christians do things with and for Him, but do they know that His call extends to them? Do they know that God is not willing that any should perish but instead desires that all people be saved and come to the knowledge of the truth? We have a mission to accomplish, and souls are waiting for us to do it. We have a responsibility to go, so we should come to God first to get prepared to do so. May this be the mission of our mission: to come to the God of love so we can take the love of God to the world.

MISSION OF LOVE

We have been invited to live and to love. How will we go about doing that? How will we accomplish this mission? When people asked Jesus what work they should do in order to be working the works of God, He told them that the work of God was to believe on Him (Jesus) whom God had sent (John 6:28–29). Later, Peter tells us that we should not be living the rest of our days in the lusts of the flesh but be living them for God's will (1 Pet. 4:2). So, if we were to compose mission statements for our lives, what would they say? What should they say? Are they based on what God has asked us to do? Are we working the works of God? Do we need help getting started? Are we thinking that God has never told us what we should be doing? The truth is, God has already told all of us what we should be doing. To begin with, He has asked us to love Him with all of our hearts, souls, minds, and strength, and then He has asked us to love our neighbors as we love ourselves. When we are following these two commandments, we are doing His work and living in His will. When we are following this basic tenet of love, we have begun to fulfill our mission, the one that exists because of His great love for people.

As we live out our mission statements, we should make sure they are aligned to bring God glory. He has designed life so that each of us spends our days uniquely, but we are all supposed to glorify Him. We have many decisions to make as we pass from birth to death, and we need to consider the impacts of each one. We have control over many things and no control over many others. For those things that we can control, we should be growing them into positive and lasting legacies. Psalm 90:12 tells us to number our days and to seek God's help in spending them as we should. Time is limited, so we need to be aware of how we spend our minutes and make sure we are spending them wisely. Since we do not know the lengths of our lifespans, we should live in such ways as if today is our last day; this much we can control. We need to focus on the meaning and purpose of the lives God has given us so that we can shape each day into legacies that will honor Him. We need to be active throughout life because now is not the time to permanently rest—that is for the time of eternity, when our work here on earth is finished. For now, we need to be working toward that final day. We begin the work by choosing salvation; we continue it by working and resting as He leads us. This is how we shape legacies that glorify Him.

What if we are not doing well at building legacies that glorify Him? What if we are not loving others? What if we have other issues too? What about the prodigal children that we are known to be? What if we have wandered away from what we know to be right? What if we have left our forms of godliness, have left the beauty that could have been ours, and have been content with bare heads instead of crowned ones (see Lam. 5:16)? Although we were created to be a little lower than the angels, to be crowned by Him with glory and honor, and to be set over the works of His hands (Heb. 2:7–8), there are times when we trade in the jewels for broken rocks, the gold for clay, and the protection of God for self-reliance. We want deliverance from someone who cannot deliver us, just as the Israelites trusted in the army of Egypt rather than the power of God. We look for political and social rest rather than God's rest. We want direction for our aimless wandering and provision for what we lack. We seek life but find death because we look for life in the wrong places. There is hope, though, because there is Jesus. He can deliver us and give us life because He died and rose again to defeat Satan, the power of death, and the bondage of sin (see Heb. 2:14–15). We just need to turn to Him. If we have left His side, we simply come back. We stop willfully disobeying and running. We come home. We know we are prodigals, and He knows we are prodigals; there is nothing to hide. He is the Father who awaits the return of His prodigal children so that He can welcome them home and celebrate their return. Let us not scorn and run away from such great love.

We have heard stories about people with cancer or other serious illnesses who "began to live" when they saw that their time was short. We have also heard stories about people who almost died in serious accidents and then changed how they lived for the better. All of these people had a change in their perspectives of life. They saw something they had not previously seen, and subsequently, made adjustments to how they were living. We can learn from their experiences. We can follow their examples to live intentionally; however, we do not need to have poor medical prognoses or near-death experiences in order to start living this way. God has given each of us a life to develop; let us be doing it in the best and most productive way, right now, today. Let's start really living, and living for Him—until He says it is time for us to rest. All for love. All for Him.

FULFILLING OUR MISSION

If God was to ask us to do anything, how many of us would immediately and willingly do it? What does this show us about the conditions of our hearts and the focus and pursuits of our lives? At times, rather than following through with God's plans and being blessed in the process, we make our own plans, and then ask God to bless them. We want to be in control, and reap all of the rewards. We want to run the show, and get all of the applause. The Bible tells us, though, that "the steps of a good man are ordered by the LORD" (Ps. 37:23). God wants us to join Him and become part of the plans that He has for our lives. Sometimes, these plans are going to necessitate making some adjustments in how we are living. How will we handle this? We will have to honestly answer the question of whether we truly want to surrender and have Him order our steps. Sometimes, we will get tired of obeying, going, and doing, and may even make excuses to avoid these things. At times, it will be very difficult to surrender to God's leadership because we may selfishly want to take a day off from obedience, or we may simply view the task as too difficult. But taking up His cross is supposed to be a daily task, and it is supposed to be about living for Him. We will have to learn how to deal with the issues of our human natures, the same as other believers have had to do.

Let's examine the lives of a few giants of the faith to see how they handled this issue. God asked these people to do some things and follow His plans, but they had excuses about why they could not or did not want to surrender. Some people would consider their excuses to be disqualifications for leadership positions or even other lesser roles, but God did not see things that way. These giants all lived for themselves at one time, but once they surrendered to what God was asking them to do, they were greatly used by Him. By the way, God can greatly use us too. We can add our names and excuses right after theirs and then promptly surrender!

EXCUSES OF THE DAY

Moses had some very large excuses that he could present:

- He was a murderer who would be going back to the scene of the crime (Exod. 2, 3).
- He said no one would believe that God had sent him to lead the Israelites out of slavery in Egypt (Exod. 4:1).
- He had a slow tongue and was not good at speaking (Exod. 4:10).
- He suggested that God should send someone else (Exod. 4:13).

But despite Moses's background and his counterarguments against a future tasking, God chose him anyway. God had created Moses, so He understood Moses's limitations. He knew what was needed and stepped in to help. He equipped Moses by showing him how to perform miracles, and He sent Aaron to be his spokesman and assistant. With God's help, Moses successfully became the leader and deliverer of the Israelites.

David had some large excuses that could interfere with his career:

- He called himself a worm (Ps. 22:6).
- He was a man of war and had taken many lives (1 Chron. 28:3).

- He had committed adultery and then arranged for the woman's husband to be killed in order to cover up the affair (2 Sam. 11).
- He ordered a census to be taken that God did not want him to take (2 Sam. 24).

But despite David's spotty past and a future that would look the same, God chose him anyway. David was the greatest king of Israel, and eventually, Jesus was born through his royal bloodline. David became known as a man after God's own heart. His songs and prayers that are recorded in the Bible are still touching lives today.

Paul had a list of excuses that could disqualify him from service:

- He had been a persecutor of Christians (Acts 7–9).
- People feared him as a persecutor, even after his conversion (Acts 9:26).
- He had persecuted Jesus (Acts 9:4).
- He called himself the chief of sinners (1 Tim. 1:15).

But despite Paul's ungodly past and his current route to commit more atrocities, God chose him anyway. First Corinthians 1:1 tells us that Paul was chosen to be an apostle by the will of God. Paul became the greatest missionary of the faith in the early years of the church. He traveled more than any other and had audiences with Jews, Gentiles, prison guards, and kings.

And then there is me. I am not a giant of the faith, but I am a person of excuses nonetheless.

- I am too busy.
- I do not know how to do this.

- I have failed in the past.
- I am walking in my sin nature at the moment.

But despite who I am, and regardless of who I am not, God has chosen me anyway. He has called me to particular tasks, and He is going to do great things in and through my life. How do I know? He is God and that is what He does.

MAKING A STATEMENT

Even though we have giant "excuses of the day," our surrenders can be greater than our excuses, and thus, our impacts in life will be greater. Instead of forcing our hands and commanding our work times and break times, we can trust that He will give us rest when it is time to rest, strength when it is time to work, and desire in our hearts to be obedient when we ask for His help to be so. Does this resonate with us and our situations? With our approaches to daily living? And how are our response times? All things are possible with God working through our surrendered lives.

We can overcome the excuses that rise up against our callings, and it is possible to prevent them from obstructing our relationships with God. One thing we can do is to be sure we have asked for forgiveness for anything that needs it. Another thing we can do is to have a time of introspection and ask ourselves the hard questions, such as why we do not want to obey what He is asking of us and why we are harboring negative emotions. Once we answer the questions, we can then act on the answers. For example, if we realize that another believer has an offense against us, we need to first go and be reconciled, and then come and offer our gifts to the Lord (see Matt. 5:23–24). If we regard iniquity in our hearts, God will not hear our prayers (see Ps. 66:18). We need to do what we know are the right things to do (see James 4:17). We need to do what is right in God's eyes rather than what is right in our own eyes (see Judg. 17:6). I could continue on with this list because there are many issues that we have to address in life and many sins with which we struggle. But whatever our particular issues and sins happen to be, it is critical that we take time to deal with them because disobedience takes us out of fellowship with God and keeps us out of it. Separation from God will hinder our callings, but connection to Him will allow us to overcome anything that could be an excuse.

Obedience is important and necessary for followers of God. We must do the works of God as we are called to do them. What good are words of loyalty if we do not put them into action? Why be hearers only and not doers? Where is the good in that? What are the benefits? We should take time to think about who occupies the driver's seats and where these vehicles are headed. We may need to scoot over to the passenger's sides, admitting that we were in the wrong seats. We may have some confessing to do about trying to be our own bosses and neglecting the work that God asked us to do while we were busy being bossy. We need to confess if we find that we have been ruling the day rather than allowing God to do it. His Spirit is available to help us live obedient lives and also overcome our shortcomings. May we let Him be the director of our steps so they will be obedient ones.

If we come to Him with hearts that have been set right, and if we take up the cross He is asking us to take up, then we will accomplish our missions, great things will happen for the kingdom, and we will represent Him well. It is important that Christians are accurate bearers of the truth, especially since Satan is working to deceive people. People will stay away if they misunderstand or are deceived, but if they see the power of God's love through our obedient lives, they may be drawn to Him. We cannot force their decisions, but we must provide them with the opportunities to make them. Our surrenders to God will impact the lives of others. For this reason, it is important that we present true pictures of God by how we live our lives.

In essence, our missions are fulfilled based upon the amount and timing of our surrenders. Are we going to give up our self-wills in exchange for the will of God, and are we going to do it at the moment He assigns us missions? Jesus fulfilled the mission that God gave Him at the exact time God wanted Him to fulfill it. As He was preparing to go to the cross, one of the things He did was surrender His will to His Father and accept His Father's will instead (Luke 22:42). I believe that Jesus received peace through that exchange, as evidenced by His reactions to the arrest, torture, and accusations, and also by His response as He hung there dying. He did not resist, argue, or accuse; instead, He was at times silent, at other times stating the truth, and at another time asking God to forgive those who were doing this to Him. If Jesus could surrender under such extenuating circumstances, what should we be able to do in our comparatively mundane lives? Jesus declared His mission statement when He said He came to do God's will. He eventually fulfilled that statement by being offered as a sacrifice for all of us, completing His life's work (see Heb. 10:5–10). This knowledge gives me peace and strength, and I will gain even more when I, too, surrender my will to God the Father and complete *my* mission.

Jesus had the opportunity and power of choice to either come to earth and die on a cross or stay in His glorious heaven. He had the power of choice to lay down His life and take it up again. He did not have to do the Father's will but chose to do it because of His great love for us. He was selfless. And because He died, there is now remission for sins. We can have boldness to enter into the holiest by the blood of Jesus, as He is the new and living way that has been consecrated for us, through His flesh, given for us (Heb. 10:18–20). We no longer need to come to a priest and a temple year after year to offer animal sacrifices—we only have to come to Jesus once, and accept that He shed His blood as the payment for our sins. He serves as our high priest and ever lives to make intercession for us (Heb. 7:25). Our acceptance of His sacrifice allows us to come into the presence of God and into the eternal life of heaven. We have the power to choose Him as He chose us.

Jesus lived up to His mission statement by doing all that the Father gave Him to do. He accomplished great things for the kingdom even though He did not preach to everyone in the world, did not heal everyone who needed healing, and did not go everywhere that could be visited. He did not try to do more than He was assigned. In fact, at times, He left the scene in search of solitude, even while needy people were clamoring for His attention. He did not fulfill every request that came His way. He did not stay busy for the sake of busyness. He focused on the work that the Father had given Him to do, and He accomplished it (John 9:4). He did not stray from His mission. There were times to say no, times to rest, times to be alone, and times to pray intensely. His life is an example for us. He showed us that we *will not* and *should not* be everything that everyone expects us to be. This means that we will not become involved in every crisis, even though we may feel sympathy or are capable of doing something fitting in those circumstances. We will not give to every cause, organization, or missionary that asks for our financial support. We will not be involved every time there is an activity. We will not be awake 24/7 waiting for the phone to ring. There are boundaries to our callings and limits to our abilities and resources. We are not God and never will be. We cannot be all and do all—but we can *be something* and *do something* as He leads us. Our missions are possible.

I once composed a mission statement to express my purpose for living. My statement was "It's all about you, God." But as I thought on it some more, I decided to revise it to "Always, it's all about you, God." Remembering that it is always about Him is what causes me to rest and also what causes me to serve. This is what guides me, molds me, and energizes me. This is what drives me, comforts me, and brings things into focus for me. This is what gives me peace and courage. This is my mission statement *for life!*

I have gone a step further and expanded my mission statement into prompts that remind me how to live. These are ways for me to "be" in life that will reflect a focus on Him and a determination to live in my purpose.

- Be His so He can be yours. Give Him all authority in your life.
- Be coming so you can go and do great things for Him.
- Be listening so you can hear His voice.
- Be dead to yourself daily so Jesus can live in you.
- Be hidden in Christ with God. Let Him be your refuge.
- Be hungry for His filling. Let your meat be to do His will.
- Be thirsty for Him and draw from His depths.
- Be strong in Him. Let His strength infuse you and carry you.
- Be lost in His love and let the desires of this world be lost on you.
- Be a treasure seeker. Seek to store up eternal treasures.

- Be still and know that He is God. Be still when He asks you to be still, and be active when He asks you to be active. Do not seek to be involved in the things that He has not asked you to do, neither be inactive in the things that He has called you to do. Be still in your soul and be anxious for nothing.
- Be on a sure path that leads to life, guided by His hand and His light. Do not be misguided by the things of this world, your desires, or Satan.
- Be extraordinary for Jesus as He has been extraordinary for you!

We all have a common purpose of sharing His love and leaving His legacy to impact future generations, but each of us also has a unique purpose to fulfill. We need to discern God's will for our lives and then act on that. Working hard does not necessarily indicate that we are accomplishing God's will for our lives. Activity for activity's sake is a pointless waste of time and takes us in meaningless directions. Trying to keep up appearances is deceitful. Trying to match what others are doing is unwise. We should be as busy as the Holy Spirit directs us to be and not be looking to anyone else but Him to determine His plans for our lives. Philippians 3:14 says, "I press toward the mark for the prize of the high calling of God in Christ Jesus." This high calling is an upward calling, and is my goal, my aim, and my mission. I am pressing on in that direction so that I will be ready when the invitation is issued to leave this life behind and enter into eternal life. Rest is coming for the people of God, and one day, we will cease from our labors as God did from His (see Heb. 4:9–10); for now, though, we are to go about the business of living for God in *this life*. Thus, I still have work to do. And I hope when He calls me to come to my eternal rest, I will be able to say that I completed the work that He gave me to do.

There will be a time of great celebration someday, when it is time to dwell with God forever. There will be much rejoicing as believers meet the most amazing host ever, the God of the universe, who loves them. I will be among this number, and I hope that you will be also! Yes, this is a most extraordinary invitation, and I am eagerly awaiting the big day! How about you? Please do not forget to RSVP!

NOTES

CHAPTER ONE

1   Hebrews 13:5 quoted from the NKJV.

CHAPTER THREE

1   *Strong's Concordance*, s.v. "come," accessed August 16, 2016, http://www.biblehub.com/greek/1205.htm.
2   *Roget's 21ˢᵗ Century Thesaurus*, 3ʳᵈ ed., s.v. "invite," accessed August 27, 2016, http://www.thesaurus.com/browse/invite.
3   *Roget's 21ˢᵗ Century Thesaurus*, 3ʳᵈ ed., s.v. "command," accessed August 27, 2016, http://www.thesaurus.com/browse/command.

CHAPTER ELEVEN

1   This quote is displayed on various items in the marketplace, such as plaques, clocks, and calendars.

CHAPTER TWELVE

1   For a study of the rabbinical meaning of "take my yoke upon you" from Matthew 11:29, see *Gill's Exposition of the Entire Bible*, accessed March 16, 2016, biblehub.com/commentaries/gill/matthew/11.htm.
2   *Strong's Concordance*, s.v. "easy," accessed August 16, 2016, http://www.biblehub.com/greek/5543.htm.
3   HELPS™Word-studies, Helps Ministries, Inc., 1987, 2011, accessed in conjunction with *Strong's Concordance*, s.v. "easy," accessed August 16, 2016, http://www.biblehub.com/greek/5543.htm.

CHAPTER SIXTEEN

1   Psalm 8:4.

You may contact the author via her Facebook page,
via email at franceestrain@gmail.com, or
via her website at https://franceestrain.com.

CPSIA information can be obtained
at www.ICGtesting.com
Printed in the USA
FSHW020058201118
53845FS